Industrial Relations in Small Companies

A Comparison: France, Sweden and Germany

P.I.E. Peter Lang

Bruxelles · Bern · Berlin · Frankfurt am Main · New York · Oxford · Wien

SALTSA

A Joint Programme for Working Life Research in Europe

SALTSA is a programme of partnership in European working life research run by the Swedish Confederations of Trade Unions (LO), Professional Employees (TCO) and Professional Associations (SACO). SALTSA was a cooperation venture of these three confederations and Swedish National Institute for Working Life until the Swedish government closed NIWL in 2006. The SALTSA programme continues in new forms.

The aim of SALTSA is to generate applicable research results of a high academic standard and relevance. Research is largely project-based.

Research is carried out in three areas:
* the labour market
* work organisation
* the work environment

The Work Environment and Health Programme

Research on work environment and health focuses instruments and methods for healthier working conditions, the effects of certain risks in current working life as well as the conditions of selected groups of workers. Projects are designed with the ambition to contribute to the political debate and decision-making, applied occupational health and work environment management as well as participatory processes involving social partners in European working life.

Chairman of the SALTSA Programme is Professor Lars Magnusson and programme secretary for this area is Charlotta Krafft.

Christian DUFOUR, Adelheid HEGE, Sofia MURHEM,
Wolfgang RUDOLPH & Wolfram WASSERMANN

Industrial Relations in Small Companies

A Comparison: France, Sweden and Germany

Arbetslivsinstitutet

LO TCO SACO

SALTSA — JOINT PROGRAMME
FOR WORKING LIFE RESEARCH IN EUROPE
The National Institute for Working Life and The Swedish Trade Unions in Co-operation

"Work and Society"
No.56

Translated by Philip Cockle, Donald Johnstone and Ann Simpson.

1 avenue Maurice, B-1050 Brussels, Belgium
info@peterlang.com; www.peterlang.com

ISSN 1376-0955
ISBN 978-90-5201-360-2
D/2007/5678/55

Bibliographic information published by "Die Deutsche Bibliothek"
"Die Deutsche Bibliothek" lists this publication in the "Deutsche Nationalbibliografie"; detailed bibliographic data is available on the Internet at <http://dnb.ddb.de>.

CIP available from the British Library, GB and the Library of Congress, USA.

Contents

Christian DUFOUR and Adelheid HEGE

CONCLUSION

Introduction

Christian DUFOUR and Adelheid HEGE

Small companies are a topical subject. While it is widely recognised that their numbers are growing and that the staff they employ are more and more numerous, the public debate on this subject has become particularly contradictory.

There are those who believe that their growth is the result of the virtues linked to their very size. Relieved as they are of cumbersome structural constraints, they are flexible and creative. They are natural breeding grounds for new technologies and for entrepreneurial ambitions devoid of initial investment resources. Others believe that their very size condemns them to operating on an infra-optimal level – incapable as they are of rationalising complex tasks, they are fragile and condemned to expand to reach a scale that gives them economic significance. The relatively arbitrary nature of their management is manifest specifically in the field of industrial relations.

I. Victims of Common Knowledge

Tucked away in myriads in the more isolated spheres of economic activities, small companies are familiar, almost transparent illustrations of the more prosaic aspects of everyday life. Big companies, which are not so intimately engrained in our social fabric, can steer away from this status if only because of their organisational complexity. Small companies, their employers and employees are seen to be readily identifiable players, both sensitive to and accessible for those who have to deal with them. Their accessibility conjures up both idealistic and realistic visions of individual experience. They are the gateway for whosoever wishes to become "their own boss". By their conspicuousness, small companies fall within the compass of public judgement based on immediate experience. The controversy that surrounds them is all the more acute. According to the rules of sociological methodology, common knowledge is often mistaken for *first impressions* and acts like an obstacle in the process of discovery that it replaces. Small companies fall victim all the more to this rule as they are hardly in a position to make their opinion of themselves adequately heard.

Among the self-evident truths is that small companies can be readily identified and that they share common specificities linked to their small size.

Concealed Heterogeneousness, a Neglected Field of Study

The players, who today belong to the category of "small companies", have, for many years, been among the most dynamic forces in the economic, political and social life of developed countries. The respective historical experience of these countries has never been short of events in which an army of small-scale entrepreneurs made itself heard and displayed its political mettle. It has only been comparatively recently, however, that a supposedly standard term has brought together a multitude of situations which for long had eschewed being lumped together. Craftworkers, shopkeepers, farmers, industrialists, members of the professions, artists, local associations and a motley collection of economic and social activities that make up the category of "small companies" cannot be so easily lumped together. What is more, the enumeration refers to the diversity of this category, as it exists in France. Why should, at a particular time in history, a juxtaposition of diverse, though not necessarily incompatible, experiences come to be recognised at another time in history as a coherent entity? How can a law firm be placed on an equal footing with a scrap dealer's business? It has to be recognised that what is lacking is a history of the very notion of a "small company", what exactly is understood by that term and the errors that this absence allows. This shortcoming has caused a structural weakness in our approach to perceiving economic reality.

Experts in industrial relations, employers, trade unionists, politicians and researchers alike never fail to involve themselves in the controversy that surrounds small companies. Whether it be in public debates or in the specialised literature, it is easy to collate firmly held views with regard to the features of industrial relations in small companies. More careful consideration will show that neither the virulence of such controversy nor the firmness of its underlying judgements are based on any sound references. Research conducted within major companies has never been matched by anything comparable with regard to smaller organisations. In this domain, the management sciences have made substantial though recent progress (Torres, 1998).[1] Nevertheless, industrial relations, involving what makes up a vast majority of companies, continue to remain in a sort of *terra incognita*. Relatively few in-depth studies and surveys have specifically focused on them whereas they

1 Olivier Torres (coordination), 1998, *PME, de nouvelles approches*, Economica, Paris.

constitute a field in which they are often referred to and challenged, either positively or negatively. Admittedly, they do feature in statistical surveys. They are the subject of evaluation criteria that are supposedly valid as much for them as for the largest companies. Once the results of these studies have been obtained, they are taken to be a legitimate basis for knowledge of all companies precisely according to the universal nature of the chosen standards. Is such a procedure justified, however, particularly with regard to industrial relations?

The Unexpected Nature of the Field

This book owes its origins to field surveys conducted in France at the hinge of the 21st century. The researchers at IRES were called upon by DARES, the research facility of the Ministry of Employment, to report on the conditions in which bargaining on the reduction of working time was being conducted. A new bargaining procedure referred in particular to small and very small companies. This demand led researchers specialising in industrial relations to investigate companies of a very small size, which they would never have surveyed otherwise (Dufour *et al.*, 1999 and 2000).[2] What were unexpected stems from an assessment in the form of a paradox? Most of the companies visited were devoid of any consultation and bargaining structures even though they were required to establish them by law. This provided confirmation of what was already known. The statistics, together with legal disputes concerning labour law, have described this situation for several decades. Nevertheless, although devoid of any *ad hoc* institutions, these companies do not seem in any way to be more lacking in capacity for consultation and negotiation than larger companies, which are perfectly equipped with the apparatus required by labour legislation. This assessment warrants a twofold enquiry. It presupposes, on the one hand, that the real effects of such specialised institutions need to be looked at; and on the other hand, it calls for reflection on the social procedures at work in these small companies, which can compensate for the absence of any institutional framework.

The convergence of this problem and a meeting with the persons in charge of the SALTSA programme led to devising a research project of an international comparative nature. The task at hand would be to investigate the production of labour standards in small companies. Are they totally outside the compass of the production of standards; do they operate according to specific regimes; is their quantitative development likely to have an effect on national labour standards?

---

2 See the bibliography at the end of the chapter France.

II. An International Comparison, the Quest for a Vague Object

In order to break out of the sphere of common knowledge on this subject, the task at hand was to study several social systems in different countries on this particular theme. Three countries were chosen for this comparison: France, Germany and Sweden.

Three Different and Original Countries

For specialists in professional relations, these three countries present varied industrial profiles, overlapping each other to a certain degree and all three undergoing a process of change. They make up what would seem to be a patchwork suggesting an easy comparison in the elaboration of labour standards. Sweden, with its virtually universal rate of trade union membership (over 92%) has experienced a change in its traditional system of centralised bargaining towards a concerted, more decentralised form, which continues to include more than 90% of the workforce. In companies, a voluntarist and monistic type of representation makes few distinctions according to size. Germany (union density of approximately 30%) serves as an international reference with regard to sector-level bargaining as well as co-determination within companies. Whereas the traditional negotiating scheme was brought into question (cover through collective bargaining approached 60% in 2004), legislative measures introduced after 2000 modified certain features of the twofold regime of employee representation; the smallest companies were specifically targeted. France nurtures its exceptional status with regard to employee representation (union membership in the private sector is below 5%); in recent years, a deliberate policy has been conducted for a negotiated reduction of working time. France has to reach a compromise with certain shortcomings of its dual system of representation and negotiation within small companies in particular. The latter were ultimately exempted from the general law on the working week.

The Requirements and Means of Viewing a Situation from a Distance

The three research teams brought together for this project were aware from the outset of the twofold necessity of maintaining distance from the subject if progress was to be made in this field.[3] It was neces-

[3] Christian Dufour and Adelheid Hege from IRES were assisted by Wolfgang Rudolph and Wolfram Wassermann, from the Büro für Sozialforschung in Kassel, and by Sofia Murhem from the University of Uppsala. Also present at the seminars held during the survey: Lars Magnusson, professor of economics, and Torbjörn Strandberg,

sary both to set aside national reflexes in making comparisons as well as analytical references focused on large companies. The researchers had references at their disposal from numerous field surveys in their respective countries. Such background knowledge needed to be compared with first-hand foreign experience. It will be noted that an exchange between the three national groups was fostered by jointly conducted surveys. The so-called "cross-country survey" method was therefore adopted (Dufour, Hege, 2002). The idea was to invite each national group to participate in its neighbour's survey and, in turn, to welcome the two foreign groups in its own country. The linguistic abilities of the researchers meant that there was no obstacle to any exchange between France and Germany. In Sweden, English was the language of communication for practical reasons. The demands of this method are closely linked to what is at stake in the research itself. The aim is to break away from the traditional interpretation of social reality in small companies, which has been influenced by the imposition of standardising models borrowed from surveys on large companies. The threefold relocation of the surveys (a) in small companies, (b) foreign companies, and (c) with foreign colleagues, can be interpreted as a research procedure and a laboratory situation.

This so-called "empirical" aspect of our research has played a key role in the comparison of analyses between the three countries. It was to focus on some ten or more companies in each country. The thirty cases chosen in this way were to make up a common fund of references for the research group. As such, the sample is very limited. It can be understood only thanks to the experience acquired by each national team. The researchers in each country could bring into play a substantially larger range of cases in order to contextualise available examples. These enable each national team to view their own achievements in more relative terms and to bear that in mind under the supervision of the other two teams. The fields of enquiry do not necessarily become part of a spontaneously common experience. Discrepancies between the researchers in their understanding of the situations revealed to them constitute one of the methods of extending knowledge. They are inevitable in this kind of situation and are sought after deliberately as heuristic principles. As any exchange of experience on these cases between the researchers is based on different societal experiences, it itself makes up fields of research. Why do the German researchers react to such and such an aspect that is "obvious" for their French counterparts? Why do Swedish circumstances appear particularly foreign to French and German researchers?

---

adviser to the LO union (Sweden), both of whom were in charge of the SALTSA programme.

III. Some Additional Methodological Difficulties

A study by social science researchers of small-scale groups is governed by specific constraints, in both methodological and ethical terms. These constraints are considerably heightened in the specific context of small companies and on the theme of industrial relations. The researchers were quite aware of this as were their various interlocutors in the companies. Establishing contact requires patience. The procedure involved and the events that provide such an opportunity should be seen as valuable data, an integral part of the survey itself. Lessons drawn from any direct contact are played out as much in hosting rituals as in explicit survey enquiries. The international nature of the team of researchers aroused curiosity and opened up a number of opportunities.

It might be thought that, by the very nature of the access, the surveys might merely reveal the positive aspect of situations in this type of company. That may well be true, even if some companies refuse any investigation for reasons that are quite honourable: small groups that are "contented" may also wish to avoid the limelight. Those companies that accepted our presence were by definition open to an external survey if not to an internal investigation. That does not mean that their industrial relations are straightforward, uniform or harmonious. Nor does it mean that the internal industrial relations processes are recognised and still less can be assimilated to those that are most frequently displayed. There is, after all, no need to conduct in-depth surveys to discover the worst possible situations within small companies. While the worst examples, in terms of industrial relations in particular, are not always widely known, their profile has been identified. The courts of justice of the various countries abound with situations of this kind. The error no doubt lies in not going beyond the situations and considering them to be practical interpretive standards of industrial relations in companies of this kind. But why retain as standards for understanding small companies as a whole those that come to light only because their working conditions are unbearable to (some of) their players?

At this stage in any sociological investigation, it would be foolish to seek to be comprehensive. Our task is to report on social phenomena that are typical of the companies that lend themselves to our enquiries. The largest companies are not treated any differently.

When Is a Company Small and for Whom?

Our working procedure was marked by a series of research group meetings and exchanges of numerous documents. They laid the ground for field visits. After a survey phase came a reflection phase which guided us on further surveys to be conducted.

Initially, it was a matter of agreeing, if not on the very subject of research, at least on the preliminary path towards that aim. What did we know as to what we wanted to study? What was lacking for us to grasp what was at stake? Inevitably, statistics are the point of departure as they provide a basis for comparison that can scarcely be avoided in a preliminary phase.

The countries provided answers that were varied but not convergent to the "straightforward" question of enumerating companies according to their size. No unified statistical material was available, either between the countries or within the countries themselves. From that point of view, an international comparison can offer a methodological aid to sociologists. The illusion of common knowledge disappears at the first attempt to establish comparative tables. Admittedly, standardised data have been established at the European level. Such data offer a common comparative minimum, but they do not promise any feedback from the international comparative towards the national situation. They lose much of their subtlety in describing national situations.

It was decided to take such diversity, if not such statistical cacophony, as a guideline on our research path rather than as an obstacle to comparison. This initially puzzling situation meant accepting the idea that "the" small company does not exist. Its definitions are the subject of social controversy. Each country knows its own definitions so the sociologist cannot overlook them. The fact should not be neglected that in acquiring knowledge, what is a central notion in one particular country may well be completely ignored in another.

This multiplicity of potential definitions required us to devise, by ourselves and in accordance with what we were seeking to define more adequately, what we will refer to as small companies. The size of a workforce on a given site is invariably related to a particular legal status and to an economic profile. The combination of variations accepted by each of these three components results in mutually contradictory outcomes. Our task was to limit our initial field of investigation in order to ensure comparability, while recognising in the process that the narrowness of our definitions was not fully justified. As our focus was on the production of labour standards, we decided that we would only investigate workplaces that had no more than 100 employees and companies benefiting from both legal as well as economic autonomy.

The three ensuing national chapters start with a preliminary section describing national appraisals of small companies in statistical terms. European data provided on this subject may serve as a reference.

Table 1. Distribution of companies by numbers of occupied persons in 2002 (%)

Employees	Germany	France	Sweden
0 to 9	82.7	91.6	93.4
10 to 19	9.8	4.1	3.5
20 to 49	4.6	2.9	2.0
50 to 249	2.4	1.2	0.9
0 to 249	99.5	99.7	99.8
250 and more	0.5	0.3	0.2

Source: Eurostat-Newcronos-SBS/DCASPL, ICS, except for recreational, cultural and sports activities (NACE 92), personnel services (NAF 93), education, health and social care (NAF 80, 85). Results for the 15 Member States as a whole had not been finalised at the date of publication.

What Is Their Status in Systems of Industrial Relations?

What status do small companies have in systems of industrial relations in each of the three countries? That is the second question raised prior to the survey, the results of which are provided in the national chapters. It raises a question of methodological focus – more precise than any statistical consideration – directly linked to industrial relations. This question seeks to identify, in terms of standards, what the networks for producing social standards are and what position small companies in such institutionalised processes actually occupy. Are they recognised as specific entities? If not, why and if so, on what specific criteria? Who are the players who have a decisive role in laying down such standards?

In correlation, this question raises another: how do small companies react with hindsight to institutionalised standards and their elaboration? It presupposes that a comparison is drawn between the various forms of collective representation of the players in such economic and social units. Which organisations classify the numerous, polymorphous ranks of small company employers? What role do the employees of such companies play in national trade union structures?

This institutional refocusing is occurring at a time when profound changes are under way in all three countries. Questions as to the role of small companies were heightened by the Internet bubble episode. That came to an end in early 2000, but contributed to stimulating reflection on possible alternative models for devising industrial rules, more adapted to high-tech companies, which develop rapidly, with highly educated, young employees. It was to have an influence on the choice of companies to be visited. It also influenced a hypothesis opposing earlier models of industrial relations to more recent ones and the possible precursory role of small companies in this domain.

Institutional refocusing also involves meetings with the players themselves. In the three countries, contact was established with collective bargaining negotiators, from among employers and workforce alike. Visits were made to the local representatives of their organisations. The labour inspectorate was called upon in France where the French researchers were, at the same time, conducting a survey on the elected employment tribunals (*Prud'hommes*) with many local interlocutors (Hege, Dufour, 2004).

The second section of the national chapters centres on the position occupied by small companies in industrial relations systems.

IV. Specific Practices, Compared Practices?

Empirical surveys have a dual objective. On the one hand, their aim is to check whether possible industrial relations practices are specific to small companies in the production of social standards. These can then be compared to what we know of larger companies. We must also focus on possible practices in small companies, specific to each of the three countries; the comparison therefore becomes international. Both of these questions can be summed up in a third, namely that of the combined identities and differences between small and large, co-national and foreign companies. Does this lead ultimately to cumulative differentiations, which make Swedish small companies incomparable with French and German small companies? Conversely, is it possible to identify practices whereby small companies possess similarities with their foreign counterparts, but are quite different from their larger national neighbours?

With this aim in mind, it was decided to draw up monographs of individual companies. Discussion of these accounts constituted one of the foundations of an exchange between the researchers. Harmonising their points of view led to devising common evaluation criteria without doing away with national inequalities or divergent points of view. The third part of the national chapters is based on a synthesis of these monographs. What is there to be learnt from each country with regard to the underlying approach to industrial relations in small companies? On what essential procedures and players are their internal regimes and their external relations based? Each national team conducted its own evaluation for which it retains responsibility, even if the conclusions were submitted for joint discussion. Their evaluations were based on essentially a shared appraisal with regard to the way industrial relations are conducted within small companies, their possible specificities and their relationship with underlying external labour standards.

V. Comparative Conclusions

If conclusions have ever deserved the status of a preliminary preparatory status in a research process, those that we can now provide may serve as a reference. The main conclusion is undoubtedly that the field of enquiry we have opened up remains both extensive and promising. New paths of enquiry have been opened up both with regard to counting small companies and the analysis of their role in general industrial relations and the internal rationale of their own industrial relations. However, a preliminary conclusion would seem to be possible. Admittedly, to avoid an in-depth analysis of small companies according to their specificity would be a blind spot as regards industrial relations by the very fact of their large numbers and their demographical features. Furthermore, that would deprive analysts of a yardstick in analysing the practices of large companies. Small companies are not large ones on a small scale (if not to refer to the notion of "hypo-companies" in their regard). Nevertheless, relations within large companies do not lie outside manifestations of industrial relations, which are more easily perceptible in smaller entities.

Our aim, therefore, is not over-ambitious. What matters is to record what we have observed and attempted to understand in economic and social entities, which are not easily perceived by professional observers when the latter have neglected them for so many years. There has been a strong feeling of dealing with a field that is not only unfamiliar but also strewn with deceptive signs. The task is to make use with circumspection of concepts, which can be presumed to be ill-adapted, while at the same time defying empiricism, which serves less to produce innovative hypotheses than to run the risk of subverting the survey through an unhelpful return to common knowledge. There again, a cross-enquiry method and discussions between researchers from different theoretical and practical backgrounds are fully justified.

Research on small companies with regard to industrial relations is thus merely at its initial stage.

France

Christian DUFOUR and Adelheid HEGE

Institut de recherches économiques et sociales, IRES

I. Small Companies, Quantitative Change and Industrial Relations

In France, two reasons justify examining small companies in depth and paying special attention to the labour standards that they produce or convey. On the one hand, the number of people they employ is on the increase and, on the other, the legal framework of industrial relations in the workplace is partially adapted to the latter's size. Involvement of unions and employers' organisations in the smallest workplaces is known, on the whole, not to be the same as in bigger companies. We will see throughout this chapter that, in a period of major changes in industrial relations practice and legal frameworks, they occupy a strategic place in the production of new rules governing industrial relations.

In the first part of this chapter, we will describe changing numbers and sizes of small companies and the specific nature of the industrial relations system that concerns them.

In the second part – on the basis of case-studies of very different kinds of small companies – we will seek to specify, in a more empirical way, the features of industrial relations in smaller companies.

A. Uncertain Identification and Sinuous Quantitative Change

Identifying the number of employees in small companies is not a simple task for both statistical and conceptual reasons. Broadly speaking, two types of calculations can be distinguished, namely by workplace (*établissement*) and by economic dependence (company (*entreprise*)). In 2003, there were more than 8.4 million employees in workplaces with less than 50 employees, i.e. 53% of the 15.8 million employees in the private sector. In the same year, there were 3.7 million employees in workplaces with more than two hundred employees, i.e. 23.4% of all employees.[1]

Table 1. Number and proportion of workplaces by size, 2003

UNEDIC	Size by number of employees							
	1-4	5-9	10-19	20-49	50-99	100-199	200-499	500 and over
Number of workplaces	962,424	295,116	133,350	89,058	27,479	13,229	6,673	1,739
(%)	62.9%	19.3%	8.7%	5.8%	1.8%	0.9%	0.4%	0.1%
Number of employees	1,923,726	1,940,936	1,790,094	2,746,085	1,885,478	1,827,746	1,984,637	1,718,246
%	12.2%	12.3%	11.3%	17.4%	11.9%	11.63%	12.5%	10.9%

Source: Statis Unedic, No.173, 3rd quarter 2004.

The figures provided by the Ministry of Industry in its document entitled "Key figures on SMEs" (*Chiffres clefs des PME*) are in terms of companies with less than 250 people in industry, commerce and services (small and medium-sized enterprises, SMEs) – not in terms of workplaces. Moreover, companies in the areas of agriculture, finance, administration, associations and letting of property, as well as some rare legal entities, are excluded. According to this calculation, in 2002, SMEs represented 99.5% of all companies in the sectors concerned, i.e. more than 2 million. They employed 58% of all employees, i.e. 8.2 million. As many of them only occupy an entrepreneur, they actually account for 63% of total employment (i.e. 10 million people).

In France, SMEs produce 45% of turnover and 53% of added value (1,300 billion and 380 billion Euros respectively). Companies with less than 50 employees provide 39% of added value. In 2002, 42% of employees in SMEs were women, which is the same as in big companies. Structural effects intervene here. Within this group of companies with fewer than 250 employees, more women work in the smallest units, which are often service companies. The proportion of women in non full-time employment is 66% in SMEs, compared with 63% in companies with more than 250 employees. Pay is on average 20% lower in

1 According to the definition used by the French unemployment insurance scheme, the National Union for Employment in Industry and Commerce (*Union nationale interprofessionnelle pour l'emploi dans l'industrie et le commerce*, UNEDIC); the scheme covers 14 million employees.

SMEs than in bigger companies – and within SMEs, women's pay is also about 20% lower than men's.[2]

Table 2. Distribution of occupied people by company size, 2002

Employees (thousands)	0-9	10-19	20-49	50-249	Total SMEs	Over 250	Total
Food and agriculture	199.6	46.4	63.8	114.2	423.9	245.2	669.1
Manufacturing and energy	363.3	209.9	448.6	740.8	1,762.5	1,902.2	3,664.7
Building and public works	700.1	191.5	241.9	190.5	1,323.9	182.9	1,506.8
Commerce	1,228.1	282.2	451.5	458.5	2,420.2	909.5	3,329.7
Transports	154.3	62.2	133.1	187.2	563.8	583.4	1,120.2
Services	1,543.6	334.8	462.4	534.9	2,875.7	1,974.5	4,850.2
Education, health, and social services	438.8	44.2	76.5	103.6	663.0	57.1	720.1
Total	**4,627.7**	**1,171.0**	**1,877.7**	**2,329.7**	**10,061.1**	**5,854.7**	**15,860.8**

Source: DGI-INSEE-DCASPL, Chiffres clefs des PME, 2005.

Data in the SIRENE file for 2004, published by the National Institute of Statistics and Economic Studies (*Institut national des statistiques et des études économiques*, INSEE), make it possible to add to the above data by including companies that were excluded from the previous calculation. This leads to a figure of almost 2.5 million companies.

The distribution of employees by size of workplace changed between 1975 and 1998. At the beginning of the period, the smallest workplaces occupied roughly the same proportion of employees as the biggest ones, namely about 20% for those with between 1 and 9 employees and the same for those with more than 500 employees. By the end of the period, a big gap had appeared with the smallest workplaces increasing their share to 26% and the biggest ones falling to 11%.

Table 3. Distribution of companies by size (thousands and %)

1-9 employees	10-49 employees	50-249 employees	Total PME with employees	Without employees	Total companies
836.6	56.1	23.7	916.4	1,465.3	2,474.7
33.8%	2.27%	0.95%	37%	59%	100%

Source: INSEE (Fichier SIRENE), 1 January 2004.

2 DGI, INSEE, DCASPL, data on companies that do not come under a "micro" company scheme. *Chiffres clefs des PME*, Minefi, 2005.

Figure 1. Changes in the distribution of employees between companies/workplaces of different sizes

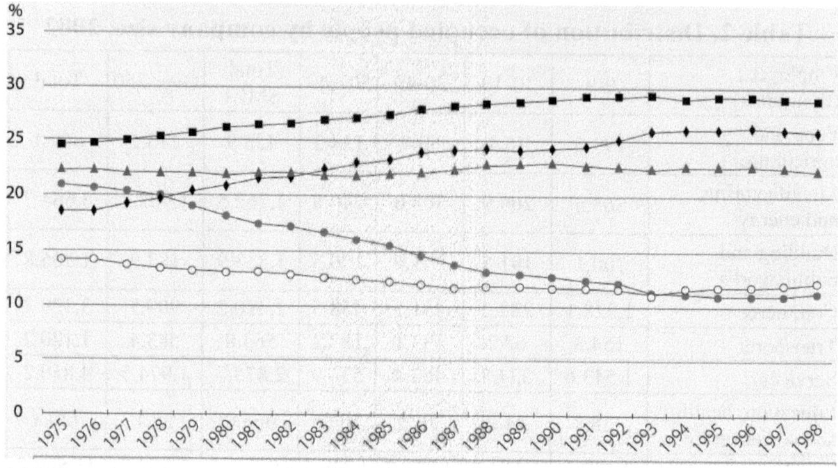

♦ 1 to 9 employees ▪ 9 to 49 employees ▪ 9 to 49 employees
▲ 50 to 199 employees ○ 200 to 199 employees ● 500 employees and more

Source: UNEDIC.

The same phenomenon is to be seen in observations of average size of long-standing companies (not workplaces) over a dozen years. Very big companies with more than 5,000 employees lost many employees very rapidly; whereas, at the other end of the scale, small companies increased their average number of employees.

Table 4. Changes in the average size of long-standing companies

Year	1-9	10-19	20-49	50-199	200-499	500-999	1,000-4,999	5,000-9,999	10,000 and over
1985	3.6	14	31	93	305	691	1,964	6,487	25,408
1991	4.5	16	36	102	327	691	1,747	4,741	19,812
1997	5	17	37	107	316	648	1,524	3,797	13,137

Source: INSEE. Field: companies, except for temporary employment agencies.

These long-term changes can also be seen *via* the relative change in numbers of private-sector employees, according to the size of their workplace. With an index with base 100 in 1980, workplaces with between 1 and 9 employees increased to almost 140 in 2003, whereas workplaces with more than 500 employees dropped to just over 70.

Figure 2. Changes in numbers of employees, by size of workplace (index with base 100 on 31 December 1980)

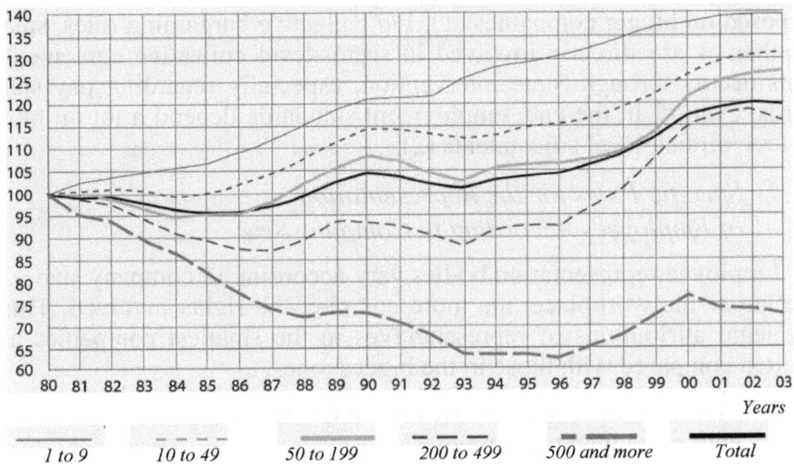

Source: UNEDIC.

This rapid statistical overview illustrates the difficulties of studying "small companies". Both terms, "small" and "company", are not easy to define. Many big companies are divided into numerous workplaces, which are more or less independent regarding human resources management. Many companies – both big and small – are attached to major groups, within which they may, or may not, be accountable to central bodies, regarding staff management. The difficulty of fixing a size for defining "small companies" leads to posing the question as to whether size itself constitutes a discriminating factor regarding industrial relations management. This initial question is even more complex, given that size is, by its very nature, an approximate and fluctuating factor. It is more realistic to accept the idea that this is an area, whose frontiers are not only vague, but also unstable, even if it seems that there is a momentary loss of precision, especially regarding issues related to labour standards and industrial relations practices. Changes in numbers of employees are, as we will see hereafter, a central aspect of the development of industrial relations and labour standards.

B. *Are Industrial Relations Institutions "Adapted" to Small Companies?*

From a certain point of view, France is solidly equipped for adapting labour standards to companies of various and varying sizes.

Several thresholds concerning numbers of employees structure a gradual increase in legal obligations regarding employee representation in companies. Small companies are not subjected to all the obligations imposed on bigger companies (1). *Via* collective bargaining rules, small companies are directly involved in sector-level collective agreements. This occurs through State intervention, especially regarding pay standards, even if, in the end, employment standards depend a lot on more or less implicit local adjustments (2).

1. Specific Rules for the Representation of Employees According to Company Size

Employee representation bodies vary according to company size, i.e. the larger the workplace, the more complex the rights involved. Thus, the legal attributions of representatives in the smallest companies are limited compared with those in the biggest ones.

a. Elected Bodies are Provided for in Companies with more than ten Employees

Employee representation is not compulsory in companies with less than 11 employees. From this size on, the law provides for the election of employee representatives (*délégués du personnel*, DPs) by all employees. Between 1 and 3 DPs with full status and the same number with substitute status are elected in companies with between 11 and 99 employees. Previously, they were elected for two years, but since a law, which was adopted in August 2005,[3] they are elected for four years. According to the legislation, trade unions that are representative nationally have priority for presenting lists of candidates for the elections – the first round of the elections is reserved for such trade union lists. A second round is organised, in which non-union candidates have the right to present themselves, if abstention is greater than 50% of registered voters in the first round or if there are no trade union lists or if some seats are still vacant.

---

[3] Law No. 2005-882 adopted on 2 August 2005. This law includes a whole series of measures aimed at promoting small and medium-sized companies. However, the changes in the length of the mandate of elected representatives concerns companies of all sizes. A sector-, group- or company-level agreement can, nevertheless, provide for mandates lasting from between two and four years in the units concerned by the particular agreement. This law was strongly criticised by the trade unions, which were not consulted about it. The law was accompanied by a decree (*Ordonnance* No. 2005-892 adopted on 2 August 2005), which stipulates that employees under the age of 26 are no longer included in staff numbers for calculating the threshold for establishing employee representation bodies. Thus a company with twenty employees, half of whom are under 26, could no longer legally elect employee representatives.

In the great majority of small companies, DPs are elected on non-union lists. The law provides for a monthly meeting between the elected representatives and the employer. The role of DPs is to monitor the individual and collective implementation of laws and collective agreements that apply to their company. In some cases, employers must consult them before taking certain decisions (regarding paid holidays, safety and so forth), but they do not have the power to make formal agreements.

Given the difficulty of having DPs in small companies, legal texts provide for bringing together several companies that are geographically close to one another, in order to organise elections of "site representatives" (*délégués de site*) with prerogatives similar to those of DPs. However, there has not been significant take-up of this measure.

In companies with 50 or more employees, there are also works councils (*comités d'entreprise*, CE). Three or four full members and the same number of substitute members are elected in companies with between 50 and 99 employees. Comités d'entreprise are elected according to the same rules as DPs and often DPs are also CE's members. Comités d'entreprise have two rather different functions. On the one hand, they manage the social fund, which is provided by the employer, for organising social and cultural activities (tourism, leisure activities and solidarity, etc.) for employees. The fund is rarely big in small companies, especially newer ones (IRES/DARES, 1998). But the fact that it is possible to organise such activities often is an incentive for employees to take the initiative of creating such a structure. Employers are not always against, as they gain from more friendly relations between members of the company. On the other hand, this function of promoting conviviality is accompanied by a very different kind of responsibility. The CE's job is to monitor the company's business, human resources and technological developments. It has the right to information and/or consultation regarding redundancies, training and business results, etc. Along with the DPs, it organises a committee that specialises in health and safety at work and working conditions (*Comité d'hygiène, de sécurité et des conditions de travail*, CHSCT), which has extensive powers. However, just as is the case for DPs, comités d'entreprise do not have collective bargaining rights.

Given the fact that often the same person has both mandates, and also in order to reduce the number of elections, it is possible in companies with between 50 and 200 employees to organise one election for electing employees who are both DPs and CE's members – their position is called "single employee representation" (*Délégation unique du personnel*, DU).

Table 5. Representation rights in French companies, by size

Company size	Representation rights	Functions
Less than 11 employees	None	
11 employees and over	Employee representatives (DP) (elected)	Representation of employees regarding existing rights and agreements; some rights to consultation
From 50 employees and over or between 50 and 200 employees	Works council (CE) (elected) + DP or Single employee representation (DU) (elected)	Management of social and cultural activities within the company; information and consultation on business, technological and human resources issues.
	Trade union representative (DS) (designated)	Collective bargaining rights

b. The Specific Place of Union Rights in Representation Rights

Employee representation in workplaces and companies is twofold: trade union rights are quite separate from employee representation rights. Legally, there is no minimum threshold for creating a trade union section (*section syndicale*) for all members within a company. The role of this kind of structure is to carry out strictly union tasks, such as membership drives, contact with members, trade union information and so forth. There is, however, a threshold of 50 employees for a union section to be able to designate a "union representative" (*délégué syndical*, DS). The latter can negotiate and sign agreements within companies on behalf of their union. The law thus puts collective bargaining entirely in the hands of the unions – not the employee representation bodies. There can be as many union representatives as there are union sections (affiliated to different trade union confederations) in the same company. This is the case in bigger companies, where there is cohabitation, if not competition, between unions. In fact, in a country, where union density is very low in the private sector, the smallest companies have not only almost no recognised union representation, but even almost no union members. It is, therefore, impossible to negotiate agreements in such very small companies in line with legal rules that are applied to big companies. In order to overcome this difficulty, legislation offers two alternatives. In companies with less than 50 employees, it is possible for a union to designate a union representative (DS), chosen amongst the elected DPs. However, as we have seen above, it is not rare for this body not to exist, even in workplaces with more employees than the theoretical threshold.

c. "Mandating" – an Original and Controversial Procedure

It is, thus, possible for an employee to receive a mandate from a recognised representative union to negotiate on a specific topic. It is worth examining in greater detail this procedure, which is quite original in the international context. It was incorporated in legislation in 1996 and involves a representative union empowering an employee to negotiate and sign an agreement in his/her company, on a particular topic and at a particular time. The mandated employee must present the draft agreement, which has been drawn up within the company, to the union, with which s/he is in contact. If the union approves the content of the agreement, s/he can sign the agreement on behalf of the union and it is, thus, valid for all the employees in the company. This possibility was used a lot between 1998 and 2001, in order to negotiate the reduction in working time, in line with the laws that were adopted in June 1998 and January 2000. Some unions see it as a potential way of making members in the smallest companies. Others consider it to be an illusory path regarding access to representation, which, in fact, legally threatens prerogatives that were hitherto recognised for purely union structures. Research on the subject shows that mandating is, in fact, a relatively effective way of concluding agreements in small companies, provided it is accompanied by good employee participation in the various stages of discussion of the draft agreement. However, it does not seem to have led to establishing lasting union contacts in the companies concerned (Dufour, Hege *et al.*, 2000).

2. Collective Agreements – Frame of Reference and Adaptations

Collective bargaining can take place at various levels, namely that of the company and nationally, both at sector and cross-sector levels. The different levels are not legally independent from each other.

Given the numerous incentives coming from the authorities, sector-level collective agreements concern almost all French employees, regardless of whether they work in small or big companies. When a collective agreement is signed at this level, it is systematically extended to all companies in the sector by government decision, provided that none of its measures infringe the general law. More than 90% of French employees are covered by such collective agreements. However, in spite of their extension to almost all employees, collective agreements do not play as big a role regarding labour standards, as might have been expected.

a. Minimum-Level Collective Agreements

In many cases, sector-level agreements only refer to labour code and simply adapt them to the specific circumstances of the type of activity covered by the particular negotiations. This is especially true of new parts of the service sector (Meilland, Dufour, 2001). As far as pay is concerned, minimum pay included in collective agreements is close to – or even less than – the legal cross-sector minimum wage (*Salaire minimum interprofessionnel de croissance*, SMIC), whose level is fixed by the government each year. Collectively-agreed pay increases are often the result of adjusting minimum levels in the agreement to government decisions and their impact on the entire pay structure.

In spite of challenges to the hierarchy of sources of rights, more general agreements still predominate over specific agreements (in line with the "preferential principle" (*principe de faveur*)). Agreements signed at company level are thus often significantly better than standards set in sector-level collective agreements. This is the case for pay, and also works schedules and social protection.[4] Being attached to a sector-level agreement is, therefore, often of no "real" significance for employees of big unionised companies – neither their pay, nor the pace of their pay increases are related to the levels and pace of the sector-level bargaining that concerns them. In fact, two parallel bargaining rationales, which are almost independent, apply, on the one hand, to big companies, and, on the other, to sectors (Barrat, Daniel, 2002).

Are small companies the main "beneficiaries" of sector-level collective agreements? On the one hand, in most specialised surveys, employers say that such agreements are a permanent yardstick for them.[5] On the other hand, external observers – namely employment tribunal members and labour inspectors – are often critical regarding their actual implementation. Collective agreements unquestionably play a role in arbitration when conflicts between employers and employees in small companies emerge into the outside world. However, as far as daily practice is concerned, their implementation involves a significant degree of interpretation, which both employers and employees can promote. Implementing a collective agreement involves adapting a text to a situation, which is always unique.

The use of job classifications contained in collective agreements – and the way their hierarchy is organised – illustrates the process of applying texts to actual practice. All surveys show that hierarchies of

4 For an illustration of this situation in the metal industry, see Dufour, Hege, 1999.

5 The survey on "Pay structures" indicates that "57% of employees are in companies, whose employers say that they use the sector-level collective agreement to establish their pay structure", quoted in CSERC, 1999: 39.

job classifications are closely respected in small companies. In other words, a specific level of pay corresponds with each employee's job classification. This is often used to assess the impact of collective agreements on employers' practices and pay structures. But, perhaps, the relationship between job classifications and pay should be interpreted the other way round, namely that job classifications correspond with pay. In practice, this means that employers attribute to individual employees the job classification that corresponds with the pay they wish to give them – not the other way round. During recruitment negotiations, an employer indicates to a future employee the pay s/he will receive. The company accountant then applies this decision, which owes little to the collective agreement and a lot to the state of the labour market at a particular time. The accountant will find references in the collective agreement making it possible to ensure that there is not a gap between company practice and the law. During any official monitoring, the accountant will simply indicate that s/he has taken the collective agreement into account when setting pay levels.

b. The Reduced Role of Collective Agreements in Determining Real Pay

The minimum wage set by government is subject to what is at stake in national elections. During the fifty years of the SMIC's existence, it has acquired the status of a labour standard. It plays a central role in determining politically acceptable labour standards. It thus plays an important role in determining pay in small companies, which extends beyond the context of industrial relations.

A quantitative assessment of its impact is complicated by the fact that there are various SMICs related to the differing schemes regarding working hours, following on from the legislation on the reduction of working time. Two groups that are administratively separate have to be combined (provisionally), in order to calculate the number of employees, who are directly concerned by trends in the minimum wage.

Table 6 minimises the impact of the SMIC, because it excludes populations, which are very much concerned by the minimum wage, such as agricultural workers, home-helps and seasonal workers.[6] However, this does not prevent us from highlighting the growing proportion of employees, who are directly concerned by trends in the SMIC and GMR. At the beginning of the 1990s, the pay increases of a little more than 8% of employees depended on increases in the SMIC. At the turn

6 20% of the 620,000 temporary agency workers, 31.8% of the 320,000 agricultural workers and 44.4% of the 580,000 people employed in the domestic sector were paid on the basis of the SMIC or GMR on 1 July 2004 (*Ibid.*). 8.1% of the 5.6 million employees in the public sector are estimated to have pay at this level (*Ibid.*).

of the century, more than 13% of employees were in this situation. This trend seems to be speeding up during the present decade and approached 16% in mid-2004. These statistics should be accompanied by an assessment of the number of employees, who are indirectly affected by increases in the SMIC, namely those who are paid slightly above this level and whose pay is increased so that the hierarchical gap between them and those who are less well-off, does not completely disappear.

Table 6. Numbers and percentage of employees paid on the basis of the SMIC or Monthly Guaranteed Pay (*Garantie mensuelle de rémunération*, GMR), by company size on 1 July 2003 and 1 July 2004

	2003		2004	
Company size	**Thousands**	**%**	**Thousands**	**%**
1-9 employees	890	28.3	1,030	32.3
10-19 employees	240	16.0	260	17.3
20-49 employees	270	14.3	330	16.5
50-99 employees	180	15.5	190	15.2
100-249 employees	130	9.9	170	13.1
250-499 employees	90	8.9	70	7.8
500 employees and over	250	4.8	320	6.3
Total	2,050	13.4	2,370	15.6

Field: employees (excluding apprentices) in the non-agricultural market sector, excluding domestic and temporary work.

Source: DARES, enquête ACEMO, *Premières informations*, June 2005, No.26.1.

The same table illustrates the dichotomy of pay practices between big and small companies. The minimum wage does not greatly concern employees in big units.

The reduced role of sector-level agreements in determining pay is confirmed by statistical surveys carried out amongst employers and union representatives (*Enquêtes Réponse*, 1993 and 1998). When they are questioned about the criteria that are used for drawing up pay demands in the workplace, only 12% of union representatives mentioned sector-level agreements (*Enquêtes Réponse*, 1993). In the same survey, employers, who quote the sector level as being decisive for their pay practices, employ 13% of employees.

In banking, chemicals and even building, minimum pay of their respective sectors hardly concerns anyone. Sectors, where the gap between actual pay and minimum pay is the smallest, are also those where local labour markets play a decisive role, e.g. minimum pay in hairdressing no doubt depends more on location and the labour market (in Paris, the Paris region, a major provincial town or a village) than on the collective agreement. But the latter takes into account least favourable situations for setting its own standards.

Table 7. Hourly pay, actual basic pay and collectively agreed minimum pay in six sectors (%)

	Average gap between actual basic pay and collectively-agreed minimum pay for the sector [a]	% of employees paid at the level of the sector's minimum pay	% of employees paid at most 10% above the sector's minimum pay
Banking	52	0	0
Building	19	3	15
Chemicals	21	2	7
Clothing	17	14	36
Hairdressing	19	14	40
Footwear	17	10	22

[a] or the SMIC if it is higher.

Source: Meurs, Skalli, 1997, quoted in CSERC, 1999, p.39.

Unfortunately, there is no analysis making it possible to measure the impact of local labour markets on pay in different sectors. However, in this respect, the differences between small and big companies are great, especially when the latter are national or international ones. Trends towards reducing the size of big companies, which were referred to above, often aim at taking advantage of the impact of local labour markets. Small companies have a very symbiotic relationship with the local community. In some cases, this forces them to increase their labour costs. In others, it enables them to reduce them and come closer to collectively-agreed standards, which, as we have already seen, take the most unfavourable local features into account.

3. Small Companies and the General Law: Signs of Unequal Treatment

Small companies are governed by general labour law with specific adaptations regarding employee representation. Legal specifications regarding other aspects of labour law – especially individual employment contracts – are generally the same for all employees, regardless of company size. However, it is worthwhile highlighting two recent developments that could signify the beginning of differing legal frameworks for employment related to company size.

In 2002, following on from the 1999 reforms regarding working time, rules were introduced establishing differences between employees in bigger and smaller companies. In 2005, a new kind of employment contract – the "New Recruitment Contract" (*Contrat nouvelle em-*

bauche, CNE) – was introduced and only applies to companies with 20 or fewer employees.

a. The Case of the 35-hour Week

In 1999, the left-wing government embarked on a policy aimed at reducing working time. Three phases were planned. During the first phase (July 1999-January 2000), all companies were invited to voluntarily negotiate agreements reducing working time. On the basis of this experiment, during which many small companies were involved in negotiations (see above: "mandating"), a law was adopted in January 2000 (second phase). It made it compulsory for companies with more than twenty employees to introduce, within 24 months, a reduction in working time on the basis of a 35-hour week. From January 2002 onwards, small companies with under 20 employees had to implement the measure (third phase). The spreading of the process over a long period of time aimed at giving small units sufficient time to adapt, as it was considered it would be less easy for them.

The three phases were respected, but many employers of the smallest companies waited for the spring 2002 general elections in order to begin implementing the law. Their wait-and-see attitude was rewarded by the right-wing electoral victory. In October 2002, the new government changed the legal measures concerning the reduction of working time. Reference to the 35-hour week has been retained, but it is no longer compulsory for companies with less than 20 employees to reduce working time. Any time worked between the 35th and 39th hour is paid as overtime, but at a lower rate than other overtime.

The law thus legalises two different sets of rules in this area of labour law – one for big companies, which must implement the 35-hour week, with the possibility of using overtime; and another for the smallest companies, whose legal weekly working time is 35 hours, but actual working time remains 39 hours (i.e. the legal weekly working time in force before the new legislation). The main employers' organisation (*Mouvement des entreprises de France*, MEDEF) supported this change, although it considered that it did not go far enough. It justified its position by referring to the difficulties that the reduction of working time would have caused small companies. The Craftwork Employers' Association, (*Union professionnelle artisanale*, UPA), which had been in favour of the transition to the 35-hour week, did not oppose the change head-on, as it satisfied those of its members, who were most reluctant about the organisation's official strategy (see below).

b. The New Recruitment Contract

Another breach of equality in the area of labour law related to company size occurred when the New Recruitment Contract (CNE) was introduced by the government in July 2005. Its aim is to help the smallest companies to take the plunge and recruit new staff. It does so by making it possible for them to take on new employees with a contract that does not refer to duration. It is, therefore, an open-ended contract, but is accompanied by the possibility of dismissal with fewer constraints for employers than a fixed-term contract. In fact, employers can dismiss employees recruited on such contracts without justification and with very short notice during the first two years of their employment.

This new type of contract was strongly denounced by the unions. They fear that small companies are being used to experiment a new labour status, which will be gradually extended to companies of all sizes. A sign of the fact that labour status in small companies is not only a national concern is reflected in the International Monetary Fund's position in favour of this measure. It considers that "the CNE's effectiveness in reducing unemployment will be the larger, the less limitations it has in duration and scope, and the sooner it leads to the adoption of recent proposals to integrate all existing contracts into a single one" (IMF, 2005).

C. Representatives – Twofold Inequality

As far as collective bargaining players – and also the involvement of representative employers' and employees' organisations – are concerned, twofold inequality can be observed. On the one hand, trade unions have very little influence in small companies, whereas some employers' organisations can play a major role, even if there are great disparities. On the other hand, employees in small companies are less well represented than employees in big companies. The State imposes itself as a predominant player in setting labour standards in small companies, while *professional* players have a secondary role in comparison.

1. Specific Employer Representation Bodies for Small Companies

Several employers' organisations are recognised for collective bargaining (Bunel, 1997). Employers' representation in France does not generally have separate structures for carrying out business and industrial relations functions. They negotiate with their employee counterparts agreements of general interest (national cross-sector agreements) and leave sector-level bargaining to those of their members, who are specialised in the particular sector. Only the three most important employers' organisations will be presented here. They differ in terms of the size of the companies they represent.

The main organisation, namely the MEDEF, plays a decisive role in French industrial relations. Structurally, it is a "union of unions" bringing together different occupational groupings, covering all areas and types of companies. Its member organisations include companies of all sizes; nevertheless, the MEDEF is generally thought of as being the spokesperson of big companies. *Via* its most powerful members, such as the Union of Metal and Mining Industries, (*Union des industries métallurgiques et minières*, UIMM), the MEDEF controls the production of sector-level collective agreements throughout the country and in all sectors. Employers' organisations' collective bargaining practices vary – history, sectors, location and composition of companies concerned all play a role. However, the various practices tend to lead to shared strategy. Apart from the occasional exception, employers' organisations aim at ensuring that collectively-agreed standards leave most decision-making on pay within companies in the hands of individual employers. They see individual autonomy as a strong prerogative and sign of their authority over employees, guaranteeing their freedom of action. However, employers' organisations prefer to leave the responsibility of setting the minimum wage to the State, thus giving it the role of guaranteeing social cohesion. Neither employers' organisations nor individual employers are accustomed to the idea that sector-level pay bargaining could be advantageous for company management itself.

There are no collective agreements whose coverage is defined by the size of the companies concerned. Sector-level bargaining is, therefore, always structurally a source of confrontation between big and small companies. This confrontation is taken on board by the existence alongside the MEDEF of two employers' organisations, which are different from their big neighbour in terms of the size of the companies they claim to represent.

The General Confederation of Small and Medium-Sized Enterprises (*Conféderation générale des petites et moyennes entreprises*, CGPME) is the second biggest employers' organisation. It originated partly from a reaction to the power of big companies within the MEDEF. It claims to bring together "real employers", namely those who directly own their companies, unlike "delegated employers" (employed managers) in big companies. The CGPME does not have the same lobbying power that the MEDEF developed a long time ago. It even seems to depend on its powerful rival regarding many topics. Since the end of the 1990s, the CGPME has been suffering from a serious internal crisis, which affects its ability to intervene and also leads to doubts about its ability in the future. It cannot stand bargaining on the reduction of working time demanded by the trade unions and has constantly campaigned against the laws on this issue that were adopted between 1999 and 2002. It has been greatly involved in the measures adopted by the right-wing government in autumn 2002, which modify the conditions for introducing the 35-hour week.

The Craftwork Employers' Association (*Union professionnelle artisanale*, UPA) has become more active in recent years. It has members in small and very small companies, especially in the building industry, hotels and restaurants. It has taken positions on several issues that are different from those of the MEDEF. It has developed a strategy of negotiating with the unions on the reduction of working time, even though the latter do not have many members – or none at all – in small and very small companies in the craftwork sector, most of which are members of the UPA. The UPA's aim is to avoid a growing gap between small and big companies regarding industrial relations practices. The UPA, whose members are often labour-intensive companies, fears that, in the long term, the craftwork sector will not have enough skilled workers, because of unattractive labour conditions. In this respect, the UPA signed an agreement along with all representative trade unions at national level providing for the development of trade union representation within companies in its province. This agreement was hotly contested by the MEDEF, which tried to mobilise opposition against the UPA's leadership. The results of this spectacular initiative are yet to be assessed.

The UPA's position illustrates the hypothesis of a change in the role of sector-level collective agreements in France. For a long time, they were considered as being a way of equalising pay conditions upwards, in order to limit competition between companies *via* pay (Saglio, 1991). Employers, who pay their employees most, seek to protect themselves from competition from low pay practised by their neighbours. The UPA's strategy is to avoid competition on the basis of high labour costs, in order to have access to better-paid employees and avoid locking very small companies in an under-valued labour market. The UPA fears that the strategy of reducing the importance of sector-level collective agreements will lead to a two-tier labour market – one being reserved for employees in big companies with better industrial relations conditions and *ad hoc* collective bargaining; while the other will be reserved for employees in small companies, with significantly less favourable labour conditions and offering big companies easy access to cheap subcontracting. The UPA's current strategy means that it is in conflict with the MEDEF and some of its own members, who do not think that it is a priority to protect themselves from a risk highlighted by the UPA's present leadership. On the contrary, they see their survival as depending on their ability to offer low labour costs – and this approach is fairly much in line with the CGPME's strategy.

2. *Trade Unions Are Almost Entirely Absent from Small Companies*

In a country, where union density in the private sector (probably) does not exceed 6 to 7% – with many members concentrated in certain areas – the most common situation is for there to be no union members at all. This is almost an absolute rule in companies with fewer than 50 employees and a general rule in those with fewer than 100.[7] This does not mean that employees do not have any form of representation. *Comités d'entreprise* seem to be present in more than three quarters of workplaces with 50 employees and over and DPs in about 35% of those with more than 10 employees. However, in most cases, these representative institutions are not unionised. Almost half of elected *Comités d'entreprise* are not unionised and almost half of all *CE's* members are not members of a union. As they are in smaller companies, they concern about 2.5 million employees, i.e. almost 40% of employees with comité d'entreprises.

Union presence in small companies may be in the form of one member, who is prepared to go public. This usually happens when the employee concerned wants to represent employees within the company or promote the creation of representation bodies. In order to protect such employees, unions can give them the status of "union representative" (*délégué syndical*, DS), even if there is not a union section in the workplace. In most cases, however, unions (regardless of which ones) are considered undesirable in internal company life – both by employees and employers. Many justifications are given for such defiance. Surveys of non-union elected representatives show that, in many cases, they carry out their mandate in difficult conditions – both because their employer may be hostile and because fellow employees do not support them very much. Latent requests for outside help are not always met by the unions in the way they would like. Links with unions often do not exist or are difficult. This distance is precisely what led to a desire to study in greater depth the situation in small companies. The case studies, which are analysed below, point to explanations for this situation.

7 For a statistical and qualitative analysis of the application of the employee representation system in French companies with more than twenty employees, see Dufour *et al.*, 2004.

Table 8. Union presence in workplaces, by size (%)

	Workplaces by number of employees					
	20-49	50-99	100-199	200-499	500-999	1,000 and over
No union presence	77	50	28	15	4	3
1 union	15	29	35	18	8	3
2 unions	5	13	18	26	13	6
3 unions	2	5	12	22	25	18
More unions	1	3	7	19	49	70

Source: Enquête Réponse, 1999.

In fact, unions can claim to intervene in the life of small companies from the outside, either *via* collective agreements or their participation in the many joint bodies that make up French industrial relations, for example, vocational training bodies and employment tribunals. They also provide advice during individual and collective conflicts *via* their local cross-sector structures. A specific feature of the French trade union movement is that it has both sector-level (vertical) and local (horizontal) structures. The latter bring together the various sectors that are present in a given geographical area (locality, *département* or region). The local (cross-sector) trades councils are often approached by employees in small companies with no union section or members, in order to obtain legal or practical advice. These structures have been very involved in the new "mandating" procedure.

From a certain point of view, unions are part of the "social public order" (Jobert, 2000), which has developed over the decades during which labour law has evolved. State recognition of trade unions and the devolution of the State's executive tasks – more than their strength in terms of autonomous representation – seem to be behind union involvement in small companies.

Employers' organisations' relations with their own members are not exempt from the same kind of remarks.

3. The State Is Omnipresent in Many Different Ways

The State is directly involved in the production of labour standards. This is a strong historical tradition, which gives it the role of guaranteeing citizens' equality in all aspects of their existence (Dufour, 1992). Employers' organisations and trade unions, which have the right to make agreements solely thanks to State recognition of their representativeness, only have a secondary role in relation to that of the State.

The majority of trade unions consider that sharing roles should not lead to less State intervention. Employers' organisations, however, never cease to stigmatise State interventionism. But, as we have seen above, they leave de facto the door open to State intervention, because of the feeble contribution of collective agreements. It should be added that, since the end of the Second World War and until recently, most big companies had to deal more or less directly with the State. Some were directly state-managed or nationalised (rail and air transport, the post office, telecommunications, energy, part of the car industry and most of banking and insurance) or had to be in direct contact with the State about their markets (aeronautics, steel industry and shipyards, etc.).[8]

The State intervenes in four main ways regarding the setting of labour standards, which theoretically apply to all companies (this declared principle will be analysed below).

The legal framework. It is a means of wide-ranging intervention that concerns the legal nature of work relationships between employers and employees, rules concerning employee representation and collective bargaining (see above), as well as issues related to work organisation within companies (labour code). Working time, for example, has been subjected to strong stipulations in French legislation for several decades: weekly hours, working time, organisation of daily schedules, length and organisation of leave, retirement age and so forth. The recent episode on the reduction of working time represents a change, less in relation to the legal framework, but rather in terms of it having led to much collective bargaining on a topic, which previously involved "simply" applying very complex legal stipulations within companies (Freyssinet, 1997).

Collective agreements. The law gives organisations that are recognised as being representative (by the State) the right to negotiate collective agreements. The latter apply to all employees if a representative trade union signs, but only to the members of the employers' organisation, if it signs. Extension to all employees by the authorities of collective agreements signed by unions and employers' organisations makes up for the weakness of the representativeness of the signatories; it also

---

8 There are many direct State employees in France (about a quarter of all employees). They are mainly employed in qualified jobs (teaching, health and administrative functions, etc.), which provide them with average pay that is higher than that of private sector employees. They have their employment for life, a status which is an implicit reference regarding social "normality". The "civil servant" (*fonctionnaire*) is a mythical image in conversation in small companies – it is both envied and disparaged.

gives the agreed compromises the same weight as legislation. The detail of legal stipulations limits the collective bargaining opportunities for unions and employers' organisations. This situation can oblige those involved in collective bargaining to be innovative, in order to come up with original standards; but it can also – as is often the case – lead to their putting stipulations into the agreements, which do not differ significantly from existing legislation.

The labour inspectorate and legal institutions. The State has decentralised resources for checking the application of legislation and collective agreements in the workplace. The labour inspectorate can ask any employer in the private sector for an explanation of the situation in their company – and, if necessary, impose penalties. Locally, such intervention differs depending on company size. Labour inspectors – who are high-level civil servants – monitor companies with more than 50 employees. Labour controllers monitor small companies, of which there are often thousands within their area. They are also civil servants, but are subordinate to the labour inspectors and are much less mobile geographically and in terms of their civil service status than the latter. The labour inspectorate is a source of advice and consultation that is used a lot by both employers and employees. However, the former often use their own legal experts, in order to avoid "being noticed" by the inspectorate's services. The latter, on the contrary, sometimes want to draw the attention of the State services to the situation in their company. In spite of its lack of resources, the labour inspectorate is a real force for intervening locally.

Employment tribunals (*conseils de prud'hommes*) are legal structures, which are composed of an equal number of employer and DPs, who are elected every five years (the last such elections were held in December 2002). These tribunals are locally based and divided into sections according to business activity (industry, commerce, agriculture and other). And there is also a special section for professional and managerial staffs. They are real arbitrators in the local labour market (Hege, Dufour, 2004). As decisions have to be majority ones, if there is not unanimity, one of the sides (employees or employers) is necessarily divided. If there is no majority, then the case is sent to another legal body, without the participation of the "voluntary" elected members. Most of those who go to employment tribunals are employees of small and very small companies. Employees and employers of bigger companies know how to find internal solutions to problems, in order to avoid using employment tribunals, which imply a negative image of the companies concerned. Employers fear employment tribunals, as employees turn to them when they are pretty certain of gaining satisfaction, i.e. when their employer has not legally respected their employment contract. Statistics show that the great majority of judgements are favourable to employees. Thus, the threat of being "dragged to the employment tribunal" by an employee is taken very seriously by their employer. Condemnation by an employment tribunal – which is a local body and composed of one's peers – is seen primarily as moral stigmatisation, which can also turn out to be very expensive. It is significant, however, that conflicts brought before employment tribunals are mainly related to conditions regarding the end of the labour contract (dismissal) – as if employees of small companies consider it taboo to use the tribunals to resolve conflicts that occur during their employment relationship. Employment tribunals have considerable powers to reinstate employees, but they rarely use them, because they know that such a decision would lead to practical difficulties, both for the employer and employee concerned.

Joint management bodies. A large number of functions are delegated by the State to joint bi-partite (employers and unions) or tri-partite (employers, unions and the State) management bodies. This is the case regarding the social security system; the unions are represented in management bodies regarding the health service, unemployment, retirement pensions and so forth. There are also specialised joint bodies for small and medium-sized companies in the area of vocational training (Blassel, Jacquier, 1997). Many of these joint bodies exist both at national and local levels or depend on local initiatives that involve local employer and union players. However, there is curiously little information about the density of coverage of joint management bodies throughout the country. No such assessment is made either by the State or the various organisations concerned, which devote considerable time and energy to these bodies.

II. Small Companies and Their Players: Survey of Industrial Relations Regulation

A. Preliminary Questions and Access to the Field

The labour code, collective agreements and the legal minimum wage constitute a dense and detailed frame of reference regarding industrial relations in the workplace and setting working conditions and pay. Although big and small companies are generally in the same situation, the legal framework imposed from the outside is, in practice, more flexible for small companies. They benefit from legal adjustments that are related to size and are often able to avoid strict application of standards, which should or could apply to them. Thus, many of them do not implement the law concerning employee representation structures.

Small companies, therefore, differ from big ones – and also vary amongst themselves – in terms of an unequal or smaller degree of conformity with the range of institutions, which are designed to also take into account some of their specific features. What are the consequences for industrial relations and the quality of standards? What are the main obstacles to unionisation in small companies? Is the hypothesis verified that the various institutions promote equality by rendering industrial relations in small companies similar to those in big companies, thus preventing them from going along different paths? Do reduced rights and obligations deprive employees in smaller companies of their means of defence? Does a lack of representation institutions have the same impact on very small companies as on relatively bigger units?

These questions (amongst others) guided the surveys that were carried out in the winter of 2001/2002 by a team of Franco-German researchers in ten small companies in western and west-central France. For the researchers of both countries, these surveys followed on from many previous ones. Cross-country analysis made it possible to add to the range of questions concerning the French situation. The small size of the sample made it necessary to use monographs. It involved identifying the coherence of each individual case and capturing its original features and its points in common with the other individual cases. Rather than using pre-determined groups on the basis of a subtle range of variables, the aim was to identify and analyse analogies and differences by comparing the rationale behind the actions of the different social groups concerned.

The surveys were carried out in two areas of France with contrasting economic and social features.[9] A feature of the west-central region of France is its weak economic fabric. High tech companies have arrived in the region recently. Both employers and employees come from rural areas and are strongly attached to the land. There is little unionisation in an environment that is marked by the influence of the Catholic Church and employer autocracy, which is often anti-union. Pay levels are low. Low unemployment rates can be partly explained by young people moving to urban areas.

The other area – Brittany – has gradually lost its former industrial centres. Unemployment is high. There is greater union presence than in west-central France; the CFDT is the strongest trade union. The union movement has its roots in a regionalist political tradition. The small companies that were studied are in a regional city and also a formerly

[9] We chose areas, in which we had already carried out surveys on mandating (Dufour, Hege *et al.*, 2000) – most of them concerned thirty or so small companies.

industrial middle-sized coastal town, which is now centred on the tourist industry.

Various intermediaries were approached, in order to identify companies for the survey – active members of employers' organisations, union officers, labour inspectors and controllers; the telephone directory was also used. As is often the case in this kind of survey, the sample was drawn up both gradually and pragmatically – the features of the first company gave an idea of the requirements for the next one. Thus, a visit to a very small company provided an incentive to then look for a relatively bigger one, while a visit to a long-standing company preceded making contact with a recent company start-up. A unit devoted to the provision of services followed an industrial workplace. Contact with a non-unionised company led to looking for a unionised one, and so forth. Our sample covered a lively and diversified field in terms of business activities and results, types of qualifications, gender distribution, employers' careers, trade union situations, etc.

Table 9. The French sample of small companies

Work-places visited	Date of creation	No. of employees	Employee trends	Status	Representative institutions / Union representatives				Contact	
					DP	CE	DS	M[3]	E[4]	S[5]
Consultancy company	1993	8	Upward	I[1]					•	
Insurance company	1965	11	Upward	I				•	•	•
CAD company	1989	30	Upward	I	•				•	
Hotel-restaurant	1950s	28	Stable	I				•		•
Garage (sales and repairs) (subsidiary)	1960s	70	Stable	G[2]	•	•				•
Garage (sales and repairs) (holding)	1988	63	Stable	I	•	•			•	
Clothing factory	1970	40	Down-ward	G	•	•	•			•
Production of electronic boards	1981	120	Down-ward	I	•	•	•		•	•
Car equipment factory	Buyout 1998	60	Stable	G	•	•	•			•
Computer-engineering company	1988	200	Upward	G	•	•		•		•

1) Independent 2) Belongs to a company or group 3) Mandating 4) Employer 5) Staff (employee).

All the workplaces that were visited are in the private sector. As far as the other criteria are concerned, the French sample sometimes diverged from the original rules that were decided upon for the transnational research. Some of the companies, which were originally small, had grown and exceeded the threshold of 100 employees. But, we were interested to learn about the consequences of such rapid growth for industrial relations. Others had been taken over or merged – former family companies were no longer independent and had become part of a (big) company or a group; but we wanted to know what effects these changes had on employees and management. Such infringements of the rules not only point to the changing nature of companies, whose features are never stable; they also reflect the perception of small companies held by those practitioners who were asked to help us in our research – their pre-selection is, by definition, subjective. By following their proposals and relying on their necessarily partial practical experience, we came up against the kaleidoscopic nature of the situation, which we were seeking to analyse. *The* small company resists unequivocal definitions and approaches that universalize. We preferred to approach them by these doors, which opened virtually "by chance", rather than meticulously respecting a rigorous catalogue of criteria, which were considered to be objective and unifying.

Our transnational specifications provided for semi-directive interviews both with the employer or their representative and, separately, with an employee representative. In France, it was not always possible to implement this principle of two interviews, which makes it possible to compare employee and employer points of view (see the table). The reasons for this varied – absence of the chosen interviewee; overloaded work programmes or difficult industrial relations situations; separate interviews were considered superfluous in very small units. We considered these recurring incidents in the course of the survey as elements of the research, i.e. pieces of the puzzle, rather than reasons for elimination, even if the absence of a two-sided view obviously constitutes a limiting factor for the survey.

The ten small French companies, which were visited, have contrasting industrial relations features. Often the intermediaries, who indicated them to us, justified their interest in them by their original nature and thus the interest they could have for us. At the beginning, it was possible to divide them into four groups, according to the kind of social dialogue existing in them – which should not be confused with respect for the official framework of standards. The kaleidoscope of "possible" industrial relations within the various groups then required more in-depth analysis of players in small companies, in order to find explanations and elements of synthesis.

B. Varied Small-Scale Industrial Relations Compromises

What is the rationale behind relations between employers and their employees in small work units? Our survey did not lead to one model that is especially telling or predominant. The case studies nevertheless do converge on one particular point, namely that the employer plays a decisive role in terms of providing impetus. The industrial relations identity of small companies seems to find its epicentre in the employer figure, even though in practice it has varying – and often contradictory – features. The entries that are used to approach our subject are thus firstly with employers, who do not analyse and organise their industrial relations role in the same way. Four types emerge from our survey, which obviously do not cover the whole range of possibilities.

1. Irreproachable Industrial Relations – Active Members of Employers' Organisations

Three employers, who are active in the regional structures of their employers' organisations, opened the doors of their companies to us – a group of consultants, a computer-aided design company and an insurance company. These employers were keen to tell us about their twofold experience as heads of companies and militant entrepreneurs. They have great benchmarking ability in the area of industrial relations management in small companies, which is nourished both by their occupational activity and their presence in employers' circles. These young men, who are heads of (very) small growing companies, want to promote in employers' organisations the ideas regarding business and industrial relations management that they are trying to implement in their own companies. Nor do they neglect the marketing and networking possibilities that participation in employers' representation offers. They are ready to criticise heads of companies, who (in their view, the great majority) are not very competent or even helpless in the area of industrial relations; whereas they set themselves targets of excellence, whose business and industrial relations aspects are almost inseparable.

The heads of the consultancy and CAD companies are both former executives of big companies. They each started up their own company with an associate at the beginning. They have differing plans for the future. The former does not exclude the possibility of selling his company once its market value has taken off. The other has a long-term plan of installing and developing a company that will create skilled employment in an area that has very little – in this case, entrepreneurial spirit and local commitment are closely interrelated. The insurance broker's business is headed by an heir and his mother, who had founded it. She persuaded him to change his occupation, in order to ensure the future of the family project.

All three companies count on the added value of a skilled and competent workforce (many of whom have managerial and professional staff status), in order to become permanently established in the market. However, they do not pay generously in order to attract and keep staff – pay is in line with the market. The SMIC is the reference for new recruits and/or the less skilled. They consider that they offer their employees other advantages, such as valorisation of externally marketable skills, the company's industrial relations climate, high quality social dialogue and an attractive concept of each person's work. The head of the CAD company knows that a job in the region is worth a certain amount of financial sacrifice in the eyes of a workforce, which is often forced to leave the area against its wishes: "We don't even try to keep the others – they are already in Toulouse or Paris". Pay increases are thus managed carefully and meticulously in the name of business development and permanent jobs.

These companies make it a point of honour to treat their staff as professionals and responsible adults, who should be allowed to say what they think and be listened to. The tiny size of the consultancy firm means that the head of the company thinks that any formal organisation of the social dialogue is superfluous – it is organised at the level of individuals. In both of the other companies, employees are regularly invited to meet with or without the employer. They have thus discussed – on the employer's initiative – the possibility of going over to a 35-hour week. Their opinion influenced the final decision. In the insurance company, they anticipated the legal obligation to reduce working time and, at the same time, gave their approval to the company's development plans, which were linked to it. In the CAD company, the employees decided to abandon – at least temporarily – the idea of reducing working time, because they considered the strict monitoring of working time demanded by the mandating union to be over the top. Employees also receive regular information about the business and financial situation of the company and management does not hesitate to tell staff about the difficulties of the business situation and their worries about it; they also ask them for their opinion, without jeopardising the hierarchy.

Although there are frequent discussions, they do not lead to the creation of representation bodies – rather, the contrary was observed. In line with the minority opinion in his employers' organisation, the head of the consultancy company is against them on principle, even if the legal threshold is reached: "These structures are not adapted to our situation in small companies". His counterpart in the insurance company seems to be much of the same opinion. The signing of the agreement on the 35-hour week required union mandating and the employee concerned joined the union (the employer paid her union dues). However, elections for DPs were not organised. Relations with the mandated employee "are sufficiently good for it not to be necessary to formalise the situation", according to the employer. This was confirmed by the mandated employee: "Here, there is not much point in holding elections – we are a bit like a family". According to the head of the CAD company, there probably would not have been a unionised employee representative in his company, if he himself had not been a union representative in the past and thought it unconceivable for there not to be any. An employee, who is very good professionally and has responsibilities in the company, had to be pushed to take on the responsibility of employee representative.

These heads of small companies say they are attentive to their employees' needs and know them well. They ensure that new recruits integrate well and look after the careers of longer-serving employees. Festivities are also an integral part of the life of the company. At the same time, employers' attention is resolutely turned towards the outside world. They seem to consider themselves to be part of a kind of entrepreneurial aristocracy as a result of their management and industrial relations qualities. They also attribute this attitude to the fact that they spend "a lot of time" outside, in order to personally promote their company: "There is no point in seeing no further than the end of one's nose. It is essential to open the door of the company and see what is going on elsewhere". This also implies fully recognising the occupational autonomy of their employees – without being either too cautious or naïve.

2. *The Door Wide Open to Representatives... with Rather Uncertain Status*

Two companies, which seem quite different, have relatively similar histories regarding bargaining on the 35-hour week *via* union mandating: a small hotel-restaurant in the centre of France and a state-of-the-art software production company in Brittany. During these negotiations, the external players, who were our intermediaries, had close relations for a period of time with both the employer and DPs. On the basis of such experiences that are considered to be positive, they plead in favour of nuanced analysis of mandating – a subject, which those around them are often suspicious of, or even hostile to. Both said they are impressed by certain mandated employees, who are not well equipped and do not have trade union links, but are totally involved in their task and achieve results, which are relatively favourable for employees. The agreements they sign are often very comparable to those signed elsewhere by union representatives.

Working time is a tricky and on-going issue in both of the companies, whose employees are quite different as far as qualification levels are concerned. In the hotel-restaurant, employees are often low-skilled. They are subjected to long split working hours, which are a feature of occupations in the kitchen, as well as waiting and reception work. The sector-level collective agreement is "poor", according to the mandated employee, both in terms of pay increases and paid holidays. The SMIC reigns. Sharp increases in workloads generate stress and tension. In some occupations, there is high staff turnover, although less than in comparable workplaces. The employers (a couple) offer their staff "human and dignified" working conditions. They facilitate internal promotion: "When someone has proved themselves, they can take on responsibility", according to the mandated employee. The employers do not take liberties with apprentices' rights, which is often the case elsewhere.

Stress is also a constant state of affairs in the software company, which grew rapidly before recently being sold and incorporated into a group. The majority of employees are highly qualified engineers. They are young and ready to be greatly involved in projects that they carry out independently. There is considerable discrepancy between the collective agreement and the employees' actual situation. Employees are individualised and labour market tensions mean that high-level professionals sometimes have considerable scope for negotiating their situation. Frequent long hours are experienced as an inevitable constraint of the job, which is counterbalanced by the fact that the work is interesting. Employees also submit to an implicit constraint of continuous self-training on top of the official training programme – it is a matter of keeping up with an occupation that is constantly and rapidly changing. Those who are not single – and amongst them, especially women (who constitute a minority in the company) – feel this implicit pressure for permanent involvement most: "We live with it and each person makes choices", in the knowledge that defending family life can be paid for at the price of slower promotion.

In the hotel and restaurant sector, there is great reluctance regarding the reduction of working time, which is considered to be incompatible with the nature of the sector. There are special arrangements for delaying the application of the law on the 35-hour week. The head of the hotel-restaurant, therefore, did the opposite of his peers – when urged by the union officer, who is a member of his football club, he accepted to anticipate bargaining on the reduction of working time. There are no DPs in this company, which employs almost 30 staff. The problem was entrusted to the young accountant, who became the mandated employee. Like the other employees, her relatively low level of qualifications and lack of work experience were not negative factors when she was recruited (nor do they affect her career negatively). It was felt that she could take initiatives and assume responsibilities. Her employer gave her great independence when preparing the agreement, as he knew that she is in constant contact with the different groups of employees and is well acquainted with the business and financial situation of the company.[10] On her side, she made sure with the labour inspectorate and the mandating union that her draft agreement was feasible. It must make it possible to recruit staff (thanks to subsidies written into the law) and reduce the overall workload of employees, while at the same time respecting the specific constraints of the occupations concerned in terms of flexibility: annually-calculated pay is the price to pay for the reduction in working time. She draws a qualified assessment of the agreement: if, on the one hand, "every minute" is counted and paid *via* the installation of time-clocks, employees in the most stressful occupations also have the feeling that they "do more in less time", in spite of more free time, which is highly appreciated.

In the software company, which was previously small and now big, the comité d'entreprise is not unionised. Union mandating is, therefore, also necessary in this company for the purposes of collective bargaining. One of the elected members of the comité d'entreprise has taken on this responsibility, but continues to work closely with the other members as a team on bargaining issues as well. In relation to the mandating union, they reaffirm the specific features of the company, no less than management does – any suggestion of "inflexibility" is considered to be inopportune. The comité d'entreprise listens to non-union experts and counterparts in similar companies, as well as seeking information on the Internet, in order to forge an opinion. Arbitration also concerns additional free time on the basis of "freely agreed" adjustments of work schedules.

Management of both companies gives the formal or informal representatives considerable autonomy. In the hotel-restaurant, the young accountant is directly encouraged to develop real "skills in the area of industrial relations" – both knowledge of labour law and the ability to listen to employees – which the employer is not sure of having without upsetting hierarchical relationships. The comité d'entreprise in the software company hardly comes up against any obstacles for implementing an ambitious training plan, in line with company practices. Its young director accepts – sometimes unenthusiastically – that it seeks to access rights that were previously neglected, such as, for example, an

10 When contacted for the survey, the head of the company referred us to the accountant: "She will be able to explain everything as well as, if not better than, me".

outside expert's assessment of the business situation of the company paid for by the employer. Given the existence of the works council over several years and their experience with the 35-hour week, members of the works council are thinking about taking the plunge and joining a union, in order to consolidate their position in relation to their employer: "The works council now thinks that we would have more weight if we were unionised". In both companies, representatives feel that they – and the employees in general – experience more open-mindedness and are listened to more than is the case in many companies in their respective sectors. This, however, does mean that, at times, they think it is necessary to add their "voice" to that of the employees – company rationale is not always in perfect harmony with staff aspirations.

Although employers say that they are neutral on these matters, they in fact adapt rather well to a situation, in which the representatives do not demand an institutionally more solid status: DP in some places; unionised comité d'entreprises and union representatives in others. Employees make their choice in the knowledge of its limits – and without saying anything about the long-term.

3. Uncertain Industrial Relations Management and Very Mediocre Compromises

The garages that we sought to contact, in order to compare them with their German counterparts, are competitors. They are situated just a few hundred yards from each other in a middle-sized town in Brittany. We found them *via* the telephone directory. We were not introduced by known intermediaries and were received with a certain degree of curiosity. However, our request to have two interviews (with the employer and an elected representative) was met with some reluctance and not satisfied – we met the works council treasurer (a blue-collar worker) in one and the chairperson and managing director (*Président-directeur général*, PDG) in the other.

One of the garages became a subsidiary of a group after a period of business difficulties that led to redundancies. Several directors appointed by central management followed in quick succession. The other garage took the opposite path. In a period of strong tension in the sector, when financial profitability and concentration were taking on greater importance, the employer, who had taken over a family company founded by his father-in-law, bought up several small and middle-sized bankrupt garages. The survey took us to the family company, which has remained the biggest unit. Increasing the size of the holding is a big ambition of the employer, who trained as a chartered accountant. In both companies, the mechanics and the sales staff constitute two somewhat separate worlds, which put other occupations into the background

– especially the administrative staff. Both the market and competition influence pay-setting more than the collective agreement, which is considered to be out of step. Professional magazines may be used to establish transparency regarding current market pay standards. Both garages have non-unionised comité d'entreprises (in fact, DUs) – in the parent company of the holding, it was created following on from the 35-hour week law; in the subsidiary, it has been in existence for longer, but with periods when it did not function.

The players concerned consider that their comité d'entreprise functions "as it should"… without producing significant results. Blue-collar workers are the driving force; professional and managerial staffs participate, but are not active. Legally-required monthly meetings are held; business information is given sparingly; paid time-off for representation functions "can be taken"; employees have a budget for social and cultural activities. The budget is calculated very precisely at the basic minimum and is thus, in fact, diverted from its original function, i.e. the budget that is legally meant for the functioning of the works council is used to pay for an annual outing and Christmas parcels. The elected members of the comité d'entreprise discuss technological developments, which are changing the nature of the jobs in the workshops – without much hope of achieving anything. Technological know-how is increasingly concentrated on a few technical advisors, who benefit from state-of-the art training. They become increasingly advanced compared with the repair mechanics, who are rarely sent on training, as "there is never enough money", according to the treasurer of the subsidiary's works council.

Workshop employees are impatient for bargaining on the 35-hour week to start. With this prospect, there was a high degree of participation in the CE's elections. However, management in both companies are reluctant. They are resigned to it, "because it's the law and, as other companies have done it, we have to, because of competition and the labour market situation". But the holding's chairperson and managing director recognises that the result did not meet employees' expectations and has led to unrest in the company. Pay moderation – the price to pay for the reduction of working time and recruitment of a few employees in the workshops – was badly accepted by staff, who considered themselves to be already low-paid; more flexible work schedules have not taken into account the needs of life outside the workplace. Nor is this flexibility really adapted to the seasonal nature of the work in a tourist town. The employer remarked: "I was afraid that people would lose the habit and taste for working if they had too much leave or periods of too little work".

Management of the garage that became a subsidiary eventually put an end to discussions, by deciding unilaterally – after consulting central management – to set new collective weekly working hours at 38 and use overtime to reach an average of 35. No one was recruited and work was not reorganised. This led to a few very angry meetings in the repair workshop, but nothing else. According to the elected representative, the staff are "calm" and stable. As there were no labour market alternatives, the employees did not do anything else, even though they were very dissatisfied.

In this sector, which is highly competitive, management is aware that any errors cost a lot – bankruptcies in the local area provide clear evidence of this. In both companies, business concerns obscure industrial relations concerns, thus running the risk of provoking latent staff dissatisfaction and demotivation. The business and financial confidence of the holding's chairperson and managing director, which enables him to consolidate his position in the market, is not accompanied by seasoned industrial relations management. He seeks in the law, the market and competition, rules that are not to be adapted to the specific features of the local labour situation, nor to be discussed with employees. There is a degree of uneasiness that can also be identified on the employer's side – he dreads inept industrial relations management in his other garages having a negative impact on results. The managers of these subsidiaries are often former marketing staff, who do not seek out social dialogue and are very reluctant about employee representation bodies. "I have to push them to accept such structures", observed the managing director.

In this context, the works council functions in a formal way, rather than really influencing the quality of industrial relations. The holding's chairperson and managing director is not unhappy to find a spokesperson, who enables him to conform to competition rules in this area as well… and who creates very few problems. In the neighbouring company, the lack of resources and success deprives the works council of greater ambitions. The treasurer, who is realistic, recognises the fragile nature of the structure, including as far as the employees are concerned: "Without the social and cultural fund, there would probably be no works council".

4. *Authoritarian Employers, Poor Standards and the Antidote of Workers' Solidarity*

Officers of the local CFDT (cross-sector) trades council served as intermediaries, in order to gain access to three companies with union representatives. These factories – a woman's clothing company, a manufacturer of electronic boards and a car equipment manufacturer – mainly employ unskilled and low-skilled women. All of the companies had undergone one or several restructuring processes involving redundancies.

At the time of the visit, the clothing company had already been sold and its staffing level reduced from 70 to 40. It was originally created by a professional dress designer and lasted longer than many of its counterparts that were struck down by the crisis. The professionalism of the owner, who had created her own brand name, retarded decline before over-ambitious plans in a context of chronic under-capitalisation led to bankruptcy. The employees were presented with a fait accompli, as was the comité d'entreprise – it had not been informed, contrary to legal obligations. The company was bought up by a competitor and continues production on a smaller scale.

The factory producing electronic boards is a subcontractor for national and foreign clients. It experienced regular growth before registering a significant drop in demand. In order to get out of this crisis situation, the couple, who own the company, partially withdrew from financial and industrial relations management, which they entrusted to professionals. Negotiations on the 35-hour week were started, which – with the public subsidies they give rise to – should lead to relaunching growth, which nevertheless remains hesitant. In order to cut costs, an increasingly big share of production is being relocated to North Africa. Information on company developments is disclosed very sparingly to staff and the works council. Management is concerned to formally respect representatives' prerogatives, but maintains a cold and distant climate between themselves and the elected DPs and union representatives. They are made to feel that employees' aspirations lie elsewhere and that their intervention is likely to worsen the company's business problems.

The car equipment manufacturer took over the site of a former food production factory and kept some of the staff. It is a subcontractor for a major company and one of several units. Public subsidies, which were paid for keeping staff after the relocation of the previous company, were a powerful reason for the buyout. At the time of the visit, the business situation was uncertain and there was high management turnover. Reducing labour costs is a major concern and in order to do so, labour law is not always respected. According to the elected representative, the many temporary agency workers are often forced to work longer hours and are not paid as they should be; safety standards are often ignored; and the comité d'entreprise is subjected to underhand and illegal surveillance. This situation of bullying and lack of respect for the law led to works council members joining a union. External players (the labour inspectorate, local authority and local health insurance office, etc.) seem to be reluctant to intervene, because many jobs are at stake.

In these companies, in which we met the trade union representatives (and only in one case, a member of management), authoritarian management makes employees feel unwanted. They have to defend themselves against the reproach of costing too much in uncertain business situations – and seem hardly to represent anything more than anonymous items on a balance sheet. Savings that can be made on pay are examined closely. Dressmakers cannot hope to be paid more than the SMIC, in spite of long service and confirmed skills; in the electronic components factory, the SMIC is only just reached, because the length of service bonus is an integral part of pay; after the buyout, the car equipment manufacturer removed all accumulated rights to length-of-service payments, which were often great, from manual workers' pay.

Elected representatives reacted to combined business tensions and their employer's authoritarianism by joining a union. This led to the appearance of union representatives (DS). Elected CE's members, who are now union members, in the car equipment company said: "Before the buyout, there were no union representatives – only a works council"... "In those days, we did not see the point – when there was a problem, we had a discussion with management and it was dealt with quickly".

However, elected representatives in neither the clothing factory nor the electronics company described the industrial relations climate as being totally bad. Manual workers do not lack cohesion: "We are united and have always supported each other", according to the union representative in the clothing factory – the same thing was said in the electronics factory. Production workshops are sociable places that play an important role in women workers' lives – they have worked together for many years and are "rather happy to come and work here".

C. External Standards – Obvious, Necessary and Adjustable Points of Reference

Although small companies in France develop very varied industrial relations compromises internally, they are similar in other ways. Reference to systems of external standards – laws, collective agreements and markets – is a common denominator. These standards play an obvious and somewhat "natural" role in daily industrial relations, as well as being put into perspective and adapted to circumstances. In small "work communities", reference to external standards tends to make players similar, more than it differentiates them.

The legal minimum wage plays a major role in determining the existential conditions of small companies. It is directly applied to many employees or is used as a yardstick. We often heard the following statements during our survey: "Here, pay is a little higher than the

SMIC"; "It is hardly at the level of the SMIC"; "It is way above the SMIC...". When fixing pay, the SMIC plays a much greater role than collective agreements, which the players concerned – both employers and employees – often criticise. Either sector-level collective agreements set minimum pay below the SMIC and are, therefore, in any case inapplicable (or coincide with legal pay and are thus superfluous), or they are considered to be unrealistically high in view of the local labour market situation. Employers are able to name the relevant collective agreement, but do not know which specific aspects directly concern their company.

Sector-level collective agreements do, however, play a role as far as standards are concerned. It is true that job classification scales are often a formal, rather than a real, reference point – they are used to grade employees according to their pay, rather than according to the profile referred to in the collective agreement and then apply the appropriate precise pay category. A particular grade is given to an individual's pay claim, rather than the other way round. However, the existence of a set of rules regarding occupations is not considered insignificant, while anomy – or a lack of standards – in labour matters, is not generally desired. In fact, there is rather a tendency to criticise collective agreements for not being sufficiently concerned about "real conditions" regarding pay on the ground. Collectively agreed standards tend to be set "at a low level" and thus are often of uncertain use and hardly useful for comparison with competitors. Players in small companies do not really identify with the idea that collective agreements are especially aimed at them, in order to try and ensure that the gap between labour standards in big and small companies does not grow wider.

In the small companies covered by our survey, there is thus a tendency not to set market forces against legal and collectively agreed standards. Rather, interaction is anticipated, whereby the market incorporates the principles of regulation provided by State and collectively agreed standards – and the standards themselves incorporate the market situation, or at least do so at the (often implicit) adjustment margins, which they seem to authorise. In all of the companies, the market – and especially the local labour market – is an essential and unavoidable point of reference. This does not lead to uniform behaviour – it is possible to align industrial relations management on that of competitors or to be different – but it highlights small companies' great dependence on the economic situation and that of the labour market. Those employers, who are most attached to their industrial relations responsibilities, are not the last to use their networks and other channels of information, in order to have detailed knowledge of the state and practices "of the market", in order to adjust their labour standards, regarding pay, bonuses and leave, etc. Generally, "the market" tends to justify careful, if not restrictive, management of pay standards in the small companies that we visited.

Labour law is another unifying element that is meant to attach individual small companies to the general framework of standards. The players concerned do not refuse to recognise the standards, according to which their practices can be judged. Often employers depend on internal accountants or external chartered accountants – more rarely on employers' organisations or the labour inspectorate – in order to help them understand "what we can, and cannot, do" regarding recruitment, dismissal, fixed-term contracts, temporary agency work and tax subsidies, etc. The laws on the 35-hour week required such mediation, in order to understand their complexity and be able to decide how to adapt them to the needs and possibilities of their own company. In this particular case, public debate and employees' expectations made it almost impossible to purely and simply ignore them.

The creation of employee representation bodies is one of the legal stipulations, which employers consider should be adjustable in line with local conditions. The legal threshold for having DPs (DP) seems to be significantly lower than the actual size of companies, in which they exist generally – regardless of employers' staff policies. Comité d'entreprises (single employee representation, DU) seem to be "more natural" in companies (with more than 50 employees) that are meant to have them. However, the fact that they exist because of legal stipulations does not mean that they exercise the functions required by the law, nor that the members, who occupy those functions, exercise the prerogatives linked to their functions (paid time-off and information, etc.).

Relatively general reference by players to external State and collectively-agreed standards is thus two-sided. On the one hand, there seems to be consensus regarding the principle of regulation, i.e. the fact that a series of constraints (protections from the employees' point of view) apply to all players does not lack legitimacy, especially as these constraints introduce an element of transparency into competition. On the other hand, the relatively formal nature of the standards is also a factor of acceptance; both employers and employees in small companies know that, as far as whole areas are concerned, standards do not have to be applied as such, and therefore there is considerable scope for flexibility. It is possible, as the example of the garages showed, to perfectly respect collective agreements and the rights of works councils without there being any visible impact on the labour standards in force in the workplace. The fact that links with representative employers' organisations and trade unions are very tenuous makes the scope for local arrangements even greater. Those serving as reference points, who would promote a unifying interpretation of the collective agreements and their underlying spirit, are mainly absent. Conversely, the fact that national players are far removed from the specific situation of small companies promotes the creation of purely formal standards, rather than ones with substance.

D. The Uncertain Legitimacy of External Industrial Relations Players

Institutional presence of trade unions in small companies is very rare. In most cases, the union (whichever one it is) is considered – both by employees and employers – to be a not very desirable participant in internal company life. Many reasons are given for such distrust. They range from ideological disagreements ("The union is primarily political") to organisational and practical reproaches ("If only they would agree"; "It leads to disagreements and fights"), as well as the feeling of their being strange ("It's not for us – it's for big companies"). Both employee and employer interviewees generally claim not to know whether there are union members in the company.

During interviews with employees, who have relations with unions (either because they are themselves members or because they are mandated representatives), such remarks do not disappear, but are less pronounced. Union members want pragmatic relations with their union, namely legal advice, practical data and sources of information. The union does not itself say how it differs from the labour inspectorate, thus reinforcing a lack of understanding of the specific identity of union demands. The main difficulty seems to come from union demands that members should distance themselves from their employer and set themselves apart from their company's interests.

As for union officers, they refer to this difficulty in a symmetrical way. Employees contacted in small companies "are under their employer's thumb". Unions have a pretty negative assessment about demands regarding job security coming from employees in small companies ("They are very vulnerable, what with unemployment…") – this kind of demand seems an insurmountable obstacle to any form of collective action. In none of the contacts we had with unions, did they seem very sensitive to, or understanding about, the priority of employment linked to the vulnerable situation of small companies. However, they mobilise fairly easily when a situation of job losses leads employees to seek their help during a conflict.[11] They also point out employees'

[11] Interviews of union officers in a coastal town in Brittany showed that they recognised that they were absent from small companies, except when there is a conflict after redundancies, but without that leading to any lasting trace in what remains of

rights to create representation structures in small companies – they refer to legislation in this area, but do not consider whether it is credible for employees, who contact them, to apply such legislation. Both of these attitudes – namely not taking into account the defence of jobs centrally, on the one hand, and reaffirming the principle of available rights, on the other – combine to render union involvement meaningless for employees in small companies.

However, "employee advisors" (*conseillers du salarié*) arouse greater interest. They are individuals, who often have very close links with a union, and can intervene when requested to do so by an employee to accompany him/her regarding contacts with the employer, in order to resolve a conflict. Candidates for this role must be registered with local State services. This activity takes up a lot of the advisors' time and, therefore, they are often pensioners. Very little research has been done on employee advisors, but they clearly occupy an important place in daily union practice regarding small companies.

The union structure concerned is usually the local (cross-sector) trades council. Occupational union structures, which are still mainly associated with big companies where they have members, are less visible than the local structures. Union officers of the cross-sector structures in both of the regions covered by the survey recognise that occupational structures are not interested in small units. "Union activists in big companies are more attracted by Paris and company structures, such as comité d'entreprises (CE), central works councils (*Comité central d'entreprise*, CCE), group works councils (*comité de groupe*), than by small companies, even if they are subcontractors working for their company. They have difficulty in finding time to be in contact with the latter, but they don't have difficulty in finding time to go to a meeting in Paris", was the reproach made by a full-time union officer in the central region.

Very few employers of small companies are active members of employers' organisations. Neither the business nor industrial relations role of these structures are used to explain internal company practices. Such active employers describe their involvement in terms of commitment, which is not shared by many of their colleagues in other such companies and even difficult to justify within their own company, when it leads to their being absent and adopting policy, etc.

Committed employers often take on several positions in both sector-level and local cross-sector structures and sometimes also in employ-

---

the company. This is exactly the same situation as that regarding employment tribunals, when unions are approached by individuals, who did not want anything to do with unions when they were in their job and who are reluctant to join, even during their tribunal case.

ment tribunals. They justify this by referring to the lack of candidates and also to the fact that it is logical. Relations with the State (labour law framework and various regulations) and also with the representation structures of big companies (MEDEF) are given as reasons for being involved. Designs regarding access to potential clients and markets *via* networking and notoriety are not always absent.

However, for the majority of employers, such organisations are not preferential contacts as far as managing their company is concerned. They quite freely admit to being quite rebellious in relation to these bodies, even when they are said to play a service role (chambers of commerce (*chambre de commerce*) and craft guilds (*chambre de métier*)). Compulsory membership is often criticised as being simply yet another tax without any real service provision, as they do the same thing as their own costly company service-providers (such as accountants and lawyers, etc.). The role of employers' organisations regarding collective bargaining is either not really understood or actually not known. In this area, the State is seen to be the main organiser, while employers' organisations and trade unions only play minor roles.

Personal demands and the objective need for a management style that is in line with the specific situation of the particular company are the main reasons for the lack of interest in collective management structures. However, this attitude is accompanied by the view that it is necessary to organise the labour market in order to avoid unfair competition. But this demand is made at the political level rather than to the industrial relations structures – both regarding business and labour issues. Nor are trade unions considered to be useful. When there is participation in one or other such structures, employers do not always feel that it is necessary to participate in the meetings. They send their accountant, number two or other close colleague in order to maintain the link and avoid losing relevant information and seeming provocatively uninterested. In many situations, especially in small towns, industrial relations are marked by close-knit local relations.

In spite of the large number of external collective standards, whose legitimacy is rarely challenged, players in small French companies have considerable freedom to determine their "own" labour standards. This partially explains the wide range of practices identified in the survey. The balance between business and industrial relations strategies, which is sought after – and achieved – in each particular company, therefore, varies greatly. The type of people and environment, as well as local labour history, often seems more influential than prescribed standards. How far does employers' freedom go in determining internal labour standards in their own way? In order to answer this question, it is necessary to examine in greater detail the relations and even the sociology of the players involved in small companies.

E. Unequal Relations and Mutual Constraints: Employers and Employees in Small Companies

Discussions and negotiations are not missing in small companies, even when they do not have representation bodies. However, the employer's pre-eminence is rarely challenged. Employees, in fact, tend to criticise unions for minimising too lightly (or because of lack of knowledge) the constraints that their employer has to deal with.

Employers are at the heart of the industrial relations system of the company, because of their distinguished position both in business and human resources terms. When they are entrepreneurs (and therefore not employed managers, who were also represented in our sample), they personally assume the business risks related to their production decisions, the vagaries of the market and also general current circumstances. Such business risks also have a human resources dimension – they have employees and want to promote the image of guaranteeing them a permanent workplace. At the same time, prospects of making their capital profitable depend on employees' good will in terms of contributing to business results. As they are *a priori* less mobile than their employees as a result of the twofold business and social link that attaches them to their company, owner-employers claim that they are doubly legitimate in their demand to be considered the predominant player as far as the production of labour standards is concerned. This is often referred to by employers, who never cease to recall the fact that the perpetuation of the company is not only a business aim, but also a moral value. Those who start up small companies and "refuse to grow", i.e. do not recruit, are severely criticised by entrepreneurs, who employ staff, accusing the former of "cheapening" or diminishing their role.

Employees acknowledge employers' pre-eminence in drawing up labour standards and thus do not only submit to a balance of business forces. They also have to adjust to the industrial relations and cultural dimensions, as well as the identity, of small companies. These dimensions are inseparable from the employer figure and are consolidated *via* close daily relations.

1. Range of Identities of Small Companies

The range of identities of small companies is built on references that occupy an essential place in the life of both employees and employers. The local, occupational and family ties of the company and their players play an important role in our case studies. They are firstly identified with the owner-employer's biography, which provide employees with many rallying points. However, identity is not just a one-way process.

The local situation, which the company is part of, strongly influences industrial relations compromises. Jobs are at stake – in regions that do not have many on offer – as is also the possibility of "living and working locally" (as the old slogan goes). Some employers base their company's identity on such roots. The head of the CAD company in the centre of France recruits young technicians from the countryside. They are proud to belong to a high-tech company, which enables them to stay in the region. The owner of the hotel-restaurant is careful to give a chance to local motivated youth to access skilled jobs, without asking for formal qualifications. The profile of local entrepreneurs also involves taking part in the local social fabric – the owner of the CAD company, who is active in the employers' organisation, has difficulty in drawing up a complete list of all the sports, educational and cultural associations he is a member of. Participation in local associations and sports activities offers his counterpart in the hotel the opportunity of developing friendly relations with clients, suppliers, decision-makers, as well as with former and future employees…

However, local shared identity does not always bring employers and employees closer together. They can have a paternalistic or authoritarian managerial style. In rural areas, employers and employees know each other well – they often went to the same school. This does not necessarily lead to reflexes of local solidarity. A labour controller told us that many small company owners in the centre of France tend rather to emphasise the gap between them, as well as their differences. They behave like "local notables", showing off external signs of wealth and success. Paternalism reveals its hard and intransigent (repressive) features, when there are problems between employer and employee(s). Employees' local ties and the fact that they are not used to protesting make it possible for employers to put pressure on pay and take liberties with labour law. Employment tribunals are used only as a last resort, when relations have become unbearable. A labour controller analysed the situation as follows: "The countryside is employees' life – they put up with what they have got".

Likewise, in companies in high-unemployment areas of Brittany, the local situation of the company, which is inextricably related to the (restrictive) conditions of their immediate environment, is strongly internalised by employees. This awareness of the local identity of the workplace, which does not mean that there is no mobility at all, no doubt goes further than the simple observation that "there is no alternative" to one's current job because of existing labour market conditions.

Employees also acknowledge that employers are objectively constrained by the situation.

The kind of occupation is also a strong reference point for identity, which produces a system of constraints and compensations recognised by both groups of players (management and employees). Heads of companies' professional excellence provide them with recognition. In the clothing company, the women manual workers accept highly subordinate relations, because of the quality of the product – in the knowledge these relations also constitute the basis for skills being passed on. On speaking about the employer's authoritarianism, the union representative emphasised: "We really do make beautiful clothes here". In the software company, working longer than official hours goes without saying in a demanding and highly-valued occupation. In the hotel-restaurant, the most skilled occupations (cooking and serving) cannot be conceived of other than in terms of split shifts and long working days, which are hardly compatible with normal life in society. However, such practices lead to occupational communities, which are proud of their differences. If, on the one hand, occupational reference points justify giving up certain things in the eyes of employees, on the other, they guarantee their autonomy. Reference to occupation is also somewhat exclusive in relation to other groups, for example, in this case, administrative staff and those in unskilled jobs in hotels and restaurants… It can also lead to conflicts between competitive occupational groups (e.g., sales staff versus mechanics), which are sometimes difficult to resolve when the employer's own occupation does not tip the balance one way or the other (as in the garage holding).

The family is a social institution that is very much present in negotiations on labour standards – as a value, a system of constraints and a metaphor, thus giving it special weight. No one escapes it – employers and employees are rarely able to organise their career paths totally separately from their family situation. Choice of occupation and career are often related to family history. For employees, who are not single, a change of job or a decision to persevere in spite of working conditions, which are considered to be bad, involves families as much as the individuals concerned. They are thus quite ready to recognise their employer's arguments and behaviour, which are justified by referring to family constraints.

Families contain the promise of permanency, which is a key value for players in small companies. When a company is passed on to children, it is not only a matter of bequeathing property and material value to one or several descendents, but also of ensuring the continuation of a line of descent. This may mean that heirs have to make decisions that involve sacrifices. The head of the insurance company thus decided to give up his military career in order to take on the company, which his mother had created. The heirs of the hotel-restaurant and one of the car dealers chose spouses, who would be compatible with managing a family firm. Other companies (because of a lack of heirs?) broke their promise of permanency, such as the clothing factory, which was sold after bankruptcy proceedings. New company start-ups rapidly come up against a choice – either their owner sees it as a personal adventure, which can be voluntarily ended once they have been successful (as was – or could be – the case of the young owners of the software and consultancy companies); or they opt for permanency with the risk (challenge) of having to take on board industrial relations discussions and conflicts that managing a company over time inevitably leads to. The owner of the CAD company took on board a kind of second family. Social integration and occupational socialisation of technicians at the beginning of their careers were, in his view, as passionate a project as that of developing high-tech tools, which make it possible to win markets.

The analogy between small companies and family circles is never far away. Here and there, employers and employees say: "We are a bit like a family". The moral responsibility and the responsibility regarding standards of this point of reference do not always have the same degree of influence, thus conjuring up both the "natural" subordination of children to parental authority and the duty of mutual support. However, it remains the case that – especially in very cohesive small companies and work processes that bring players together every day – employees do not escape such twofold allegiance, which links them in a somewhat fusional way to the community (the company "family") and also encourages them to find their autonomy (liberate themselves) in their work. We will see below that the involvement of (official and unofficial) DPs in small companies is also situated in this area of tension between fusion and autonomy.

Small companies' identities are, thus, built on concepts, which surpass by far the short- and medium-term business horizons of their productive activities. Behind local ties and family sagas, there is history, which transcends individuals – and even their generation. They find their place also *via* occupational socialisation. These implicit reference systems concern both groups of players, namely employers and employees, and on recognising themselves in them, they also recognise each other. At the same time, implicit standards are a source of great legitimacy for what employers do. And as we have already seen, they involve both risk management and autonomous decision-making. The influence of implicit references seems in some way to remove constraints related to employers' actions from open debate and turn them into factors that cannot be avoided. As they have less autonomy, employees seem less able to take advantage of these reference points for identity. The influence of implicit standards on the players involved clearly does not produce homogeneous business and industrial relations strategies. The family analogy also springs to mind here. This shared system of standards creates many links between the players – although they are not named as such, they play an important role – and can promote equalitarian or authoritarian industrial relations, cooperative or hegemonic ones, or even humanist or tyrannical ones, just as family life can be marked by subordination or respect, affection or indifference and tolerance or proscription.

2. Small Employers, Charismatic Power and Autonomous Decision-Making

Community spirit seems strongest in very small companies (under 50 employees). This kind of company is characterised by the obviously central position of the owner-employer, who is an emblematic figure and whose traits merge with the specific way in which they manage industrial relations. Family, occupational, political, religious, union ties, as well as psychological traits, temperament, charisma, relationship with the occupation, local integration methods and so forth all mean that small employers themselves, and also their companies, are unique social configurations.

The above holds provided the employer is, indeed, ready to link his or her destiny to that of the company. With distance, the specificity that employers are able to bring to the identity of their company is less marked. Because they see themselves as promoting the permanent nature of their company and its history, two company heads – a grandson of a military serviceman and himself a former serviceman and heir of his mother's start-up and a farmer's oldest son in an arid region – turned their own biographies and family histories into elements contributing to the "name" of the company. The situation is quite different for the company head, who is active in the employers' organisation and comes from a family linked to the labour movement – managing a company he started up is a stage on the way to something else, rather than an end in itself. In this case, his biography is part of his personal life and does not contribute to building collective identity.

The employer's central role leaves little room for employees to speak out independently. The employer's character determines the way young employees are greeted and integrated – but, in any case, they have to obey the rules that are in force. The CAD company head, who was tempted by the job of trainer, combines management concerns, employer's demands and "older brother" attention helping new technicians in the long process of training required before achieving professional fulfilment: "Here they have the right to make mistakes – it is important". The former owner of the clothing factory demanded silent obedience from those who had just finished their training. The employees concerned said: "We were dead afraid". But any idea of mutiny was in vain ("Ms. X just had to come into the workshop..."); yesterday's beginners were very thankful to her for having taught them "loads of things"; they emphasised that contact with an authoritarian person "also forges characters". In the hotel-restaurant, apprentices and new recruits cannot count on any indulgence or pity from management regarding the difficult and tiring working conditions, but they know that they themselves and their rights will be respected and their professional qualities recognised...

The way in which employees are involved – or not – in business discussions also highlights employers' differing temperaments, as much as their various management concepts, which do not, in the end, always lead to significantly different results. "Business" culture plays an important role in the insurance company, which has a strategy of regular and continuous information. However, no business information is given to the employees of the hotel-restaurant. The accountant heatedly said: "But people have eyes and, even if they have not had much education, they are not stupid". The women manual workers in the electronic components company talk rather ironically about the data they are given on the state of orders: "We have been twiddling our thumbs for weeks in the workshops". In the clothing factory, the manual workers heard about imminent bankruptcy from the bankers – they had not been informed about it at the works council meeting.

Behind employers' tendency to consider business reports as a more or less taboo topic, their approach to links within the community of their company can be identified. In the CAD company, many meetings are held around the huge central table in the meeting room; discussion and information have a place and often occur during festive moments. The arrival of the employer's last baby was thus fittingly celebrated: "That is part of the things we celebrate together – just like marriages, moving house and new cars". Informal relations predominate in the management consultancy company. According to the head of the company, its small size means that everyone meets everyone else at one time or another – and therefore it is unnecessary to regard discussions in plenary sessions as being "sacred". In the clothing factory, authoritarian relations are also related to a generational hierarchy, which is an additional reason for reserving strategic knowledge for a restrictive circle.

The "name" that employers give to their company also depends on an unstable balance, given that it is related to themselves. The central and emblematic person can leave. After the sale of the clothing factory, the owner was not greatly missed after her departure, but the manual workers felt rather abandoned: "It created a vacuum". Company growth can also lead to a redistribution of power, which makes it possible for other players to contest the employer's "charismatic" authority. This is what happened in the CAD company, when the company head spent more and more time outside the office to implement his development plans. Some of the board's members tried to "force their way", in order to break with a management style that they considered to be too friendly and open to discussion.

3. *The Social Order of Small Companies – in the Process of Becoming Bureaucratised*

Formalised hierarchical structures are not the preserve of companies above a particular size (50 or more employees) – the very small consultancy company uses it for managing complementary skills. The appearance of the bureaucratic principle leads to making business management autonomous, with human resources management (whether humanistic or repressive) seeming to depend less mechanically on it. Intermediate employees with specific responsibilities become more important, such as foremen and project supervisors, human resources directors and so forth. The reduced role of the employer as a force for integration seems to result from the growth of the company, without this being the only reason. Employees are thus partially freed from aspiring to the permanency of their employer's project, without this state of affairs promising improved labour standards or securer employment. The introduction of representative bodies and their routine functioning can also be seen as a response to the disintegration of the former close relationship between an employer's business and human resources management activities.

The rapid growth over fifteen years or so of the company producing electronic boards at first led to the consolidation of the business – in a favourable period for the electronics sector, a subsidiary was created. But the industrial relations equilibrium, which was characterised by authoritarian management, did not survive a period of stagnation and crisis. New players arrived in the company (associates and a human resources director) and criticised the "management errors" of the owners (a couple). The company founder's wife was removed from her position as accountant. The current human resources director considers the employer's methods to be "obsolete" and advocates radically subordinating human resources issues to business and management rationality. A union representative remarked on the growing isolation of the owner: "A few years ago, he was still highly thought of. He used to talk with everyone and organise meetings. Now, he comes into the workshop and hardly even says hello".

The garage holding is another example of the difficulties, in industrial relations terms, of a growing family firm. The managing and financial skills of the owner give him competitive edge and also contribute to consolidating his position in relation to the car manufacturer, who subjects growing dealers to increasingly precise criteria. At the same time, strong competition leaves little leeway for original human resources policies or an approach that promotes integration. Organisation of the cohabitation of the various occupational groups is not based on firm principles. Former sales employees, who have been promoted to the position of garage directors, hesitate to fully take on the industrial relations responsibilities entrusted to them. During bargaining on the reduction of working time, they did not dare introduce an explicit exchange between free time and reorganisation of work, which could have been understood and appreciated by employees, without reducing their productivity.

Company growth changes the industrial relations equilibrium, but does not necessarily threaten it. The computer experts in the software company owe their relatively appreciated industrial relations situation partly to their favourable position in the labour market, but also to a feeling of belonging to a community that is related to their age and occupation. After a period of rapid development and significant turnover, employees have had the time to free themselves from the charisma of their employer, who founded the company. Employee representation bodies have won a place as an obvious and important element of industrial relations management.

4. When Representation Appears

(Very) small companies with a community spirit seem to be most reluctant to create employee representation institutions. However, from a trade union point of view, they would perhaps be most useful in such companies. We have seen that employers are at the centre and able to create support for themselves and their management constraints. As employees have to willingly or forcefully "play the employer's game", they seem to have to put up with all the disadvantages, namely limited pay policy, poor working conditions, union repression and so forth. The creation of representative bodies under trade union auspices thus seems to be a necessary antidote to submission resulting from close contact, as well as being a lever for developing an opposition force capable of dealing with conflicts. But such institutions often seem out-of-reach. How was this dilemma reflected in our case studies? They tell a story, which is not inconsistent, in spite – or because – of their diversity.

There is nothing to stop one from thinking that, in (very) small companies marked by the employer's "charismatic power", the absence of

DPs and union activists is in line with the more or less explicitly formulated wishes of the employer. It seems clear that there is also significant reluctance on the employees' side. They have difficulty in finding candidates – and also perhaps find it even more difficult to authorise one of their colleagues to demand a certain distance and differentiation in relation to themselves – both of which are features of being a representative. Elections simply do not seem to make sense in very small units. They imply that elected representatives can, in a relatively autonomous way, carry out and take on board arbitration concerning all employees. In small (and not quite so small) companies, where elections of DPs and even works councils have been organised, representatives generally tend to minimise the influence of the structure and the significance of being singled out: "In fact, it doesn't make a big difference".

Although the employer's recognised pre-eminence is a barrier to the appearance of a declared opposition force, the opinion of the employees and that of the employer are not entirely the same – and both parties are aware of this. Bargaining in small companies on the introduction of the 35-hour week was no doubt very telling, rather than actually leading to a really new approach. It brought employees' expectations directly up against their employer's management rationale – at least employees know that there is little chance of them always coinciding perfectly. The 35-hour week – in the same way as other issues that do not get so much publicity – led to discussions amongst employees that also constituted a warning for the employer. Even before representative structures appear, employees find a way of "having a clear understanding" of what they should or should not "ask the employer for". Market constraints and those related to the employer's personality both affect decisions regarding explicit and implicit demands. In some cases, employers will stop any discussion from taking place and make a unilateral decision; in others, discussion amongst employees will be encouraged and resources provided (in terms of time-off for meetings and external expert reports).

With the 35-hour week issue, small non-unionised companies discovered mandating, which requires both designating an employee, who is given a trade union mandate to negotiate and sign an agreement, and also contact with an outside union structure (see the first part of the chapter). The industrial relations and representation rationales of small companies do not seem to be significantly affected by this. Reluctance for a colleague to be separated from the group is no less than it is in relation to the "obligation" to elect DPs; minimising the event is also for show. As if to emphasise its purely formal character, union mandating is often sought after, not before, internal discussions and negotiations. This situation is similar to observations made in a previous survey (Dufour, Hege *et al.*, 2000). However, mandating also makes it possible to become aware of informal forms of representation in small companies, which no doubt existed before it did.

There are few volunteers for taking on a union mandate. However, there is often consensus as to who it should be. When certain employees play an informal mediating role between the employer and employees, and are recognised as being credible in this role, it seems natural that they should be mandated. The accountant is often perceived as being the "ideal type" of this kind of informal representation in (very) small companies, which are open to social dialogue. They have two qualities, which seem at first sight to cancel each other out, namely spokesperson for some of the employees' aspirations *vis-à-vis* the employer – the informal representative owes their status of being trustworthy of tacit cooptation; at the same time, the employer's influence on them is probably greater than that of the employees. We will return to this aspect below.

As companies grow in size, the presence of representative bodies becomes commonplace. Prospects of having a works council and a social and cultural budget, which benefits all employees, can play a role in its being created. Gradually, the elected members get to know about the works council's other functions and procedures. In older companies, neither employees, nor employers remember exactly how the bodies were created. It feels as if they had always existed. The rules regarding the functioning of the works council (or single employee representation, DU) – namely, regular meetings, formal agendas and minutes, etc. – seem to make small companies (as well as both small and big ones) similar to each other, rather than the real impact of the body on industrial relations. "We manage to be pretty much present", say some; while others retort: "There probably would not be a works council, if there wasn't the social and cultural fund".

Recently-created representative bodies are rarely unionised. Reluctance does not come only from employers; employees and elected members also distrust the destabilising effect that union involvement might have on the company's industrial relations and even business equilibrium. Internal cohesion and external references seem to be rather incompatible in the smallest companies. Unionisation seems heavy-going or even absurd, as it requires assuming and promoting internally the positions and identity of a distant outside player. Open anti-union repression, which did not exist much in our case studies, is probably not the most frequent reason for not joining a union. Once again, the 35-hour week and mandating contributed to bringing the issue out of the shadows. The works council member in one of the garages explained why contact made with a union by the works council – *via* a client – "led nowhere. They (the union) asked for impossible things. They were too unrealistic and demanding. What is in the company's interest is in ours as well".

When initial contact is made with a union – in the context, for example, of mandating – employers, notably of very small companies, often tend to consider that it is an event which concerns the company (community?) as a whole. Both the heads of the insurance company and the hotel-restaurant have union officers amongst their acquaintances. They contact them (or are contacted by them) about mandating and are convinced that this particular union – more than any other – is compatible with their company's rationale. They do not hesitate to recommend it to their counterparts once their own negotiations have finished. The idea that employers cannot stand on the sidelines when union presence is at stake implicitly guides employers' actions, who are also concerned to respect their employees' autonomy. Following on from the mandating process, the head of the insurance company paid union dues to one of the small French confederations for a few members (and even renewed their membership without the employees concerned asking him to do so). His counterpart in the CAD company encouraged an employee representative to join a union – the latter was less keen than his employer. In this particular case, the union, which was chosen by employees as being best adapted to the needs of small companies, was in fact the one that their employer had been a member and union representative of previously… in a big company. Elsewhere, the desire to avoid "terile discussion" if not open opposition to the employer's strategies, is more evident. One employer thus urged an employee, whom he trusted, to join a union, in order to oppose during works council elections – on a different union list – a colleague who had become the union representative (DS). According to the employer, the works council is now composed of people, "who have proved themselves in the company" and the first DS, who "blocked the development of the company, has been marginalised".

Older companies that have grown seem less impervious to the creation of a union group, but its arrival on the scene is no less of an event. The appearance of a union group formalises and highlights the distance between employers and employees, more than elected representation bodies do so. Members of the software company's works council are aware of this and hesitate to take the plunge. They have the feeling that, in order to be effective in the long-term, representation should be turned towards the outside world, thereby emphasising more clearly their differences with their employer. Over time, the disadvantages of self-sufficiency are measured: "Sometimes, we feel a bit isolated. We need an outside opinion". If, on the one hand, they continue to fear a change that would expose internal arbitration to external assessment, they expect, on the other hand, more solid status internally. The works council could be considered to be just an "events committee" – and this is what management, who is in fact open to dialogue, sometimes, makes it out to be. "We are now beginning to think that if we joined a union, that would give us greater stature".

Taking the plunge and joining a union can be helped by a conflict. During conflicts, the local (cross-sector) trades council (*union locale*, UL) in Brittany made contact with groups of employees interested in joining a union. Here and there, employees say: "We didn't see the point of unions" when problems could be resolved directly with superiors; here and there, people say that the appearance of authoritarian management led to joining a union. The DPs at the car equipment factory joined a union, after having approached two different unions, each of which designated a union representative. Union pluralism is considered useful: "It enables us to have two different opinions". Each of the three union representatives at the electronic components company is a member of a different trade union confederation. Everyone gains from the situation, according to one of the union representatives – the representatives have complementary qualities and there are, thus, "more people for discussions with management".

In these companies in Brittany (where working class history plays a bigger role than in the centre of France), the small group of union members plays an indisputable role in worker sociability – by contributing to a friendly atmosphere in the workshops and sometimes leading colleagues to take action. The union representative in the clothing factory was very proud of managing to win a collection bonus "for the girls" in a bleak economic situation and in spite of their new employer's reluctance. The union representatives in the electronics factory are still very pleased with the fact that, during bargaining on the reduction of working time, they did not give in on daily schedules that fit in with working mothers' obligations. However, the representatives' union membership does not attract many other employees to the union, but that is often not the aim.

In small companies, the emergence of representative bodies and figures is, thus, the result of an uncertain and thwarted process. The sociology of the players involved explains this situation more than direct employer resistance. The closeness of employees to employers and also that of the small number of employees to each other is an effective barrier to creating an intermediate player. There is no doubt that the long-term nature of the players' involvement also greatly influences collective identities. In big companies, teams of representatives have often been in the company longer than management teams. They can thus have a real identity as a group that is difficult to ignore.[12] In small family companies, the situation is radically different. The employer's charisma forces any competitive charismatic inclinations into the background. The bureaucratic option, which is limited to creating essentially formal bodies (without really intending to create any substantial labour standards), only seems realistic once the company has begun to grow. However, representatives do not allow themselves to be totally powerless, even if it is difficult to identify what is the direct result of representatives' involvement, given the complexity of discussions between players, which are often of an informal nature.

5. Employee Spokespersons' Search for Limited Autonomy

In small French companies, representation, whose status is not clearly perceived, comes up against employers' strong desire for permanency, which tends to be supported by employees (and their representatives). The young accountant in the hotel-restaurant, who is competent, available, discreet and persistent, has managed to become a key figure at the heart of the industrial relations system – but it is not at all certain that this position of mediator, who is listened to, will survive after her departure. In the car equipment factory, return to less repressive management, which respects employees more, will perhaps sound the death knell of the small union sections. In the garages, the little influence that elected representatives are able to have on their employers, but for which they are likely to be criticised by their colleagues, may mean that there will be no one who is willing to take over from them at the next workplace elections. Representation – regardless of whether it is institutionally orthodox or not – is centred on immediate issues and not concerned about its own succession or the continuity of the representation bodies. Transmission of history or collective memory is not considered to be part of their remit. Therefore, when representative bodies appear in small companies, people are far from thinking that they will be automatically accompanied by the prerogatives (appeals, consultation and bargaining) that are normally associated with them – representation necessarily reflects the image of the particular individuals concerned.

The latter do not appear entirely by chance. Those in "marginalised" occupations, such as office staff, dishwashers and chamber maids, have hardly any chance of representing their colleagues and speaking for

12 During comparative surveys on the way representative bodies function in middle-sized and big companies in four countries, a workplace director, who had just arrived, spoke as follows about the union team: "Some of the union members have been in the company for thirty years, whereas management has changed. They are solid union members and excellent workers. One could even say that they have governed the factory more than we have" (Dufour, Hege, 2002: 146).

them. Representatives may even be quite hard on such "separate" groups. The women workers in the clothing factory stigmatise the haughtiness of office staff in relation to the workshops: "The office people do not talk about their pay. It must mean that it is higher than ours". In the hotel-restaurant, the cleaners' squabbles are considered to be rather petty and throw considerable doubt on the validity of their complaints and claims.

In the companies covered by the survey, elected representatives are from the predominant occupational groups: skilled workers, production workers, technicians and professional engineers. In both of the companies without employee representative institutions (*Institutions représentatives du personnel*, IRP) (the insurance company and the hotel-restaurant), an informal role of mediator is bestowed upon the company's accountant. This representative figure, who has already been met in surveys on union mandating (Dufour, Hege *et al.*, 1999 and 2000), intrigues external players and observers – and clearly makes his or her presence felt amongst players in the (very) small companies themselves.

Accountants are close to employers' power. Employers, who have often directly urged them to take on this mediation role, are sure of their loyalty and know they are tied to them, as a result of the confidential nature of the information they possess. They also appreciate their ability to "calm things down" (as the accountant in the insurance company says herself) and defuse conflicts "before they explode" (in the words of the hotel-restaurant's accountant). They support their employer's plans and rigorous financial management – and can be asked to "get messages across to the staff".

But these accountants also say they act as confidants for the staff. Different occupational groups in both the insurance company and the hotel-restaurant talk to them about both trivial and important problems. Staff counts on them to speak to management – and they do so when they are convinced of the relevance of the issues raised. But it is common knowledge that they know how to be discreet: "Management does not know everything and one mustn't tell them everything". Even though forced or voluntary submission to the employer's will cannot be excluded, our survey shows that it is not mechanically related to the role.

This hybrid status of "accountant-representative" sheds new light on the issue of the closeness of representatives and employers in (very) small companies. Employees, who are unofficially represented by accountants, seem to do more than just gladly or reluctantly accept a compromise with a status that guarantees privileged access to their employer – in fact, they implicitly make it a criterion of selection. This hypothesis is relevant, accountants are preferred more autonomous representation, not in spite of, but because of their closeness to the employer's world. The role they play in ensuring the company's business viability does not count against them; on the contrary, they contribute to the permanent nature of the employer's plans, which are also identified with a place of work and sociability. Their proven loyalty to the employer gives more weight to the demands of the employees, on whose behalf they are spokespersons. The insurance broker said: "When our accountant tells me about something (on behalf of the staff), I really have to listen".

Thus, the situation of representatives is not so different from those in bigger units, who can also be singled out for their occupational responsibilities. Employees seem also to expect their representatives – the union representative (DS) in the clothing factory who is responsible for making prototypes and the employee representative (DP) in the CAD company who is a technician with great autonomy in his work – to be taken notice of by management, as the latter is convinced... of their professional loyalty. In these companies, support for professional values, which is sometimes combined with relationships of local solidarity, brings employees and heads of small companies close together. Uninhibited defence by employees and their elected representatives of labour standards that unions and the labour inspectorate have learnt to be wary of – professional and managerial staffs' long working days and unorthodox organisation of work breaks – reflects the vitality of closely-knit communities.

In small companies, representation that develops in a close-knit context thus tends to tone down its differences and make sacrifices, in order to preserve internal industrial relations equilibrium. This pragmatic withdrawal, which could be thought of as being a necessary precondition for the appearance of representation, does not mean that the representative role is abandoned. However, a real change in industrial relations is rarely involved. What is sought is a reminder (of fair labour principles) and "industrial relations monitoring". There is a place for demands, but their effect on internal relations is almost always taken into account upstream. In the hotel-restaurant, the accountant thinks she can acquire a good idea of employees' concerns by often going around the different services. She is not unaware of the effects of low pay on her colleagues' lives. She knows that working conditions and requirements in terms of flexibility can "push staff to the limits" from time to time. She is also aware of the poor protection provided by the sector-level collective agreement. Employers have to be reminded of these things, even when they are concerned about respecting their staff, and at the same time they have to ensure the rigorous implementation of employees' rights – an area where their professional expertise and representative mandate coincide: "Labour issues are too serious – you mustn't get it wrong".

The accountant, who is not a union member and pleads close relationships, is thus not so very different from union representatives, whom circumstances push to promote differences. The union representative (DS) in the clothing factory emphasised: "We must, after all, defend ourselves. We must say things... We are not there simply to listen". Her counterpart in the electronics factory recalled the confrontation on the 35-hour week in the following terms: "I could not give in to management – I had to defend the employees".

F. What Players Do with Labour Standards

This survey of small French companies reveals extremely varied industrial relations situations and compromises – and behind the compromises, the predominant power of employers regarding labour standards.[13] Small employers seem to be able to apply external collective standards very flexibly and also keep their distance from those who produce them. Heads of small companies thus have great autonomy in creating their own industrial relations. The absence (or precarious presence) of an institutionalised employee opposition force can consolidate the impression that employers are in charge. This observation must, however, be qualified.

It has to be qualified to the extent that industrial relations in small companies give great scope to implicit agreement and informal arbitration. The specific nature of such companies, namely their small size, means that they are not very suited to formalising many procedures, which, in bigger units, involve explicit discussions and the creation of official structures. There is also a more widely shared phenomenon – implicit and informal relations, which imply that relations between players affect official institutions (employee representative institutions, IRP and hierarchical systems, etc.) more than the latter are able to change the course of tacit agreements, which exist in small – and also big – companies.

The informal nature of compromises often means that it is difficult for the players themselves to interpret them. They may take the form of "arrangements". The ability to make arrangements is often referred to as a prerogative of small companies and is of interest to employees, compared with bigger companies, which are seen as being more bureaucratic and less tolerant of individual cases. Even though they can see the financial advantages of working in a bigger company, employees of

13 The small sample, of course, limits the impact of this observation, but also gives it depth.

very small companies often speak of the constraints and less "human" nature of organisational processes in big units. They thus value the possible arrangements that make up their daily working life – even if it is only to justify them.

Selective implementation of external standards often involves half-implicit/half-explicit compromises in small companies. Employees are not encouraged to elect DPs, but they are able to meet during working hours either regularly or when major changes have to be made. The 35-hour week is introduced with a pay freeze, but other forms of remuneration are sought, in order to meet staff's urgent expectations concerning pay (profit-sharing, luncheon vouchers and so forth). It is not just a matter of a short-term strategy using devices to prevent conflicts; it is rather an attempt to harmoniously combine a long-term system of mutual recognition and ever-changing management needs. In this respect, implicit compromises call upon the imagination and intuition of the players concerned.

Many factors intervene in strategies of implicit adaptation and exchanges between players – they include: daily relations; acquired situations; versatility required of employees in companies that see themselves as being flexible in spite of their small size; occupational ethics and cohesion; as well as the vulnerability of small companies in the face of competition and that of employees in the labour market. Employers weigh them up (when they have long-term strategies) at every change in the market and in their entrepreneurial plans. Employees sacrifice part of their power of protest because of them, but also use them to nourish the idea that they have "fair" compensations and recognition of their work. And representatives refer to them when they assess employees' claims, expectations and rights.

References

Barrat, O., Daniel, C. (2002), "La négociation collective, le statisticien, sa lanterne et le débat social", *La Revue de l'IRES*, No.39, 2002/2, p.3-32.

Blassel, H., Jacquier, J.P. (1997), "La représentation sociale territoriale, premier essai de mesure et d'évaluation", *La Revue de l'IRES*, No.25, Automne, p.89-115.

Bunel, J. (1997), "Représentation patronale et représentativité des organisations patronales", *Travail et emploi*, No.70, p.3-20.

CSERC (Conseil Supérieur de l'Emploi, des Revenus et des Coûts) (1999), *Le SMIC, salaire minimum de croissance*, Paris: La Documentation française.

Dufour, C. (1992), "France", in IRES (collectif) *Syndicalismes Dynamique des relations professionnelles*, Paris: Dunod.

Dufour, C., Hege, A. (1999), "Frankreich Tarifverhandlungen in der Metallindustrie", in Schulten Thorsten, Reinhard Bispinck (eds.) *Tarifpolitik unter dem Euro, Perspektiven einer europäischen Koordinierung: das Beispiel Metallindustrie*, Hamburg: VSA-Verlag.

Dufour, C., Hege, A. (2002), *L'Europe syndicale au quotidien, la représentation des salariés dans les entreprises en Allemagne, France, Grande-Bretagne et Italie*, Bruxelles: P.I.E.-Peter Lang.

Dufour, C., Hege, A. (2004), "Des institutions et des acteurs, pour quelles politiques sociales, post-enquête Réponse", IRES, rapport à la DARES, avril 2004, 102 pages.

Dufour, C., Hege, A., Vincent C., Viprey M. (1999), "Le mandatement dans le cadre de la loi du 13 juin 1998", Rapport à la DARES, IRES.

Dufour, C., Hege, A., Vincent C., Viprey M. (2000), "Le mandatement en question", *Travail et emploi*, No.82, avril, p.25-36.

Fonds monétaire international (2005), *France – Consultations de 2005 au titre de l'article IV Conclusions de la mission.* www.imf.org/external/np/ms/ 2005/ fra/071105af.htm.

Freyssinet, J. (1997), *Le temps de travail en miettes: vingt ans de politique de l'emploi et de négociation collective*, Paris: Éditions de l'Atelier.

Hege, A., Dufour, C. (2004), "La place des femmes dans les prud'hommes", Rapport final, service du droit des femmes, ministère du Travail, avril.

IRES-DARES (1998), *Les comités d'entreprise, enquête sur les élus, les activités et les moyens*, ministère de l'Emploi et de la Solidarité, Paris: Éditions de l'Atelier.

Jobert, A. (2000), *Les espaces de la négociation collective, branches et territoires*, Toulouse, Octarès.

Meilland, C., Dufour, C. (2001), "Services in France: Heterogeneity of Employment Systems within Common Institutional Frames", in Dølvik Jon Erik (ed.), *At Your Service? Comparative Perspectives on Employment and Labour Relations in the European Private Sector Services*, Brussels: P.I.E.-Peter Lang, p.341-382.

Meurs, D., Skalli, A. (1997), "L'impact des conventions de branche sur les salaires", *Travail et emploi*, No.70, p.33-50.

RÉPONSE, 1993, RÉPONSE 1998, DARES, ministère du Travail.

Saglio, J. (1991), "La régulation de branche dans le système français de relations professionnelles", *Travail et emploi*, 1/1991, No.47, p.26-41.

Sweden

Sofia MURHEM

Uppsala University

I. Small Swedish Companies in a Wider Context

During the 1980s and 1990s, small companies were increasingly perceived as engines of economic growth, as well as a way of increasing employment. In public debate, small companies are considered to be an alternative, when large corporations in heavy industry are moving factories, and thereby work opportunities, abroad. A transfer of the workforce to the service sector also means a shift towards more employment in small companies. Moreover, political ambitions to promote self-employment and entrepreneurship, as seen for instance in the European Employment Strategy (EES), have reinforced the interest in small companies.

At the same time, the Swedish model of industrial relations has been based on large companies and little research has been conducted on small ones. In fact, industrial relations of small companies have been a neglected research field in Sweden. We do not know if employment conditions and working conditions differ in companies of varying sizes. From international studies, we might assume that there are differences, but it is hard to say to what extent, as those studies took place in a different industrial relations context. Swedish research indicates that small companies are less unionised, and belong to a lesser extent to employers' organisations, but also that there are large differences between sectors.

This chapter aims at studying the characteristics of industrial relations in small companies in Sweden. Do they differ from large ones concerning industrial relations? Are both the formal and informal institutions, which regulate the everyday life of employers and employees in small companies, different? What are the consequences of these differences? The companies studied are situated in Uppsala, the fourth largest city in Sweden, located about 65 kilometres north of Stockholm.

There are two different views of industrial relations in small companies. The first one is based on the notion that there are fundamental differences between small and large companies – differences which are evident in industrial relations and are caused by the very size of the company. This view is, for example, held by Goss (1991). The other, which is put forward by Chapman (1999), is that small companies – as well as large ones – are foremost enterprises, i.e. capitalist organisations acting in a market. Thereby, the similarities between small and large companies will be far bigger than the differences. Diversity is more likely to be greater between sectors than between companies of different sizes in the same sector. Hence, the possible differences between small and large companies are the result of their responding as rational players chiefly to institutions and transaction costs. Which of these models is most adequate is still an open question.

The Swedish model is based on central collective bargaining, high coverage of collective agreements, formal conflict-resolution through negotiations and high membership rates, even if there have been some changes especially from the 1980s onwards with increasing decentralisation. High membership is partly the result of organisations being influential at both local and central levels. In general, membership rates, both for trade unions and employers' organisations, are considered to be lower in small companies. The particular aspects studied here are chosen since they form part of the fundamental conditions of the Swedish model.

The following aspects of industrial relations are studied in this chapter: membership rates, collective agreements, labour legislation, leadership and work organisation, conflict resolution, working hours, gender relations and the role within the Swedish industrial relations system and society. The study concludes with implications for further research. The role of managers, their relationship with employees and the mode of workplace organisation are examined. How conflicts within the companies are resolved and whether the method is formal or informal is considered. Membership rates of trade unions and employers' organisations and other business organisations, as well as workplace presence and attitudes towards the organisations are studied. Coverage and content of collective agreements are examined, as are levels of negotiations, i.e. central or local and individual or collective. The perception of labour legislation, such as employment protection – both in theory and practise – is explored, as are working hours and type of employment, i.e. permanent or temporary, full-time or part-time. A gender perspective is also present in the study.

The chapter is organised as follows. The first part on business structure and working conditions is intended as background information for readers. It is followed by a brief overview of the research field, the aim of the study, variables studied and methodology, as an introduction to the study. Thereafter follows a description of Swedish industrial relations and then the material from the case studies. In the final part, conclusions are drawn from the case studies.

A. Small Companies – Business structure and Working Conditions

Earlier research indicates that small companies differ from large ones in important respects regarding working conditions. For instance, Brown *et al.* (1990) showed that small employers employ more women, pay less, and provide worse health and pension plans and less further education. However, most studies refer to British and American companies, and the results may not hold true for Swedish ones. As approximately 75% of Swedish private-sector employees are covered by collective agreements, which include pay and pensions, while health plans are part of the public welfare state, it is most likely that such differences are negligible. Even if most formal institutions are the same for employees in both small and large companies, there might be differences in actual practices. Such differences may both be visible, such as trade union presence in the workplace, or invisible, such as the pattern of conflict resolution.

In this section, the development of small companies in Sweden during the 1990s will be examined. Compared to most other European countries, large corporations have always been more dominant in Sweden. Very large and small companies dominate the business structure, while there are few medium-sized enterprises. This is evident in all sectors of the economy, but there are variations between them (Magnusson, 2000: 30-31).

As shown in table 1, small companies are important as employers in Swedish business life. However, the importance of small companies varies between sectors of the economy. Small and medium-sized enterprises are most important as employers in wholesale and retail trade, hotels and restaurants, and in construction. In these sectors, more than 50% of the workforce are employed in companies with less than 100 employees; approximately 15% are in companies with 1 to 4 employees. In manufacturing, the percentage employed in small companies is significantly smaller, for example in transport and communications. Amongst the sectors in the following table, banking and insurance have the smallest proportion of employees in small companies.

Table 1. Percentage of all Swedish private-sector employees employed in small companies (less than 100 employees), 1993-2002

Year	Percentage
1993	29%
1994	30%
1995	31%
1996	32%
1997	32%
1998	33%
1999	33%
2000	34%
2001	34%
2002	34%

Source: SCB database, own computations

Table 2. Percentage of companies and employees by company size in different sectors in Sweden, 1993-2002

	Year	1-4 empl.	5-9 empl.	10-19 empl.	20-49 empl.	50-99 empl.	Total
Manufacturing	1993	3.40%	4.13%	4.95%	8.64%	8.09%	29.21%
	2002	3.38%	4.19%	5.93%	10.01%	9.25%	32.76%
Construction	1993	13.39%	9.78%	10.65%	11.08%	5.54%	50.44%
	2002	15.24%	12.78%	14.84%	14.04%	6.61%	63.51%
Transport and commu-nications	1993	6.86%	5.06%	5.17%	5.68%	3.67%	26.44%
	2002	7.68%	6.46%	7.09%	8.63%	5.77%	35.63%
Wholesale and retail	1993	15.57%	13.12%	12.47%	13.65%	7.86%	62.67%
	2002	13.97%	12.88%	12.69%	14.52%	8.10%	62.16%
Hotels and restaurants	1993	13.64%	14.36%	15.16%	18.30%	9.31%	70.77%
	2002	14.48%	14.69%	15.02%	20.56%	9.43%	74.18%
Banks and other financial services	1993	1.85%	1.41%	1.84%	4.25%	5.06%	14.41%
	2002	3.92%	2.53%	2.49%	5.34%	5.24%	19.52%

Source: Statistics Sweden's database, own computations.

Nevertheless, the figures show that the proportion of employees in small companies is growing. Increasing deregulation in the 1990s in certain sectors, such as transport and finance, partly explains this trend.

Table 3. Average number of employees per company (with at least one employee) in different sectors in Sweden, 1993-2002

	Year	Employees per company
Manufacturing	1993	31.96
	2002	30.26
Construction	1993	10.19
	2002	8.58
Transport and communications	1993	19.42
	2002	16.50
Wholesale and retail	1993	8.92
	2002	9.55
Hotels and restaurants	1993	9.44
	2002	8.75
Banks and other financial services	1993	59.86
	2002	31.60

Source: Statistics Sweden's database, own computations.

Almost all sectors, with the exception of wholesale and retail, show a decrease in average size, measured as number of employees per company. In spite of the increase in the average number of employees, commerce remains, on average, the sector with the smallest number of employees. Manufacturing has the second largest average size, due to comparatively high costs of production plants, etc. To afford the necessary investments and make them profitable, a certain size is usually needed. The service sector, which needs less fixed capital and for which its employees are its most valuable asset, is not surprisingly dominated by small companies, except for finance. Finance, in fact, shows the largest drop in average company size (which almost halved), probably as a result of the deregulation of banking and financial services that took place during the 1990s. Of the other services, the average size of companies in transport and communications is about 50% bigger than the others, but is still comparatively small.

According to American studies, small company employees have had less education than those in larger companies. A Swedish study, based on 1999 data, indicates that this holds true for Sweden as well. More than 40% of the employees in workplaces with more than 500 employees have been to university, compared with only 25% of employees in small companies with less than 50 employees. Workplaces with 50 to 499 employees have a percentage of employees with university education, which corresponds to the labour market average. The differences in knowledge intensity between large and small workplaces increased considerably during the 1990s.[1]

[1] Under- och överutbildning på 2000-talets arbetsmarknad, 2001: 10, 41, 48.

While about 50% of the positions in large workplaces (more than 500 employees) require university education, only 38% of the positions in workplaces with less than 50 employees do so. The figure for workplaces with 50-499 employees is 41%.[2] The required level of education increased significantly during the 1990s in large workplaces, most notably so for employment requiring longer university education, from 11% in 1990 to 20% in 1999. The changes for small workplaces have been small, for instance the percentage of positions requiring longer university education increased from 8.5% in 1990 to 9% in 1999.[3]

B. Industrial Relations in Sweden

The Swedish model, in the sense used here, originated in the 1938 Saltsjöbaden agreement, in which employers and trade unions established their relationship. The social partners agreed that labour market issues should be negotiated between the employers' federation and the trade union, without the government's involvement. The Swedish industrial relations model was based on the large export industries, in combination with central unions and central negotiations. An important part of the model was the pay policy with solidarity, i.e. employees would receive the same pay independent of company profitability. The policy caused many companies to go out of business and restructuring of the economy to more profitable companies and sectors, which was a process considered beneficial to the country. Employees, who were made redundant, were retrained in active labour market policy courses by the Labour Market Board (Arbetsmarknadsstyrelsen, AMS), founded in 1948. The concept of full employment, crucial for the social partners, was thereby upheld.

The mutual understanding between employers and trade unions, which had been such an important factor for preserving the Swedish model, was increasingly replaced by legislation in the 1970s. The labour movement became more radical and tension between trade unions and employers emerged. A shift in employment from the 1970s onwards towards the service sector meant that more people were employed in small companies. During the 1980s, on the other hand, employers became more profiled in a neo-liberal way. Sweden was forced by the recession in the early years of the 1990s to abandon full employment, and unemployment figures rose to levels unheard of since the 1930s. At the same time, negotiations became more and more decentralised, resulting in more influential individual trade unions and sector-level employers' organisations. These developments continued until the 1997

2 *Ibid.*: 64-65.

3 *Ibid.*: 70.

Co-operation Agreement on Industrial Development and Pay Formation (*Industriavtalet*), which might be a restoration of the Swedish model's centralised bargaining, but at sector level. Elvander (1998, 2000, 2002) considered that this was the most important agreement in Sweden since the *Saltsjöbaden* agreement in 1938. New production processes, such as project work, were developed. Many researchers think that such changes present a challenge to the Swedish industrial relations system.

Jelle Visser (1996: 202-203) has described the Swedish industrial relations system and compared it to other European countries. One of his conclusions is that the level of organisation is extremely high in Sweden, but that the Swedish model, based on a tri-partite coalition between the trade unions, the employers' federation and the government began to erode in the 1970s. However, many important characteristics, such as the high degree of membership, still exist.

Kjellberg (2001: 43, 309) has found that trade union membership in Sweden, as in most other countries, is lower in small companies, and thereby, an increased percentage of the workforce employed in small enterprises would mean a lower union density. This is further supported by the findings of Furåker and Berglund (2001: 11), namely that employees in small companies find individual negotiations with the employer more useful than trade union negotiations. Kjellberg (2001: 204) states that, in order to reach groups with low unionisation, trade unions need to change their activities. Among the target groups are employees in small enterprises. There are also differences in collective agreement coverage. A lack of collective agreements is found chiefly among small companies in the private service sector, operating for instance in flight transport, media and wholesale and retail trade.

1. Trade Unions

All employee representation in Sweden is organised through the unions, and there are no independent channels. There is, nevertheless, an exception, namely the law on European works councils (SFS 1996: 359). While the works council represents all employees, the Swedish union section (*fackklubbar*) only represents trade union members. The central level is undoubtedly strong, but so is the local. The *fackklubb* is an important part of the union structure, as it is the face of the trade union for individual members (Kjellberg, 2001: 31). Using data from 15 European countries, Visser (2002: 32) also concludes that workplace representation has a positive effect on unionisation. However, many smaller companies do not have a *fackklubb*. Most of the employer-employee relations have been carried out through negotiations, not only on pay, but also concerning the Co-determination Act of 1977. If there is no *fackklubbar*, a regional union representative (*ombudsman*) will act for the employee, if s/he is a trade union member. There are no closed shops in Sweden.

Sweden has the highest union density in Western Europe. The corporatist tradition has probably contributed to this, as well as making trade unions influential. Also the fact that, according to labour law, trade unions are legal entities, and not the employees themselves, is likely to have increased unionisation. Since trade unions are strong both on a central level, thus making them influential politically and in negotiations with the employers, and also locally, they get the best of both worlds, by keeping in touch with every member (Kjellberg, 1998: 76-77). The system described above, with *fackklubbar* or contact persons (*fackrepresentant, fackombud*), has obviously worked well. A feature of all Western European countries with high union membership is also that the unions administer the unemployment insurance scheme, and Sweden is no exception (Rothstein, 1986).

There are three major national trade union confederations in Sweden, the Swedish Trade Union Confederation (*Landsorganisationen*, LO), the Swedish Confederation of Professional Employees (*Tjänstemännens Centralorganisation*, TCO) and the Swedish Confederation of Professional Associations (*Sveriges Akademikers Centralorganisation*, SACO). LO is for blue-collar workers, TCO for white-collar workers and SACO for employees with higher education.

Swedish trade unions have a hierarchical mode of organisation. First, there are the local sections (*fackklubbar*), which cover one or more workplaces. They organise meetings for members, in which every member has the right to participate, make his or her voice heard and participate in decision-making. Secondly, there are regional/geographical structures. At this level, democracy is representative and they, in turn, elect representatives to the third and highest level, namely the congress. The congress is the highest body and makes long-term decisions. It also elects a board and chairpersons (Hansson, 1996: 49).

Within many sectors, trade union density increased during the 1990s, as shown in table 4. However, unionisation in general shows a slight decrease during the last decade. Generally speaking, white-collar employees have lower union density than blue-collar workers – as do private-sector employees compared with public-sector employees. Also young people, under 25, tend to be less unionised than older employees. Despite this, the percentage of young trade union members playing an active role in their trade unions has actually increased. In the last decade, women – especially blue-collar women – have increased their unionisation rate, while men have decreased theirs (Kjellberg, 2001; Nelander and Lönnros, 2000).

Factors such as workplace size affect unionisation, as does the type of employment, i.e. small workplaces are less unionised and temporary or part-time employees tend to be unionised to a lesser degree. However, the fact that no statistics on unionisation by size of workplace or company are available is in itself interesting. It may be an effect of the importance of large companies in the Swedish economy and debates.

Not only size, but also traditions within a particular sector such as the presence of *fackklubbar*, affect unionisation. Among the cases studied later, there are two extremes. One is among metal workers, where they have a hundred-year-old tradition of *fackklubbar*, the other is wholesale and retail workers, where *fackklubbar* evolved in the 1960s. In Hansson's study of trade union careers, the majority of those who have reached the highest levels started in the *fackklubbar*, usually in a minor position (Hansson, 1996: 93).

Today, there are approximately 240,000 shop stewards (union representatives) in Sweden. They are elected by the trade union members in each workplace and represent them on various occasions Shop stewards have a strong legal position, which is described in more detail in the next section. If there is not a *fackklubb*, then union members can elect a union representative in their site. About 25% of the shop stewards are safety representatives. Every Swedish workplace with more than five employees has, according to law, to have one or more safety representatives responsible for the working environment. The safety representative may even close the workplace down if the working environment is too hazardous. The representative is elected by the trade unions of the workplace. However, the position is low-status and it is increasingly difficult to recruit safety representatives generally (Pilemalm, 2001: 571-575).

Both the metal industry and wholesale and retail trade are also extremes when it comes to differences in unionisation rates. Table 4 clearly shows the considerable differences between different sectors. It is nevertheless evident that union density in Sweden is very high in all sectors.

Table 4. Union membership in Sweden, percentage of all employees 1990-2002, first quarter

		Manufac-turing	Construc-tion	Wholesale and retail	Private service sector (except retail)	Govern-ment	Local govern-ment
1990	Blue collar	89.9	89.7	68.1	69.9	91.9	87.4
1992		91.4	88.7	70.4	71.7	94.9	90.0
1994		92.7	89.9	74.8	75.7	96.8	94.1
1996		92.0	9.08	73.8	76.8	95.7	94.3
1998		91.3	89.9	72.6	75.1	95.2	93.3
2000		90.4	88.9	71.4	74.5	95.7	92.3
2002		90.5	86.3	68.2	74.1	93.7	90.6
Difference		0.6	- 3.4	0.1	4.2	1.8	3.2

		Manufac-turing	Construc-tion	Wholesale and retail	Private service sector (except retail)	Govern-ment	Local govern-ment
1990	White collar	82.2	80.0	60.1	66.1	93.6	93.3
1992		83.8	70.0	64.8	68.7	94.7	93.3
1994		84.4	76.7	64.2	73.8	93.2	94.8
1996		82.6	84.4	63.2	71.5	93.0	94.9
1998		81.3	80.7	61.0	69.4	92.4	94.6
2000		81.0	77.4	61.3	66.0	90.1	93.9
2002		79.5	76.7	62.7	66.6	89.9	92.0
Difference		- 2.7	- 3.3	2.6	0.5	- 3.7	3.2

Source: Nelander and Lönnros, 2000.

2. Employers' Organisations and Other Business Organisations

Employers' organisations are influential in Sweden and have a substantial membership rate. About 46,000 companies, which cover over 1.3 million employees, are affiliated to Swedish Enterprise (*Svenskt Näringsliv*). It is a new organisation, which was founded in 2001 by the Swedish Employers' Federation (*Svenska arbetsgivareföreningen*, SAF), and the business organisation, Swedish Federation of Industries (*Industriförbundet*). They have 52 member organisations – both business and employers' organisations. Individual companies are, as was the case with SAF, members of an organisation, which in turn is a member of *Svenskt Näringsliv*. The latter recognises SMEs as a special target area, and has assigned a specific officer for SMEs.

Svenskt Näringsliv has 22 regional offices – 21 in the largest cities in Sweden and one office in Brussels. The regional offices work in direct contact with member companies, but also as a pressure group locally and regionally. Uppsala has its own office.

Alongside *Svenskt Näringsliv*, there are other employers' organisations in Sweden, such as *Arbetsgivarverket* for public employers, and some independent organisations, most notably for banks, publishers and co-operatives. This means that the vast majority of Swedish employees are covered by employers' organisations, but the percentage is lower in the private sector, especially in the service sector. Still, in the private sector, about 75% of the employees work in a company affiliated to an employers' organisation (Murhem, 2001: 395).

SAF was founded as an industry-based organisation, but when the service sector became increasingly important in the 1960s and 1970s, most of the employers' organisations in the service sector decided to also join. From then on, *SAF* covered most of the Swedish private sector. The changes in membership structure also meant a change in average company size, from 120 in 1930 to 35 in 1980 (De Geer, 1992; Kuuse, 1986). However, as shown in table 5, large companies are still considerably more interested in joining an employers' organisation.

To begin with, *SAF* was not interested in admitting small companies. In 1907, it declared that the interests of large and small companies were so different that it was inappropriate for them to belong to the same organisation. The reasons were that small companies, mostly craftsmen, were not sensitive to higher labour costs, since they were not exposed to foreign competition. In addition, SAF feared that small employers would have less resistance during lockouts (Kjellberg, 2000: 57-58).

What might be the reason for such an, in a European perspective, unusually high affiliation rate? Probably, the main reason is that trade unionism is very strong in Sweden and the growth of employers' organisations was a response to the growth of trade unions (De Geer, 1992). In addition, Swedish society is itself thoroughly regulated and has a tradition of corporatism, which may reinforce the tendency to organise, both for employers' organisations, as well as trade unions.

Why do companies join an employers' organisation? One reason is, of course, representation in negotiations, another is access to advice. Also, actions designed to influence public opinion in a more employer-friendly way may attract members. Employers' organisations also represent a social environment and a collegial framework within a particular sector (Westholm, 2000: 78-79). That social environment may be stronger in some sectors and, therefore, be a reason why membership rates in employers' organisations vary between sectors.

The hypothesis of rationality in choosing to join an employers' organisation has been tested regarding the Confederation of British Industry, CBI. The results of the study, with reservations given the small number of respondents (90), was that it may hold for small companies, but for middle- and large-sized companies, additional explanations are necessary. Most of them had not evaluated the options very clearly since the cost was so small, which in itself might be rational way of acting

(De Geer, 1992). Such an explanation means that size is important if small companies evaluate possible benefits. A small company with few employees might not consider the expense of belonging to an employers' organisation worth the benefits. A complicated structure of employment contracts (many and varied contracts) will increase the gain from an employers' organisation's expertise. Studies have indicated that large companies are more interested in belonging to employers' organisations (Lundquist, 1998).

Apart from the employers' organisations, there are also other business organisations, the largest being the Federation of Private Enterprises in Sweden (*Företagarnas Riksorganisation*, FR), which had 60,000 member companies in 2001. FR was founded in 1991, when the Federation of Enterprises (*Företagareförbundet*) and the Swedish Federation of Small Enterprises (*Småföretagarnas Riksorganisation*) merged. An additional 30,000 companies are affiliated *via* 30 trade organisations. Altogether they cover about 450,000 employees. FR has its base in small companies, in fact only about 30,000 of the member companies have employees, and 54% of the total number of employees covered by FR are employed in companies with less than 20 employees. Their main task is to act as lobby organisations and try to influence public opinion and politicians. FR is actually the largest business organisation in Sweden, in terms of the number of affiliated companies. Regarding employees, they have only a fraction of the number of employees that *Svenskt Näringsliv* covers. There are also other organisations for small companies, such as *Företagareförbundet Företagarforum*, an organisation that was founded in 1991, by entrepreneurs, who did not want to join the new FR.

It is clear that the smaller companies do not consider it beneficial enough to join an employers' organisation. The differences between sectors are surprisingly small, except for other private services, which are considerably below the others. This sector includes the new economy and also newly deregulated areas in Sweden, such as banking and telecommunications.

By comparing tables 2 and 4, it is evident that there is no clear connection at sector level between a high percentage employed in SMEs and low unionisation. While the percentage employed by small companies actually has increased, unionisation has also increased. However, when comparing tables 3 and 4, more connections appear. In many instances, sectors, which have a high proportion of small companies, also have lower unionisation rates. There is little doubt that company size matters, but probably also in combination with sector-level traditions.

Table 5. Percentage of companies that are members of employers' organisations by company size and for certain sectors in Sweden, 1996-1999

	Percentage in employers' organisations		
	1-9 employees	10-49 employees	50-199 employees
	Production		
1996	13%	54%	83%
1997	11%	54%	85%
1998	13%	53%	80%
1999	13%	53%	84%
	Construction		
1996	18%	51%	79%
1997	19%	56%	70%
1998	24%	55%	67%
1999	22%	63%	77%
	Wholesale and retail		
1996	14%	53%	83%
1997	14%	55%	85%
1998	14%	59%	87%
1999	15%	63%	77%
	Other private services		
1996	12%	46%	57%
1997	12%	48%	68%
1998	13%	47%	63%
1999	11%	44%	60%

Source: Tegle (2000), Nelander and Lönnros (2000), SCB, own computations.

It is interesting to note that when LO-members were asked an open question about what they considered to be the most important reasons why fellow workers did not join their union, just 1% answered that no one or few people in the workplace were unionised and only 1% that there was no suitable union structure for the workplace. Instead 49% considered the size of membership dues to be the main reason and 40% that non-members perhaps had doubts about the benefits of membership. Among non-members, who had chosen to have just unemployment insurance, more gave political reasons and fewer the size of membership dues as reasons for not joining (Nelander and Lindgren, 1998).

3. Collective Agreements

Many issues, which in other countries are covered by law, are decided upon in collective agreements in Sweden. For instance, there is no statutory minimum wage in Sweden, instead minimum pay is agreed to in the collective agreement. Thereby, the largest differences between employment conditions might be between employees covered by collective agreements and those without. Virtually no research has been carried out on companies lacking collective agreements. It may be that such companies abide by the stipulations in the collective agreements or have even better conditions, but the other way around may also exist. Most of the companies lacking collective agreements are probably to be found among small and medium-sized companies.

The law recognises collective agreements as written agreements between an employers' organisation or employer and a trade union concerning employment conditions for the employee or the relation between the employer and the employees (23 § SFS 1976: 580). This means that they include both what usually in Sweden are called 'collective agreements', i.e. agreements between employers' organisations and trade unions, and 'substitute agreements', i.e. agreements between an individual employer, who is not a member of an employers' organisation, and the trade union.

A collective or substitute agreement signed in a workplace is valid for all employees, not only trade union members. An agreement will be signed if at least one employee so demands, but there is no extension to other companies.

The first cross-sector agreement was concluded between SAF and the trade unions in the 1930s and collective agreements are still very important. There are, surprisingly enough, no statistics on collective agreements in Sweden, but an estimate made in 1995 holds that about 95% of the Swedish workforce are covered – 72% by direct agreements and the rest by substitute agreements. However, the figure is rather uncertain (Kjellberg, 2000b: 204). In the case studies, an estimate of coverage of collective agreements, as well as substitute agreements, will be attempted.

In spite of this, collective agreements are extremely important in Sweden. For instance, as mentioned above, there is no statutory minimum wage, apart from what is concluded in the collective agreements. Usually the agreements are valid for the entire country at sector level, but there is no statutory extension to cover the whole country, as is the case in many other countries. Collective agreements traditionally cover pay, working hours, overtime and additional benefits to legislation, regarding insurance and holidays, etc.

Compared to, for instance, British collective agreements, Swedish collective agreements have traditionally covered many detailed issues. Tolliday and Zeitlin (1991: 302-304) argue that this is due to SAF's tradition of highly centralised decision-making, because of the mutual strike funds. Also the very important export industries, which have dominated both the Swedish economy, as well as the employers' organisation, have contributed to successful central cross-sector bargaining. The system of bargaining was beneficial both for the employers, who gained control over pay-setting and low pay increases, and for the trade unions, who saw it as a means of supporting pay policy based on solidarity.

The importance of large-scale companies, which were always influential in SAF, increased after 1976. From the beginning of the 1970s onwards, reduced economic growth and productivity gains made pay bargaining more complicated. Pay increases for some justified pay demands by others and this process contributed to inflation. Politicians aimed at full employment, which led to high pay expectations and the policy of pay solidarity contributed to what was then called the "wage-drift". New unions appeared and the bargaining system became increasingly complicated, especially as there were many conflicts between public and private sector employees concerning pay increases. Trade unions in the profitable export industries craved for higher pay and a larger share of the profits. Large manufacturing companies considered that decentralised bargaining had become vital. The centralised bargaining system thus threatened to collapse. SAF strongly opposed LO's redistributive ambitions and said it would no longer negotiate at the central level; however, many small companies thought central collective agreements were crucial for workplace negotiations. The decentralisation of negotiations caused SAF's focus to turn to lobbying. Membership fees were also reduced considerably. Crouch (1996) also points out that while large corporations in Sweden are able to negotiate without the help of an organisation, small firms find it more difficult. The late 1990's may have been the starting point of a return to more central agreements, but at the level of a single sector (Thörnqvist, 1999; Tolliday and Zeitlin, 1991: 305-307; Kjellberg, 2000: 182; Crouch, 1996: 361).

Elvander (1998) emphasises that if an employer does not want to sign a collective agreement, the trade unions have different paths to choose between. The more militant ones, like blue-collar commerce union (Handelsanställdas förbund) or transport union (*Svenska transportarbetareförbundet*) try, if negotiations fail, to force the employers by blockading the workplace, usually with widespread media coverage. This happened to the American retail chain, Toys 'R Us, when they started up in Sweden. Finally, they agreed to sign a collective agreement. Others try to negotiate and convince employers peacefully – sometimes over a long period of time – of the advantages of collective agreements. However, there is always the possibility of making it public and launching a blockade.

4. Labour Legislation

The Co-determination Act (*Lag om medbestämmande i arbetslivet, MBL*, SFS 1976: 580) was adopted in 1976 and contains the right to unionise, the right for trade unions and employees to negotiate on issues concerning employees, recruitment and dismissals, as well as reorganisation. Also the right to information in negotiations is included, as are collective agreements, strikes, damages and court procedures. The right to unionise and belong to an employers' organisation is unconditional. Every person, employer or employee, has the right to belong to an organisation, to create such an organisation or to work for it and that right is not to be violated in any way. Trade unions and employers both have the right to negotiate. The right for union officers to carry out their duties in their workplace is protected. Employers are not to interfere and union officers have the right to paid time-off work for trade union activities and also to an office (§3, 7 SFS 1974: 358).

The law on representation of employees on company boards (*Lag om styrelserepresentation för de anställda i aktiebolag och ekonomiska föreningar*, SFS, 1976: 351) was also adopted in 1976. It gives employees in companies, i.e. joint-stock companies, banks, mortgage banks, insurance companies and financial associations, with more than 25 employees, two representatives and two substitute members, on the company board. The equivalent also exists for public bodies. The decision to take advantage of such representation lies with the *fackklubb*, which has a collective agreement with the employer. The representatives should work in the company of the board. They do not make decisions regarding collective agreements, strikes and so on (SFS 1987: 1245). Levinsson *et al.* (1999) made an evaluation of the law on employee representation in 1999. A survey was sent out in 1998 to board representatives from LO and TCO's PTK (*Privattjänstemanna-kartellen*, Federation of Salaried Employees in Industry and Services, now known as Förhandlings- och samverkansradet PTK, Council for Negotiation and Cooperation (PTK)), as well as managing directors and chairmen of 660 randomly-selected companies. Between 51% and 69% of the representatives of these categories answered the questionnaire.

The companies were divided into three groups according to size, 25-99, 100-499 and 500 and above employees.[4]

The survey shows that the majority of managing directors and board chairmen have positive experiences regarding employee representatives on the company board. Approximately 80% do not wish to reduce employee representation. However, managing directors and chairmen of large companies, with more than 500 employees, were least happy. Many of the employee representatives keep a very low profile on most issues, except for staff, production and work-environmental issues and general reorganisation. The majority found their activities important for their trade union work. About two-thirds of the employee representatives receive no remuneration for their work on the board (Levinson *et al.*, 1999). Below, the answers to the questionnaire are used to discover possible differences between small companies and the general opinion.

Managing directors of small companies tended to be more inclined to want to keep the number of employee representatives on the board than managing directors in general: 87% compared to 80% in general. Also, none of the small company managing directors wanted to diminish the number of representatives, as compared to 20% in general.[5]

Managing directors' experiences regarding the Co-determination Act (SFS 1976: 580) are as positive as those of employee representatives, according to a 1996 survey by Levinsson (2000). Over three-quarters of the managing directors find co-determination very positive or quite positive and the major reason is that it results in more concordant decisions. Local officers have adjusted their relations to employers over time and mix negotiations and co-determination. Levinsson views this as vitalisation of the relationship and reinforcement of local-level industrial relations.

Even if most employment conditions are stipulated in collective agreements, there is some legislation on, for instance, protection of employment, holidays and parental leave. Employees are not to be dismissed without objective reasons and if they are made redundant, because of a shortage of work, they are to be taken back on, if a need for labour should occur within a certain amount of time. The minimum amount of paid holidays is 25 days per year. The law stipulates that parents have the right to full parental leave until the child is 18 months

---

4 However, only a small percentage of the respondents answered the questionnaire. Therefore the results may only serve as an indication and may not be considered statistically valid.

5 Data from Levinsson's survey, own computations.

old, but reimbursement from the national insurance system is for a maximum of 450 days for both parents taken together.

II. Small Swedish Companies from Within: Visiting the Players

The sectors chosen for the interviews were selected so as to cover a wide variety of sectors, sizes, gender and employment forms, etc., but also to fit in with the companies selected in the other two countries. The companies chosen are located in the Uppsala area, one of the more prosperous parts of Sweden, about 65 kilometres north of Stockholm. Uppsala has about 185,000 inhabitants, of whom about 140,000 live in the city itself. It is the fourth largest city in Sweden. During the last ten years, Uppsala experienced severe unemployment from the beginning of the 1990s, as was the case throughout most of Sweden. However, Uppsala, together with the entire region around Stockholm, has had a booming economy. Uppsala is a city dominated by services, while the industry sector is comparatively small. It is a university city, home of Uppsala University, the oldest in Sweden, and the Swedish University of Agriculture. The main employers are all public, namely the two universities, the university hospital and Uppsala city. The university presence has left an impact on the business structure, the bio-technical industry being especially important, but also other companies founded on new research. Uppsala is suitable for trade union density studies, which one of the three largest cities in Sweden would not have been, as the largest cities had a distinctive pattern of low unionisation among young men during the 1990s, which is different from the rest of the country. A smaller city may have caused other problems, because it may have been difficult to find suitable companies for interviews.

The interviews were used to provide additional information on membership rates, level of organisation, agreements and as the only source of information on relations between employers' and employees and ways of resolving conflicts. As interviews are very time-consuming, only a few were conducted. Seven companies were interviewed, of which three management interviews were conducted in English together with colleagues from France and Germany. The results from the interviews can only serve as examples of actual conditions. They are, nevertheless, a valuable contribution, and the sole contributor to some information, which otherwise would have been inaccessible, or, at the very least, difficult to obtain.

The aim was not to give a general picture, but rather to provide more knowledge. The companies were, therefore, chosen so as to give the opportunity to study certain aspects. They were selected from a free database put together by *FöretagsFakta*,[6] which gives information on numbers of employees, sectors and contact persons. A number of companies were selected, and studied more closely, in order to see whether they were members of an employers' organisation and their length of existence, etc. to provide a diversified picture. Very small companies, with less than five employees, were not chosen, as they could be expected to mainly be companies employing only family members or very new start-ups, and therefore less interesting from an industrial relations point of view. Only companies, which were not part of a group of companies, were chosen, unless the group itself had less than 100 employees. From previous studies, it is known that such companies, even if small themselves, tend to have unionisation in line with the size of the group, i.e. unionisation in a small company forming part of a large group is usually higher than in other small companies Kjellberg, 2000).

Some companies chose not to participate in the interviews, due to lack of time, current reorganisation or because they in fact were bigger than the 100 employee limit.

The employees were selected by management as being elected trade union representatives, or if such representation was missing, an employee usually acting as a representative or otherwise some other employee. The selection process may thereby be biased, especially as most companies lacked formal representation, but it was the only way of having easy access to the employees. It should, however, be kept in mind. Employees were given the same questions as employers, and were interviewed in the same fashion, but as they were interviewed after the employers, they could also be asked questions raised by the previous interview.

The interviews were conducted on the basis of a series of questions, which were sent beforehand to the interviewees. They included information on background variables, such as results, balance sheet totals and numbers of employees for the last five years. Partially, the questions were designed to gain knowledge of facts, such as membership and contacts with organisations, etc., but the purpose was also to find out what the interviewee thought of industrial relations. That is, his or her notion of organisations, collective bargaining, legislation, how all this related to the individual workplace, and how s/he experienced the situation in the workplace and the relationship between employees and employers. One of the aims was to investigate the current "regime" of the organisations – trade unions, employers' organisations and other

6 FöretagsFakta is a commercial company which provides information on companies to potential clients. It is free to join the database, and to use it. The size of companies vary, between very large, such as ABB, and firms with none or just one employee.

business organisations. The regime notion has been used by Hancké (1993), when speaking of trade unions, meaning that the regime is the strength of the organisation at both central and local level and the interaction between them, and that it explains variations in union density (quoted in Hyman, 2001: 212). The background variables were used for relating industrial relations to economic conditions.

As work councils, in contrast to many other European countries, do not play a part in the Swedish industrial relations system, until the introduction of the European works council (valid only for large firms), a discussion of the differences between small and large companies in shaping labour standards has to take other factors into account. In Sweden, the degree of unionisation and existence of a union section (*fackklubb*) or elected trade union representative (*facklig representantant, fackombud*) among the employees are important factors. In fact, strong union presence at local level, in combination with powerful central organisations, has been thought to be one of the reasons for the uniquely high union density.

Traditional emphasis on social dialogue makes it also meaningful to take into account possible membership of employers' organisations. In addition, membership of an employers' organisation would also mean that the workplace is covered by a collective agreement. Collective or substitute agreements, as well as individual agreements, will also be studied. The mode of organisation in the workplace, how conflicts are resolved and if the pattern is formal or informal will de discussed in the interviews. The attitude of employers and employees to labour legislation will also be investigated, as it tells about the institutions of today and in the future.

The cases were a supermarket, a garage (car sales and repairs), two hotels, two computer consultancies, of which one was into software production and the other IT, and finally one company in dental technology using new research.

The case studies were chosen both to provide a picture of the small business sector in Sweden and to match the other country studies. The service sector is the sector where small businesses are most important. In addition, the service sector is the least organised, and the lowest figures are to be found in hotels and wholesale and retail trade. In wholesale and retail trade, one company that was part of an independent chain and one that was not were chosen. Independent chains dominate Swedish wholesale and retail trade and are hence very important (Gerentz and Ottosson, 1999: 420-421). They also tend to encourage their members to join the employers' organisation, according to previous research, and therefore it would be more interesting to have one of each kind (Murhem, 2001: 401). Wholesale and retail trade is dominated by women. However, men typically work in car sales and services. It is part of the retail sector, but with very different working conditions. Other types of retail companies have a high proportion of part-time workers, whereas work in car sales is full-time. Car repair shops are organised by *Metall*, the second largest and very influential engineering and metal industry blue-collar trade union. Engineering workshops are the traditional home of the Swedish model of industrial relations. However, its base is in the large companies which dominate business life in Sweden, and, therefore, it is interesting to examine how the model works in small firms. Computer consultancy is a new sector and it is, therefore, a concern to study to what extent they have adapted to the traditional model. We could also expect it to be a sector in which new models may appear, partly due to its novelty and lack of traditions, but also partly due to new production methods, if they, as many researchers have thought, affect industrial relations.

Table 6. Case studies

							Interviewed	
Activity	Date of creation	Size (annual empl.)	Main employee group	Trade union repr.	Union density (approx.)	Collective agreement	Employer	Employee
Supermarket	1983	20	Blue-collar	Yes ?	80%	Yes	X	X
Car sale and garage	1954	35	Blue-collar	Yes	70%	Yes	X	X
Hotel	1997	25	Blue-collar	No	100%	Yes	X	
Hotel	1993	20	White-collar	No	70%	Yes	X	
Software production	1996	65	White-collar	No		No	X	X
IT and consultancy	1997	13	White-collar	No	50%	No	X	
Dental technology	1987	25	White-collar	No		No	X	X

Data was primarily collected from *Statistiska centralbyrån*, SCB, Sweden's database, which gathers material both from compulsory company reports and from surveys. Information from the databases used here includes, for instance, the number of companies and number of employees per company for different sectors. The quality of the material collected is generally good. Trade union membership rates are computed from a survey conducted by the SCB, which should be sound. Unfortunately, no information is available on membership rates for different company size categories. However, there are some company studies available, which will be supplemented by interviews. The statistics on employers' organisation membership required a special compilation of different SCB registers. As some of the information is the result of surveys, it is not possible to break it down into smaller categories. Information on trade unions and employers' organisations was provided by the organisations themselves. Klas Levinsson kindly provided data from the survey on attitudes towards employee representation on company boards.

A. The Employer

Goss (1991: 73-91) identifies four types of employee relations, ranging from high dependence of employers on employees to virtually none: 1) fraternalism, 2) paternalism, 3) benevolent autocracy and 4) "sweating" (sweatshop approach). Fraternalism means that the employer is highly dependent on the employees and may even work alongside them. An example is the building industry. Paternalism arises when the employer is less, but still to a certain extent, dependant and the employees are also dependent. Goss has borrowed the term from Newby, who found paternalism among agricultural workers. Benevolent autocracy is characterised by friendly relations between employers and employees, but at the same time a clear definition of hierarchy. A sweatshop approach means that the employees are substitutable and kept at as low a cost as possible (Goss, 1991: 73-91).

The retail business is owned by two partners, both of them men. They both work along with the employees in the supermarket, while an administrator is responsible for accounting, etc. Thus, we might assume that the business should be classified as a case of fraternalism. However, fraternalism has a strong touch of equality, and while some of the employees may be difficult to replace, many are not. The supermarket is probably more a case of paternalism in most instances, while the relationship with the accountant probably should be known as fraternalism.

The garage is a typical family firm, with the entire family working in the company. Employees' tasks are rather fixed. Many of the customers have been buying their cars from the company for a long time, at least one since the 1950s and two since the beginning of the 1960s. It is owned by a married couple, and both their son and daughter work with them – he as sales manager, and she within central management. The managing director declares that the car business is very unprofitable at the moment, only the repair department is really profitable. Hence, the future of the firm is not clear, even though he is over 70 years old. Their daughter shows an interest in management, but the outcome will depend on the profitability of the business. The employees find the uncertain future discomforting, not knowing what will happen. There is a certain amount of paternalism in the attitude of the employer, when he speaks of the firm and the employees, but probably it is more a question of benevolent autocracy in the typological sense.

One of the hotels is managed by the owner, the other by a professional manager. The owner emphasises the paternalistic structure of the hotel and that all employees are like a family. However, there are considerable differences between the relationship with the trusted housekeeper, which is of many years' standing and more fraternal, and that with the students, who are employed on an hourly basis in a sweatshop-type relationship. The latter are fully exchangeable, while the former has a key position. The hotel manager emphasises his more professional role in terms of benevolent autocracy.

Both of the directors of the IT-companies – one is a co-owner and the other an employed manager – point to the fact that they work with colleagues in a collegial fashion. Nevertheless, there is no doubt about the hierarchical order.

All the directors/managers in the companies studied are men. Women are found in a minority of middle-management positions. For instance, the supermarket has five department heads, two of whom are women and three are men. Of the remaining staff, about 70% are women, and ages vary between 18 and 62 years.

One or two of the managers consider the lack of women in higher positions to be a problem. In one of the IT companies, the managing director wants to appoint a woman for the next free position on the company board, there are none at present. Also, the dental company manager sees equality as a problem. The employee representative of the company reflects on the division between men and women due to society's norms, but says that equality is not discussed in the workplace. All managers are men, while the percentage of men and women employees is about equal. The managing director claims that it is a problem that there are too few women managers.

B. Employer-Employee Relations

Most service sectors tend to have a low degree of unionisation. The retail and wholesale blue-collar trade union *Handels*, the Swedish Commercial Employees Union, which is affiliated to LO, has about 170,000 members. It is, however, rather powerful, due partly to the militant action used against employers refusing to sign a collective agreement. A majority of the members work in companies with less than 10 employees. *Handels* cover 40,000 workplaces and has almost 1,600 *firmaklubbar* (which are the same as *fackklubbar*), 840 *ombudsmän* and almost 5,900 contact persons/shopstewards (*fackombud/fackrepresentant*). However, the tradition of *fackklubbar* is rather short, compared to industry trade unions, beginning only in the 1960s. They also have 29 regional divisions, including one in Uppsala. The TCO-affiliated union, HTF (Tjänstemannaförbundet, Salaried Employees' Union), has about 160,000 members, of whom some are employed in wholesale and retail trade. They have members in approximately 31,000 workplaces, of which 80% have less than 20 employees. Locally, there are company union sections called *företagsklubbar*, (which are the same as *fackklubbar*), but members employed by companies with more than one workplace come together in regional (*regionalklubb*) or national union structures (*riksklubb*) for that particular company. For workplaces with less than five members and which lack regional or national structures, there are general structures (*allmän klubb*). HTF has 13 regional offices and 6 local ones. Uppsala belongs to the Stockholm regional office.

The supermarket used to have a trade union representative, but the employee, who held that position, left the company, and since then, no-one has wanted to take over. The trade union representative is now replaced by help from the local trade union office.

The workers in the repair shop are members of the Swedish Metalworkers' Union, *Metall*.[7] The union, which is a member of LO, is the second largest in Sweden, with 420,000 members, covering 12,000 workplaces. In every workplace, where they have members, they have *fackklubbar*, or if it is a very small one, a contact person. Altogether, they make up 118 local divisions, numbered in order of creation. Uppsala is division number 50. 73% of the employees in the repair shop are members of *Metall*; the others are not unionised. The company did not have a union representative, but the local *Metall* trade union visited the workplace, encouraging them to elect a representative. No-one had really wanted to devote his or her time to the task before. The representative says that he does not spend very much time on the task, but finds the local trade union very helpful and valuable.

The LO trade union for employees in hotels and restaurants, HRF, has more than 60,000 members. The number of members has increased by 20,000 since the mid-1980s. About 70% of the members are women. Local organisation takes the form of workplace representatives (*fackombud/fackrepresentant*), who combine both trade union and working environment functions, and *fackklubbar*. In communities with many small companies, *fackklubbar* may be replaced by a larger one for the entire community or city, or occupation. The *fackklubbar* join a local

7 In 2006 (i.e. after the end of this research project), *Metall* merged with *Industrifacket* (the Swedish Industrial Workers) and formed a new larger trade union, *IF Metall* (*Industrifacket Metall*).

structure, which in turn belongs to a regional division. Uppsala has its own regional division.

All employees in the first hotel of the study are trade union members, which is common among blue-collar hotel workers, but not among white-collar workers. The manager explains this by saying it might be "because the white-collar union is known to be weak". Trade unions may be perceived as powerless, but there has been a tradition of being a trade union member, which may be reinforced by reading so much today in the newspapers about dismissals.

The majority of the employees in the second hotel are members of the LO the Hotel and Restaurant Workers Union (HRF), including temporary employees. Two employees in the first hotel are trade union representatives, while the former trade union representative of the second has left her position and no replacement has been elected.

Computer consultants and computer services employees mostly join LO's *Grafiska Fackförbundet Mediafacket*, TCO's Sif (*Svenska Industritjänstemannaförbundet*), Union of Clerical and Technical Employees in Industry, or SACO's CF (*Civilingenjörerne*[8]), Swedish Association of Graduate Engineers, or Jusek, Swedish Association of Graduates in Law, Business Administration and Economics, Computer and Systems Science, Personnel Management and Social Science. White-collar workers are usually members of the TCO union Sif, which has 350,000 members. It has about 22,000 trade union officers and the usual structure with *fackklubbar* or contact persons (*fackombud*). Sif is divided into 23 regional divisions, including one covering Uppsala county. The Uppsala county division co-operates with the Stockholm and Södertälje divisions in arranging courses, etc. and the three divisions even have their own magazine, which is sent to members. The Uppsala office has eight employees. About 7,000 employees are members of the Uppsala county division, covering some 750 companies. A local Sif *fackklubb* is found in 60 of those companies. Graduate engineers are members of the CF, a SACO-union, with some 85,000 members. CF has only a central office, but some 1,300 *fackklubbar* and 4,500 local officers in companies, which employ CF members.

Computer consultants have, according to workplace studies, low levels of unionisation. However, during the crisis of the Swedish IT business in autumn 2000, computer consultants started to change their mind about trade unions. Redundancies became frequent and protection obviously seemed more interesting than individualism. Jusek increased its membership by more than 20% in just a few months, while Sif made more than a thousand new members. A survey indicates that about 58%

---

8 Now called Sveriges Ingenjörer.

of employees in the IT industry were members of a trade union in 2000 (Kjellberg, 2001). As Sweden is one of few countries which have retained the Ghent system,[9] this might be what to expect (Visser, 2002: 420). The employee interviewed is a member of Sif. There is no *fackklubb* in the workplace for any trade union, which she considers to be disadvantageous. A *fackklubb* would be useful helping out in personnel issues, and to pursue further education and working environment issues. As it is now, when she wants to get in touch with her trade union, she contacts the local district, one of Sif's 23 districts. About a year ago, staff from the company contacted the district for help. At that time, the company revised their employment contracts, and the employees wanted help with how to formulate the contracts. A special case of clauses on limiting competition was at stake. They found the contact positive; they were provided with the information and expertise they needed.

The dental company falls, in a way, outside the established trade union picture. The managing director does not know about trade union members in the workplace, but the employee estimates between 15 and 20% membership. Most of unionised employees are members of Sif. Further, two safety representatives have been elected, but there is no trade union representation in the workplace.

All companies interviewed emphasise informal ways of resolving conflicts. Managers claim to resolve conflicts mainly locally and in co-operation with the employees. As employees and managers work quite closely together, this is easy and works very well. Most of the companies have not had any major conflicts, which of course may help. On the other hand, unresolved small conflicts may very well grow.

C. Pay, Working Time and Social Dialogue

1. Coverage of Collective Agreements

Wholesale and retail trade is covered by a number of different agreements. The employers' organisation has 15 with the LO trade union *Handels* and 3 with the TCO trade union HTF. Altogether, they had 35 agreements in 2000. Most of the private retailers prefer a mutual national agreement rather than an agreement for each company, as many of them are small. A strike would be very dangerous for individual companies (Kjellberg, 2000: 236-237). The collective agreement between *Handels* and the employers' organisation, *Handelsarbetsgivarna*, includes a highly unusual clause for Sweden, namely that the collective agreement does not cover a particular company unless the trade union

[9] Whereby the trade unions administer the unemployment funds.

demands it for their members in that company. Normally, collective agreements, which are signed nationally, cover all the companies, which are members of the employers' organisation, and all of their employees. The coverage of collective agreements in this particular sector is approximately 50% of all employees (Murhem, 2001: 401-402). Management of the supermarket in this study finds the collective agreement unproblematic. All employees are paid according to the collective agreement.[10] Starting pay is according to the agreements, but heads of departments receive extra pay, in order to keep them up to the business. 10% of profits are shared among the employees (all employees, including temporary staff, for whom the company is the main employer), depending on how well they have performed according to the employer.

Both hotels are covered by national collective agreements, but due to the hard competition, "they can't pay less than the agreement anyway, so it really doesn't matter", explains the employed manager. Altogether, the HRF collective and substitute agreements cover approximately 13,000 workplaces. The second hotel actually pays a little more than the basic agreement. The owner claims that "the collective agreement makes it easy to be an employer; you do not have to keep everything in your head".

The employers' organisation aims to increase the pay of high-performing employees, while the trade union prefers equal pay increases. However, the trade union is turning more to result-oriented pay. Today, they get pay rises, which are the same for all employees, to which is added a sum (a percentage of pay) in the form of individual pay increases. The individual increases are negotiated by the trade union for trade union members, while non-members negotiate for themselves. The second hotel pays one level of pay for reception staff, and another for breakfast and cleaning staff.

The car repair employees are covered by the agreement between *Metall* and their employers' organisation. The company interviewed has collective agreements, but pays somewhat more than the agreement. However, they pay less than others in the same business in Uppsala. Interestingly enough, pay does not seem to be a major incitement in employment, as higher pay does not cause employees to change companies. Many of the employees have been with the company a long time.

The collective agreement, which was valid from 1998 to 2001 and signed by *IT-företagens Arbetsgivarorganisation* covers about 30,000 employees, which comes to 54% coverage, as mentioned above. The 1998-2001 agreement does not cover pay and working hours, which are

---

[10] They receive extra for working inconvenient hours: after 6 p.m. – 50% extra; after 7 p.m. – 70% extra; Saturday afternoon – 100% extra.

agreed locally. This is unusual in Sweden and the press release published by the employers' organisation actually called it the "collective agreement for the future", clearly showing that they prefer this new type of agreement (Murhem, 2001; Kjellberg, 2001).

Neither of the IT companies in the study have collective agreements. So far, the employees have not made any demands for them, but they may eventually, according to the employers. Some customers have asked for them, among them government agencies. Also, the employers view collective agreements as providers of a positive image of the company as a serious business, and as safer for the employees. The employee interviewee provides a somewhat different picture on the introduction of collective agreements. Even if the company does not have collective agreements, the employee considers them to be valuable and better than individual contracts. Her opinion is that, so far, collective agreements have not been a high priority issue for management.

The dental technology company does not adhere to any collective agreement, nor is it a member of an employers' organisation. Pay both for blue- and white-collar employees is set by individual agreements. Pay levels are set on a demand basis, and, according to the chairperson, they pay "rather well". According to the employee interviewed, neither pay, nor negotiations are discussed among employees.

2. Working Time and Redundancies

In the grocery retail business, competition is hard. It runs in cycles, which employers have tried to overcome by having longer opening hours and Sunday opening as well. However, they have never been forced to dismiss anyone during down periods, partly by adapting working hours and partly by developing the business in new fields, such as selling hot dogs, acting as a representative for football pools and other gambling areas, etc. Redundancies are bad for business, as they lead to a bad reputation among customers. There are both part-time employees and employees employed by the hour, all of whom have chosen that particular form of employment. Usually, they are younger and some are students.

The staffing structure is very different between the hotels. But the total amount of annual employment is about the same – 25 in the first hotel and 20 in the second. However, the first hotel only employs full-time staff and outsources cleaning, though aspiring in the future to do cleaning as well. The employees work eight hour per day. Work schedules are made public at least four weeks ahead, and any changes have to be made at least two weeks in advance – all according to the agreement. If there are to be changes in the schedule system, there are negotiations. The employer draws up the schedule. The shifts are 7-15.30 and 15-23.

He does not think they need any part-time employees. The hotel's own employees have a stronger feeling for the hotel and their work than do sub-contractors, while temporary employment agencies are too expensive.

The second hotel employs about 55-60 employees, of whom 14 are full-time. In contrast to the first hotel, there is an abundance of temporary and part-time workers. Such non-standard work – if by that is meant non-permanent, non-full-time work – is quite common in the hotel and restaurant business. The hotel's temporary workers are mostly employed as cleaners and in the breakfast restaurant. Employment by the hour is not approved of by the trade union, but they have agreed to it through negotiations. Temporary employment is sometimes discontinued, as Swedish labour legislation states that employees, who are temporarily employed longer than a certain period of time, automatically become permanent staff. To avoid this, their temporary employment is ended by the hotel owner before the period expires. The average employee is 25-35 years old, but temporary employees, many of whom are students, are younger. Usually employees work six hours a day and they try to be flexible with working hours. Parental leave has worked out well. New employees are usually recruited among friends and acquaintances of the present staff, but sometimes they have advertised as well.

The first hotel has high employee turnover, but turnover is lower for managing positions. Those employed in managing positions usually have higher pay, and they are also a few years older. Most of the staff of the second one, except for those employed by the hour, have worked in the hotel since it started.

The situation in the dental technology company is different. The majority of employees works full-time and is permanently employed, but they have some PhD-students from the university working with research on a project basis. There are also some part-time workers, but they have voluntarily chosen that status, according to both the employer and employee interviewees.

Among the companies, we find different working hours, ranging from employment by the hour to permanent employment. These differences partly depend on which sector the company works in and what kind of work the employee is carrying out, but also on other factors, such as employer's preferences and the age of the employees.

3. Positions in Relation to Work Regulations

The two companies in the computer business, which, at least earlier, was known in the media for being unconventional and hostile to the old trade unions, labour legislation and collective agreement system, do not seem to correspond with that widespread belief. Both the employee and the managing directors seem to be rather fond of the traditional Swedish model of industrial relations. This goes especially for the managing directors, while the employee representative sometimes presented a more employer-oriented view on labour law, a view not shared by her employer. Contrary to the popular picture, the managing directors actually take a positive stand on trade unions and may also consider collective agreements. In general, the opinion has been that these are unpopular with the business, and ill-suited to modern business life. Labour legislation is viewed not so much as a hindrance, but as a way of making employees safer. The trade union membership rate is higher than one might expect at about the Swedish average. This may reflect a positive view from management or an effect of the general decline of the sector.

The employers in this study tend not to have a problem with labour legislation, which in public debate has often been criticised for being rigid. In fact, one of the employed managers says: "It would be dangerous if the companies could dismiss employees at will".

Also the IT-companies are embellishing this view. They find it important to have rules to make it safer for employees, especially concerning cases of redundancy. The rules may be somewhat complicated, but that maybe better than making it too easy. One of the managing directors actually thinks that nothing particular in labour law needs to be changed, while the other one suggests that the exception rule in the case of redundancies should be extended. Today, in companies with ten employees or less, two employees may be excluded from "the last in, first out rule", meaning that the employee that has been employed the longest within that particular work category stays longest, when employees are made redundant because of a lack of work. This exception may, however, be extended if the trade unions agree so in negotiations. The employee finds labour law to be valuable. There are few negative aspects about it. However, from an employer's point of view, she finds that, for instance, the legislation on redundancies and whose turn it will be may affect the company negatively. Especially businesses dependent on the competence of their employees may find it difficult. It may be disadvantageous for the growth of the company.

Even the dental technology company, which, of the companies studied, is least part of the traditional Swedish industrial relations system (as neither it, nor the employees to any larger extent, are organised and it does not adhere to a collective agreement), agrees on the weight of labour legislation. Labour legislation is very important, claims the managing director. When they had to make an employee redundant, he got help from a human resources consultant he knew, as "it is crucial to get it right". The employee in question was also informed of his rights, including the right to trade union representation, but the employee did not choose to do so.

4. Modes of Internal Company Organisation

The companies covered by this study are organised in different ways. However, they all claim to have a flat (non-hierarchical) organisational mode, with informal ways of resolving problems and conflicts.

Work tasks in the supermarket, for instance, are flexible for most of the staff. One person is working as an administrator. The business partners want to spend their time in the store and have contact with staff and customers.

The hotels' mode of organisation is described as being flat, but is, in fact, divided into small groups, each of which have a manager. However, it does not seem to be very hierarchical, but rather as most of the other small companies interviewed here. Both hotels have regular staff meetings. Every month the first hotel holds a meeting, when the budget, finances and how the hotel is doing at the moment are discussed during work hours, while the second usually combines the meetings with food and drink.

The mode of organisation is flat in both IT companies. Most conflicts – although there have not been very many – tend to be solved informally and bilaterally. The employee representative states that the organisation is flat, with few decision-making levels.

According to the manager of the dental company, organisation is flat, even if it may seem hierarchical on an organisational chart. They work with delegation of decision-making. The employee finds that whether the organisation is experienced as flat or hierarchical may depend on the individual employee and whether s/he speaks up for him/herself. She herself finds it rather flat.

5. Employee Representation

As stated earlier, in joint-stock companies with more than 25 employees, employees have the right to two employee representatives on company boards. However, none of the companies interviewed have employee representatives on their board. Some of them are too small; they do not in fact have more than 25 employees. When asked, they also give their small size as a reason. The informal way of running the company and problem-solving is also one explanation given for the lack of employee representatives. As conflicts are resolved informally, there is no need for a more formal system of co-determination.

Other forms of informal co-determination are also used. In one IT company, for instance, the employees have regular meetings in their project groups. Through these meetings, they can effectively affect their projects and work. The employee interviewed considers their influence on business to be substantial, due to the small size of the company and its flat organisation. Both employers and employees share the view of the company as a flat organisation, which has a built-in system for genuine co-determination, if not any formal company board representation.

6. *The Legitimacy of Employers' Organisations and Trade Unions*

Handelsarbetsgivarna is the employers' organisation for employers in commerce. When joining *Handelsarbetsgivarna*, the company automatically joins The Swedish Federation of Trade (*Svensk Handel*), which is both an employers' organisation and a business organisation, and the overall organisation, Swedish Enterprise (*Svenskt Näringsliv*). The Federation has more than 20,000 member companies, but not all of them are members of *Handelsarbetsgivarna*. *Svensk Handel* has 19 offices, of which seven provide employers' services. The Uppsala office provides only business services. 40 business organisations are represented in *Svensk Handel*. *Svensk Handel* claims to work hard to recruit small businesses as members and the wholesale and retail sector does have a higher percentage of employers' organisation members than other service sectors Olsson, 2000). The supermarket is a member of the employers' organisation *Svensk Handel*, which they can contact if problems occur. Usually, the need arises only about once in five years.

The garage is both a member of the employers' organisation, *Motorsbranschens Arbetsgivareförbund*, MAF and the business association for garages, *Motorbranschens Riksorganisation*, which provides customer guaranties. MAF is a member of the Swedish Enterprise Transport Group and deals with employer, training and working environment issues. It has 2,084 member companies, covering about 36,000 employees. MAF has collective agreements with Sif, *Ledarna* (Swedish association for managerial and professional staff), CF, *Metall, Transport* and *Svenska Målareförbundet* (Swedish Painters' Union). However, the employer is less enthusiastic about the employers' organisation, as he does not feel he has any particular use for it. He only joined to balance negotiations.

Sveriges Hotell- och Restaurangföretagare, SHR, is the business and employers' organisation for hotels and restaurants. It has about 4,000 member companies, of which the vast majority are small companies. In fact, 68% of the members have ten or fewer employees. SHR has five regional associations, and works with about 60 local networks of hotel or restaurant employers. There are both formal restaurant and hotel employers' organisations and business associations, as well as local informal groups of businessmen meeting regularly.

Both the hotels are members of the employers' organisation. In the middle of the 1980s, the owner of the second hotel was actually a member of the leadership. The managers do not use the employers' organisation much, but do so when they have questions about legislation or require help when having to dismiss someone. Also, they can help with legal expertise and provide ombudsmen. However, if there is a problem, the manager of one of the hotels prefers to call the local trade union in Uppsala. But the need has only occurred three times during a decade. Co-operation between the hotels in Uppsala is good, although there is a certain amount of competition on prices. They work together in a project group of the Uppsala Tourist Office, called "Uppsala Congress", which has plans for a congress centre in Uppsala, and they pay 50,000 Swedish crowns (€5,500) a year for this.

The main employers' organisation for IT companies was *ALMEGA Business Service Associations*, sub-division *ITA*. Since 2000, it is now constituted as *ALMEGA IT-företagens Arbetsgivarorganisation* (the IT companies employers' organisation), but some have chosen to join *Media- och Informationsarbetsgivarna*. *IT-företagens Arbetsgivarorganisation* is one of seven organisations in ALMEGA. ALMEGA has seven regional offices, which provide services and networks for member companies. Uppsala belongs to the Stockholm office.

In 2000, only 2% of computer consultants and computer services businesses were members of an employers' organisation. These were almost exclusively large companies. This is in accordance with the popular view of the sector as sparsely organised. However, as the largest companies were members, this means that many employees were covered. In fact, about 54% of the employees in the sector were employed by a member company (Murhem, 2001: 408). In addition, the economic problems many IT employers faced during the sector's recession in 2001 have caused many former non-members to turn to the employers' organisation. The first task for organisation has often been to help them regarding redundancy procedures. The number of employees covered by companies in *IT-företagens Arbetsgivarorganisation*, more than doubled, from 30,000 in 2000 to 66,000 in 2001, and from 400 to 600 companies.[11]

Neither of the companies is a member of an employers' organisation. The managing director of one of them feels that *Svenskt Näringsliv* is too much of an organisation for large companies, and that they do not take into account the special situation of companies managed by their

---

[11] Det här är ITA 2000 (2001).

owners. Up until 2002, they were members of *Småföretagens Riksorganisation* and from 2002 onwards of SAO. They are active in local business life.

The previous board of the other IT company, before the arrival of the new managing director, discussed the issue, but considered collective agreements regarding pensions to be too rigid. As ALMEGA-ITA provides the opportunity of service membership, that was also discussed, but considered too expensive (it is more expensive than regular membership). A renewed discussion has not so far been a priority, due to the precarious state of the business. The managing director, however, says that he thinks that the company should join in due time. The companies, for whom he previously worked, were members of an employers' organisation. They are, nevertheless, members of GEA-*Gemenskapen för Elektroniska Affärer*, the Swedish Alliance for Electronic Commerce. Among the organisers of GEA are the Federation of Private Enterprises in Sweden, Swedish Federation of Industries, the Association of IT Companies and Swedtrade. The main reason for being a member is to keep the company updated on the business. The second company is also a member of Uppsala Chamber of Commerce. Their experience of membership is that it has not proved to be business-enhancing, but that it provides a pleasant social environment. Another reason for being a member of business organisations is that customers want to know that the company contributes to the improvement of the e-commerce business. Membership thereby contributes to the marketing process. The employee's view on employers' organisations is that they form an important part of the industrial relations system as counterparts to the trade unions.

The reasons for the dental company not joining are not ideological, according to the managing director – it is just that they are still too small, but they may, in the near future, come to a point where they may be big enough to need more formal institutions. They are, however, members of the business association for dental companies, but it is more of an information-sharing organisation, than a lobby organisation, as is the case of many business associations.

According to Phelps Brown (1959), the average small size of shops is a crucial factor for explaining why trade unions have been weak in the retail sector. He attributes this mainly to the attitudes of managers/owners working alongside their employees.

The employer interviewed in the wholesale and retail sector preferred all employees to be trade union members. He claimed that both employers and employees have rights and duties and being organised makes it safer. Contact with the trade union had so far been limited. However, together with the trade union, the employer has discussed and tried to prevent work-related health problems, which have affected two or three employees.

The manager of the second hotel feels he has got a good relationship with the trade union and makes an effort for it to be that way, as he feels it is a win-win situation. His contact with the trade union is mostly when problems with the staff occur. If they cannot agree within the hotel, then the employee contacts the union. Employees do not always get what they want from the union; the latter may sometimes agree with the employer. The trade unions should, in the employer's opinion, certainly play a role, but should, on the other hand, also act responsibly.

The other manager has, just like the first one, a positive view of trade unions. He finds them necessary: "If it was not strong, the sector would be awful". It at least guaranties that the big hotels, if not the smallest ones, are run in an orderly and legal fashion.

Both of the managing directors of the IT companies interviewed share a positive view of trade unions. In one of the companies, about 50% of the employees are trade union members; in the other about 60%. Those figures are well in line with the sector level of 58%, found by Kjellberg. One of them clearly states that he prefers employees to be union members, as it makes all procedures easier, as they are more predictable. Also the employee finds trade unions important. It is vital to be a trade union member.

III. Summary of the Main Results

The interviews showed that the leadership role is generally somewhat paternalistic, with the managing director as the benevolent father, to whom everybody can go when there is a problem or a dispute. This can be related to Goffee and Scase (1995), who claim that the role of the business leader is based on images both of the entrepreneur and of their gender – the perceived specified qualities being linked to a particular gender.

The businesses studied here show evidence of all four types outlined by Goss, but the two extremes are scarce. Fraternalism, the most equal of the four types of relationships, is rare. Virtually all employers were very clear on the fact that they were, after all, the manager, in spite of declarations of flat organisations: "Well, the organisation is very flat, I am the boss, and besides that there are no different levels". Moreover, there was no doubt about the leading position in their own mind, even in relation to their closest employees/middle management. A sweatshop approach is certainly rare, but may be found in relation to those employees in the hotels and grocery store who are employed on an hourly basis. Usually, the term sweatshop has a very negative connotation. If, however, the relationship is voluntary, as we may assume is the case with students working extra hours, it is not negative. Many such employees work only for a limited period of time with the company, for instance when they are students, and are certainly fully exchangeable. If the work relationship lasts for a longer period of time, or the employee would prefer permanent or full-time employment, then exchangeability may put the employee in a difficult position for negotiations.

The two middle types are definitely the most common. Non-professional managers tend to be more paternalistic, while employed managers are more benevolent autocrats. This may be caused by the higher financial dependence on the business of employer-owners. The difference is thus also related to company size, as shown below. The pure type according to the typology is rare. Judging from the case studies, an employer may fall in more than one category, depending on the position the employee holds. For instance, the owner of the second hotel in the study is paternalistic towards the old and trusted employees, with whom he has been working for years, even in the hotel he owned before. His attitude to most of the employees fall into the category of benevolent autocracy, since the interdependence is less pronounced, while those employed on an hourly basis have a sweatshop relationship with the employer. Nevertheless, employers tend to fall into one major category.

The entrepreneur is undoubtedly a very important person within companies. Even in research-based companies, such as our dental technology company where a professional manager has been appointed and the founder/scientist still is the largest individual shareholder, while working as scientific manager, and thereby has no direct managing responsibility on a day-to-day basis, he is the base of the company. The importance of the employer/entrepreneur is clear when it comes to succession, and the difference between small and large companies is highlighted. Dependence is most evident at times of succession, when no decision has yet been made, as was the case with the car dealer. In a small business, when the owner becomes older and until a successor is chosen – be it a family member or someone else, for instance a competing firm – employees experience insecurity. The future of the company and that of the employees' future job availability are in the hands of one person or one family. This naturally causes a certain amount of anxiety amongst employees, who are more or less powerless in such situations.

There is one fundamental difference between the smallest and the somewhat larger companies when it comes to managers. Most of the companies were managed by the owner, or when there was more than one owner, either jointly by the owners, or by one of them. Non-owning managers were found in about half of the companies, ranging from the dental technology company, where the founder/partial owner occupies a function in the company, without being the manager, to one of the hotels with an employed manager. According to Storey (1997), they are usually found in companies with more than twenty employees. This is true also for the companies studied here, if we calculate in terms of numbers of annual jobs. One of the hotels, the computer software company, the dental technology company and the garage all have more than twenty employees. Of those, only the garage is still run by the owner. However, he takes together with his wife about four months' holiday a year, from June to late September, when the financial manager runs the company. Even when the managing director is there, he does not take a very active interest in the daily life of the business, according to the employee interviewed. So the assumption also holds even for that company.

We should not, however, underestimate the interdependence of employers and employees in small firms. Many employers emphasise the fact that they depend on good and reliable employees, and many of the relationships with the company have lasted a very long time.

The conflict resolution pattern in all the small companies studied here is informal. Most conflicts tend to be resolved early. Solutions were found between the manager and the employee or the employee and lower management. The employees interviewed did not complain about problems regarding conflicts, but that does not mean that they do not exist. Possibly, the manner in which employees were chosen for interviews may affect this result. As the managers gave the names of employee representatives if elected, or someone who acted as an employee representative, or otherwise another suitable employee, employees experienced by managers as argumentative or opposed to management were probably less likely to be chosen, unless they were elected representatives. In addition, employees experiencing serious trouble with management may have chosen to leave of their own free will or might have been forced to quit their employment. The possibility of forced resignation was to some extent counteracted as managers and employees were asked to talk about previous conflicts and dismissals and redundancies. As most of them had been with their respective companies for a large part of the company's life, they were likely to know about such occurrences and it was unlikely that both parties would fail to speak about them. There seems to be a strong norm of informal conflict resolution. Both employers and employees expect conflicts to be resolved informally.

However, in a few cases, mostly related to redundancies, conflicts needed more formal resolution. The most common way in cases of redundancy was for employers to contact the employers' organisation and employees the trade union. In one instance, the employer in a company that was not a member of an employers' organisation contacted a human resources management consultant he knew of previously, to make sure the dismissal was carried out by the book. It seems that in every-day life trade unions and employers' organisations do not play a large role in small companies, but that they rather are used for expertise and help when something goes wrong. Informal solutions are usually tried first, but when something is going to happen that is regulated by labour law, then the formal way may be used first.

The reason why an informal way of solving problems is chosen may not only be that the workplaces are small and the manager is close and, therefore, it is the easiest and most convenient way. There may also be a lack of alternatives, as there are few formal institutions in the workplace. This is certainly different from larger workplaces, where trade unions tend to play a bigger role, as they are present in the workplace everyday. Probably, the possibility for employees to influence managers may be bigger in larger companies, due to better formal representation. The lack of formal influence may be counterbalanced by closer informal contacts in small companies. However, this calls for further research.

Looking at the employer/employee relations from a gender perspective, the structure is clearly biased towards male domination. Employer/owners are men, even in companies/sectors, where women predominate. In companies, where there is lower management, they are in most cases also men. Even in companies, where the owners are a couple, living and working together, the man is the managing director, while the woman is working as controller or marketing director. This is not a question of terminology, but reflects the actual positions, according to the interviews. Some of the employers displayed some concern about the situation ("The next new board member will be a woman"; "Women are better managers than men"). Others took the male hierarchy for granted ("Somewhat surprisingly, my daughter is more interested in managing the business than my son"). None of the employers, however, seemed to view the unbalanced gender situation as a vital problem, since – in spite of words that sometimes expressed concern – it is still there. Even if organisation in many small companies is rather flat, there are still managers and top managers – and often also lower managers – are men. The social norm of male domination – of men as leaders and women as subordinates – is, therefore, both evident and reinforced in the small businesses studied here.

In some of the companies, full-time employment was the rule, while others had a high proportion of part-time or temporary employees. The percentage was clearly dependent on which sector the business was in, as part-time employment is common in hotels and the retail sector.

Nevertheless, one of the hotels interviewed worked only with full-time employees, so probably this situation is caused less by necessity rather than custom. Part-time or temporary employment is usually viewed by employers as a voluntary arrangement, chosen by employees, due mainly to studies or family responsibilities. Hardly any of the interviewees had considered the question. The employers had not thought about the issue of family responsibilities in a larger context, i.e. who is responsible and why. They only saw it as natural that women had most family responsibilities and thus preferred part-time employment. However, one of the employees answered that part-time work was chosen voluntarily, but that only women had made the choice. She had given the subject of women's so-called voluntary responsibility quite a lot of thought – an awareness of the importance of structural conditions that otherwise was missing.

The high coverage of collective agreements, which are also followed at company level, means that basic working conditions and industrial relations are the same for most employees, including in small companies. For a small company, adhering to a collective agreement is certainly a way of diminishing transaction costs. Decentralisation of Swedish negotiations during the last two decades has been opposed by many small businesspersons. Collective agreements were found in all companies, except those in new technology sectors, i.e. the computer services and dental technology companies. All three companies did not have anything against collective agreements. They saw it only as a practical issue, that none of the employees had wanted collective agreements, or that there was no need for such a thing in a small business. One of the employers was positive that collective agreements were beneficial, and also that customers asked for the company they dealt with to have them. All of them may well consider collective agreements in the future. The reasons were all perfectly rational, but that does not explain the differences between the sectors. We can assume that traditions within the particular sector may have quite a lot to do with it. In addition, possible actions taken by trade unions to force those who refuse to sign a collective agreement may naturally affect an individual employer's strategy and may differ between sectors and trade unions. In one instance, the choice of not joining an employers' organisation was also a way of not adhering to a collective agreement. The reason was not the collective agreement as such, but that both it and the employers' organisation were seen as too formal ways of organising the company.

Labour legislation is to a considerable degree thought to be relevant. Phrases, such as "predictable", "somewhat slow, but maybe it should not be easy to dismiss people", are used by employers. The person, who was most negative towards labour legislation, was an employee in an IT company, who, in general, found labour law to be valuable, with a few negative aspects. However, looking at it from an employer's point of view, she found that, for instance, legislation on redundancies and who will be next in turn might affect the company negatively – especially businesses dependent on the competence of their employees may find it difficult, and it might be disadvantageous for the growth of the company. One employer thought that the present exception from "the first in, first out-rule" concerning two people in companies with ten or less employees, should be extended to larger companies as well. That was the only real voice suggesting any improvements of labour law in this study. This is certainly not in line with Swedish public debate, in which labour law is depicted as a major obstacle for small businesses and their growth. FR advocates, as one of its main goals, that: "Labour legislation should be modified into individual and local solutions".[12] *Svenskt Näringsliv* advocates in its "Call for Economic Growth" that: "Labour legislation is to be thoroughly reformed... aiming at a reasonable protection for both employers and employees".[13] This view is certainly not evident among the employers studied here. The fact that most of the companies were at least moderately profitable and that they had only experienced a few redundancies may of course be one explanation for the discrepancy, but it cannot explain the entire difference.

In spite of the Co-determination Act, employee representation on company boards does not exist in any of the companies studied here. After all, some of them were large enough, but both employers and employees answered, when questioned, that there had been no demand for company board representation. One might suspect that employers would not welcome the idea and that employees, therefore, do not put the suggestion forward, but there is no particular evidence pointing in that direction. The author's computation of Levinsson's data showed that small employers were satisfied with the employee board representation of their companies, but there may be a difference between those, who have experience of employee representation, and those, i.e. the employers in this sample, who do not. The employers without experience may be sceptical as to how it would work out. This could point to a patriarchal leadership-style, where the employer is very friendly towards his employees, but wants to remain the indisputable leader nevertheless. Employee board representation may then be perceived as a threat to that position. It is evident that the right to company board employee representation is not an internalised standard in these small companies, neither among employers nor employees.

---

12 Företagarnas Riksorganisation (FR), 2002: 2.

13 Svenskt Näringsliv, 2002: 26.

All the managers interviewed claim that their company organisation is, if not on a chart, in fact, in reality, flat. They seem to be about the same, organised in small groups with few lower managers. One might nevertheless ask whether the terms "flat" or "hierarchical" are subject to fashion. Flat organisations have, after all, been the thing to have in organisational literature in recent decades, while hierarchical ones are despised. However, since the organisations are so small, they tend to be rather flat anyway, with the manager working close to the employees.

Employees and employers seem, to a large extent, to share a common view on the industrial relations system. Trade unions are viewed as something positive, which makes the relationship easier and more predictable. They are experienced as helpful and competent. Overall, the opinion is positive, both from employers and employees, even from employees who have chosen not to join. One reason given for not joining is because of holding a middle management position. However, the rate of unionisation is, as expected, in most instances lower than the Swedish average. Nonetheless, the two companies working in computer services have about the average rate, as do the hotels. Among those not unionised are many employees, who work part-time or on a temporary basis. This certainly is not unexpected, as it is the case in many Swedish workplaces, as shown by earlier surveys. It may reflect rational behaviour, if, for instance, you are a student working part-time for a limited period in order to earn some extra money, then you may not have a need for a trade union. But it may also be caused by trade unions' inability to attract these groups and make their benefits from trade union membership clear.

The last-mentioned argument, namely lack of visible benefits, is probably important, as studies have shown that ideological reasons for unionisation are not as important as instrumental ones. This has also been considered a reason for union members being less prone to be active (Pilemalm *et al.*, 2001: 575). The problems of attracting members to trade union positions as shop stewards or safety representatives are a known fact, which was evident in this study as well. Formal trade union representation in the company is not permanent, even in those which have had one for a period of time. If the individual trade union representative leaves the firm, s/he may not be replaced. The lack of *fackklubbar* or local trade union officers was thought by both employers and employees not to be a problem as such, but it would have been beneficial and useful to have a *fackklubb* or representation in many instances. We may, however, note how trade unions at regional level may affect the existence of shop stewards or *fackklubbar*, by the example of *Metall.* By visiting the garage repair shop, and encouraging them to elect a representative, formal trade union representation was established in the workplace. This points to the importance of regional and local players and their actions for the industrial relations pattern in small companies.

An important consequence of there being few shop stewards in small companies is that it is usually a step towards a trade union career. Employees of small companies, therefore, run the risk of being under-represented in higher trade union positions. Thereby, the discrepancy between small company employees and trade unionists may be reinforced. Also, trade union officers, usually coming from larger companies, may find it difficult to understand the problems of small company employees and also what it would take to involve them in trade union activities.

One of the reasons, why there are few local trade union representatives within companies, may be that the trade union network in Sweden is well-organised and encompassing. Therefore, employees may have the feeling that they are well protected anyway and, therefore, there is less need for individual involvement and local shop stewards. If that is so, it may well, in the long run, be problematic for the trade unions. It is somewhat paradoxical that one of the reasons for the high degree of organisation is that the trade unions are strong at both local and central levels. In a way, trade unions in Sweden are perhaps seen more as a part of society's social security network, i.e. a concern for society at large, rather than individuals. Therefore, if an employee finds him- or herself in conflict with their company, the natural thing to do is to call the trade union, just as s/he would call a doctor when they are ill.

The attitude towards employers' organisations is more mixed than that towards trade unions. Employees are usually indifferent, while opinions among employers vary from positive to negative. Among positive opinions are employers who find their expertise useful and feel that there is a need for balance in negotiations. Among negative opinions is the perception that *Svenskt Näringsliv* is not suited to small owner-managed companies. This opinion is well-known among *Svenskt Näringsliv*'s representatives and they have tried to counteract it with, for instance, press releases declaring that only 1.7% of their member companies have more than 250 employees, and that small companies have their own committee.[14] However, that the vast majority of members are small is obviously not the same thing as feeling that they are influential enough or that the organisation is well suited to small enterprises and speaks for them.

The decision to join or not to join seems to be based on a rational calculation of weighing benefits against the cost, which fits well with Lundqvist's (1998) study. Of Westholm's (2000) four reasons for

[14] Svenskt Näringsliv 27 August 2002.

joining an employers' organisation – representation in negotiations, access to advice, influence of public opinion in a more employer-friendly way and a social and a collegial environment – the first two seem to be the most important. The public relations function of employers' organisations was not mentioned by any of the interviewees. The importance of a social context was comparatively more important, but there are many ways to have that – by joining business associations, informal groups and chambers of commerce, etc., which probably make that aspect of membership less prominent. One reason, not mentioned by Westholm, but by the employers, was the need for a balance in, not only negotiations, but in society as a whole. So when there are trade unions, there should also be employers' organisations. Here, the traditions of the corporatist Swedish society are obvious.

Many of the companies in the study are active in local business life, meeting both with colleagues and other employers. Some try to act as role models and encourage entrepreneurship. Meeting with other managers and owners, and being members of business associations, is a way of gaining knowledge, sharing information, and also supporting and promoting business and their particular sector. Most of them are part of a social context of small and medium-sized businesses and their owners and managers, even if the context does not play any considerable role in their everyday life. Thereby, being a businessman and/or an entrepreneur is part of their individual perception of themselves.

It seems, judging from these seven studies, that in many respects small companies fit in rather well with the industrial relations model in Sweden and that both employers and employees share the values of the model. If we use the term "regime", the Swedish industrial relations regime appears to be rather well incorporated in employers' and employees' norms. They seem to be traditional and conventional in terms of industrial relations, adhering to the overall pattern of the regime. The small companies studied here may more accurately be described as followers of the industrial relations system, rather than as players who reshape the regime. New ideas and divergences from the model have, to a great extent, to be found elsewhere than within these companies. Probably the large companies are the ones that push the regime forward and change the direction, rather than the small companies studied here. Players in small companies tend to stick to informal relations within their company, but formal ones in their relations outside the company. Clearly, interdependence on the surrounding society is very high.

However, there might be a discrepancy between full- and part-time employees. Full-time employees are more often men, permanently employed, have more often worked longer within the company and are also more often trade union members. This may emphasise the fact that the Swedish industrial relations model, even within small companies, is made for the "typical worker", i.e., the worker with whom the model once originated. This unquestionably underpins the differences within the system, not so much between small and large companies as between women and men, permanently or temporarily employed, full-time or part-time employees.

The largest difference between small and larger companies is probably the flat organisation and comparatively easy access to management, which means that most conflicts are resolved in an informal way. Both employers and employees speak about how comparatively easy it is to talk to each other if a problem arises. However, the lack of formal institutions in many of these small companies may be a risk if a conflict arises, which is hard to resolve. It is easier to resolve a conflict *via* the *fackklubb* than having someone external from the trade union.

Due to their small size, many of the companies lack expertise on labour legislation and standard procedures and may also be inexperienced regarding issues such as redundancies, which occur infrequently in small companies. This may explain why many employers interviewed speak highly of labour legislation and the help they can get from trade unions and employers' organisations.

The question, as to whether differences in industrial relations are caused by company size or whether differences between sectors are more important, could be answered as follows. The differences between sectors are considerable, when it comes to traditions of unionisation, employment conditions, etc. However, there seem to be fundamental differences between large and small companies, whereas small companies are clearly alike as a result of being small organisations with close relationships between employer-owners and employees.

References

Statistical sources and legislation

Företagsfakta database

Statistics Sweden's database

Klas Levinson's survey

Legislation:

SFS 1962: 381
1974: 358
1976: 580
1987: 1245
1995: 584
1996: 359

Bibliography

Brown, C., Hamilton, J. & Medoff, J. (1990), *Employers Large and Small.* Cambridge, Mass: Harvard University Press.

Brown, P. (1959), *The Growth of British Industrial Relations. A study from the standpoint of 1906-14.* London: Macmillan.

Chapman, P. (1999), Managerial control strategies in small firms, in *International Small Business Journal*, Vol.17, No.2, p.75-82.

Crouch, C. (1996), "Revised Diversity: from the neo-liberal decade to beyond Maastricht", in Van Ruijsseveldt, J. & Visser, J. (eds.), *Industrial Relations in Europe. Traditions and Transitions.* London: Sage Publications.

De Geer, H. (1989), *I vänstervind och högervåg. SAF under 1970-talet.* Stockholm: Publica, Allmänna förlaget.

De Geer, H. (1992), *Arbetsgivarna: SAF i tio decennier.* Stockholm: SAFs förlag.

EIRO Observer (2002), "Non-permanent employment, quality of work and industrial relations". Issue 5, supplement, p.I-VIII.

Elvander, N. (1998), "The Swedish Bargaining System in the Melting Pot", in Elvander, N. & Holmlund, B. *The Swedish Bargaining System in the Melting Pot. Institutions, Norms and Outcomes in the 1990s.* Solna: The National Institute for Working Life.

Elvander, N. (2000), *Industriavtalet i tillämpning.* Sandviken: Almegas Förlag

Elvander, N. (2002), "The New Swedish Regime of Collective Bargaining and Conflict Resolution: A Comparative Perspective", in *European Journal of Industrial Relations*, Vol.8, No.2, p.197-216.

Furåker, Bengt & Berglund, Tomas (2001), "Anställdas syn på sin relation fack och arbetsgivare". *Arbetsmarknad och Arbetsliv*, No.1, p.5-14.

Företagarnas Riksorganisation (2002), *Småföretag skapar tillväxt. Näringspolitisk plattform.* Stockholm: Företagarnas Riksorganisation.

Gerentz, S. & Ottosson, J. (1999), *Handel och köpmän i Stockholm under ett sekel.* Stockholm: Ekerlids Förlag.

Goffee, R. & Scase, R. (1995), *Corporate Realities. The dynamics of large and small organisations.* London/New York: Routledge.

Goss, D. (1991), *Small Business and Society.* London: Routledge.

Hansson, C.-G. (1996), *Fackliga karriärer.* Umeå: Boréa Bokförlag (diss).

Hyman, R. (2001), "Trade Union Research and Cross-National Comparison", in *European Journal of Industrial Relations*, Vol.7, No. 2, p.203-232.

Kjellberg, A. (2000a), "Facklig organisering och partsrelationer i Sverige och Danmark", in Ibsen, F. and Scheuer, S. (eds.), *Septemberforliget og det 21. Århundrede. Historiske perspektiver og framtiden.* Copenhagen: Jurist- og Økonomforbundets Forlag.

Kjellberg, A. (2000b), "Arbetsgivarstrategier i Sverige under 100 år", in Strøby Jensen, C. (ed.), *Arbejdsgivere i Norden. En sociologisk analyse af arbejds-*

giverorganiseringen i Norge, Sverige, Finland og Danmark. Copenhagen: Nordiska Ministerrådet, Nord 2000, p.25.

Kjellberg, Anders (2001), *Fackliga organisationer och medlemmar i dagens Sverige*. Lund: Arkiv Förlag.

Kuuse, J. (1986), *Strukturomvandlingen och arbetsmarknadens organisering. SAF och dess motparter i en förändrad omvärld*. Stockholm: SAF.

Levinson, K., Ragnar, B. & Tengberg, B. (1999), *Anställdas represenation i företagsstyrelser- en enkätundersökning av Swedish Enterprise*. Stockholm: LO-report.

Levinson, K. (2000), "Co-determination in Sweden: Myth and Reality", in *Economic and Industrial Democracy*, Vol.21, No.14, p.457-473.

Lundqvist, T. (1998), *Arbetsgivarna efter 1945- arbetskraftsbrist och kartellstrategi: Verkstadsföreningen samt Bryggeriarbetsgivareförbundet och SAF*. Solna: The National Institute for Working Life.

Magnusson, L. (2000), *Den tredje industriella revolutionen- och den svenska arbetsma*rknaden. Stockholm: Prisma.

Murhem, S. (2001), "Sweden- Stability in a Turbulent Environment", in Dölvik, Jon-Erik (ed). *At Your Service*. Brussels: PIE-Peter Lang.

Nelander, S. & Lindgren, V. (1998), *Röster om facket och jobbet. Synen på fackligt medlemsskap och fackets uppgifter*. Stockholm: LO report.

Nelander, S. & Lönnros, E. (2000), *Facklig organisationsgrad 2000*. Stockholm: LO.

Pilemalm, S., Hallberg, N. & Timpka, T. (2001), "How Do Shop Stewards Perceive Their Situation and Tasks? Preconditions for Support of Union Work", in *Economic and Industrial Democracy*, Vol.22, No.4, p.569-599.

Rothstein, B. (1986), *Den socialdemokratiska staten*. Lund: Arkiv förlag.

Storey, D. J. (1997), *Understanding the Small Business* Sector, London: Thomson International Business Press.

Svenskt Näringsliv (2002), *Upprop för tillväxt*. Stockholm: Svenskt Näringsliv.

Svenskt Näringsliv (27-08-2002), *98.7% småföretagare*. Stockholm: Svenskt Näringsliv, press release.

Tegle, S. (ed.) (2000), *Har den svenska modellen överlevt krisen? Utvecklingstendenser i arbetslivet inför 2000-talet*. Solna: The National Institute for Working Life.

Thörnqvist, C. (1999), The Decentralisation of Industrial Relations: The Swedish Case in Comparative Perspective, in *European Journal Of Industrial Relations*, Vol.5, No.1, p.71-87.

Tolliday, S. & Zeitlin, J. (eds.) (1991), *The Power to Manage? Employers and Industrial Relations in Comparative-Historical Perspective*. London/New York: Routledge.

Under- och överutbildning på 2000-talets arbetsmarknad. En förstudie av matchningen mellan utbildning och kvalifikationskrav. ITPS report A2001:006.

Visser, J. (1996), Corporatism beyond repair? Industrial relations in Sweden, in Van Ruijsseveldt, J. & Visser, J. (eds.), *Industrial Relations in Europe*. Traditions and Transitions, London: Sage Publications.

Visser, J. (2002), Why Fewer Workers Join the Unions in Europe: A Social Custom Explanation of Membership Trends, in *British Journal of Industrial Relations*, Vol.40, No.3, p.403-430.

Westholm, C.-J. (2000), Varför behövs arbetsgivarorganisationer?, in Tegle, S. (ed.), *Har den svenska modellen överlevt krisen? Utvecklingstendenser i arbetslivet inför 2000-talet*. Solna: The National Institute for Working Life.

Germany

Wolfgang RUDOLPH and Wolfram WASSERMANN

Büro für Sozialforschung, Kassel

I. Small Companies Industrial Relations in Germany

A. *The Importance of Small Companies in the German Economy*

In Germany, there exist some 2.1 million workplaces, of which hardly 40,000 have 100 or more employees.[1] In other words, nearly 98% of all workplaces may be classified as small companies and about 60% of employees work in such establishments.[2]

The official economic statistics of the Federal Republic of Germany are incomplete where the classification of companies by size is concerned: annual updating is available only for manufacturing industry and hence for the industrial and industrial craftwork (*produzierendes Handwerk*) sectors.

1. Industry and Craftwork

Although small companies with 100 or fewer employees make up nearly 90% of all workplaces in the mining sector, they account for less than one employee in six. The sector is still dominated by a few large companies, with two thirds of employees working in workplaces of 500 or more employees. The construction and public works sector continues to be dominated by small entities, with 85% of workplaces employing no more than 20 persons and about 95% of them employing fewer than 100. Some 60% of employees in the sector work in small companies of that type. Here the weight of large companies is much less than in industry and mining: less than 12% of employees in the sector are employed in entities with over 200 employees.

1 Original text in German.

2 Data from IAB (*Institut für Arbeitsmarkt und Berufsforschung Nürnberg*) as at 30 June 2001.

Table 1. Workplaces and employees by company size in the mining industry, in manufacturing industry and in the construction industry

	Sector			
	Min. Ind.		Industry and Craftwork	
	Workplaces	Employees	Workplaces	Employees
All workplaces	1,341	92,559	46,559	5,956,050
1-49 employees	87%	18.5%	51%	11.2%
50-99 employees	6.4%	6%	22.6%	12.2%
100-199 employees	3.6%	7.8%	16.6%	19.9%
200-499 employees	1%	5.9%	6%	15.9%
500-999 employees	1%	10.5%	2.5%	12.9%
1,000 or more employees	1.5%	55%	1.4%	27.4%

Proportion of companies and employees (%).
Source: Statistisches Bundesamt, end of September 2004.

According to available statistics – albeit incomplete – almost three quarters of workplaces in industry and productive craftwork employ fewer than 100 persons. A bare quarter of all employees in manufacturing industry are thus employed in these small undertakings. Over 40% of employees work in large units of 500 or more workers that account for less than 4% of all workplaces. In 2000, specific statistics focused on small industrial companies showed, for the category with less than 20 employees, some 50,000 additional workplaces with nearly 300,000 employees not counted in the official statistics mentioned above. To these must be added the approximately 500,000 craft industry workplaces (*Handwerkszählung*, 1995) with roughly 6 million employees.

2. Wholesale and Retail, Trade and Services

So far, there exist no similar statistics for the services sector using a classification by size. In September 2002, the Federal Office of Statistics for the first time presented data concerning certain sub-sectors in the private services sector (excluding financial services). According to this compilation, there were in 2000 about 476,000 companies providing services that employed some 4,830,000 persons. The average size of these workplaces was about 10 employees (for comparison, in 2000 the average size of workplaces in manufacturing industry was 133 employees). Consequently, the services sector is not only tending to dominate both the structure of the economy and the structure of the labour markets, but, with the expansion of private services, it is the small company that is becoming increasingly the dominant form of organisation of work.

The statistics dealing with certain services sectors, but based on rather old compilations, confirm the predominance of small firms in the private services sector. This is true, for example, for wholesale and retail trade and for the hotel and restaurant sector: 75% of such companies have less than 6 employees. Between a fifth and a third of employees, depending on the sector, work in such very small companies.

More than 95% of the companies employ fewer than 50 persons and over half those employed in the sector work in them. The proportion of companies employing 100 or more persons is minute – less than 1%. However, about a third of employees in the sector work in companies of that size – with the significant exception of the catering industry in which larger companies are practically non-existent. In particular, retail trade is characterised by highly contrasting structures – over half of those employed in the sector work in hundreds of thousands of small and very small companies while the rest (40%) are employed in large stores and shopping precincts.

Table 2. Companies and employees by size of workplace in wholesale and retail trade, hotels, and restaurants (compilation for 1993)

Sector	Number of companies/ employees	1-5	6-19	20-49	50-99	100-199	200-499	500-999	1000 +
Garages (car sales and repairs)	54,873	62%	28%	7%	2%	0.6%	0.2%	0.04%	0.00%
	519,099	15%	30%	23%	13%	8%	6%	3%	3%
Wholesale trade	178,304	75%	18%	5%	1.4%	1%	0.3%	0.07%	0.03%
	1,592,511	18%	20%	15%	11%	10%	12%	5%	9%
Retail trade	388,414	79%	18%	2%	0.4%	0.2%	0.1%	0.05%	0.05%
	2,865,963	25%	23%	8%	4%	3%	5%	5%	28%
Hotels and restaurants	222,746	78%	19%	2%	0.5%	0.1%	0.05%	0.01%	0.01%
	1,228,113	36%	32%	13%	6%	3%	3%	1%	6%

Proportion of companies and employees (%).

3. *The* Mittelstand

In general, the sector of small and medium-sized enterprises (SME) is known in Germany as the *Mittelstand.* There exists no clear unambiguous definition for this form of company organisation. The feature they have in common is probably the close link between the owner and the company. Unlike managers, the entrepreneur (*Unternehmer*) is responsible for running the company and taking strategic decisions regarding its development. The overlapping of ownership and responsibility or, in other words, the close relationship between the economic identity of the owner and that of his or her company generally presupposes economic independence of a kind often likened in specialist literature to the independence of major groups (*Konzernunabhängigkeit*) (cf. Richter, 1977).[3]

According to a study published in 1999, Germany had 1.1 million companies in the *Mittelstand* with an annual turnover of over DM 250,000 (€125,000). Some 40% of these companies belong to the private services sector and more than a quarter of them are craftwork companies. Traditionally, the centres of gravity of the *Mittelstand* economy are the building industry, manufacturing industry (industry and craftwork) and retail trade. The up-and-coming sectors, such as transport, information technologies, health, and social services have only a marginal presence, at least currently. The category of firms with a family tradition is particularly well represented. Some 35% of the companies are over 30 years old whereas the 200,000 or so new arrivals – 18% of the total – have a less important role among small companies than is often attributed to them.

Table 3. Companies in the *Mittelstand*, by size
Number of companies and percentage of total

	1-5 employees	6-9 employees	10-19 employees	20-49 employees	50-499 employees
Number of companies	1,458,843	255,937	262,617	127,969	83,180
Percentage of total	68.4%	12%	9.5%	6%	39%

Source: (MIND, Mittelstand-in-Deutschland-Studie, 2002).

In 2002, almost 80% of *Mittelstand* companies belonged to the category of very small companies, with under 10 employees. Over 90% were small workplaces with under 20 employees. Less than 4% of *Mittelstand* companies employ 50 persons or more.

The 1999 study also provides information on the management structure of *Mittelstand* companies. About 60% of them are run by the owner

3 In Germany, companies generally defined as Mittelstand companies are small and medium-sized companies with less than 500 employees, with an annual turnover not exceeding 50 million euros and run by their owners (definition by the Deutsches Institut für Mittelstandforschung in Bonn). Different limits are used at the European level in the context of economic development aid by the European Union. SMEs are defined as those with an annual turnover not exceeding 40 million euros and employing a maximum of 250 persons. Companies may belong to one or more other companies up to a maximum of 25% (cf. Institut für Mittelstandforschung, 1997). In this chapter, small companies (Kleinbetriebe) refer to workplaces with no more than 100 employees.

in person or by a managing partner. In 17% of other cases, the company is run by the owner or his/her family. About 55% of the companies have no more than one level of employee below management. In companies with more than 50 employees, the organisation tends to be more varied and to make more use of the division of labour. Three companies in four have two, three, or even more levels of authority. Nonetheless, a highly formalised hierarchical structure is much rarer than in large companies. Only half the surveys conducted assert that managerial staff exercise explicit hierarchical responsibilities and is empowered to give orders; in other cases, they act essentially as team leaders or serve simultaneously as leaders and as supervisors. This shows that small companies rarely make use of a rigorous Taylorian division of labour, with a strict separation of managerial and other activities. The organisation of a small company requires all employees to be polyvalent, personally involved and relatively self-disciplined.

When questioned about their motivation in the management of a private company, almost nine *Mittelstand* entrepreneurs out of ten highlight their economic independence: "Being an entrepreneur is important for me because I want to be free and independent". Nearly half those surveyed intend to carry on a family business tradition. However, a little over 20% of the companies covered by the survey spoke of being forced into setting up business by the outsourcing of certain sectors of a company by a former employer or by the risk of unemployment.

The proportion of *Mittelstand* entrepreneurs, who are members of a collective organisation, varies greatly. About 70% of those questioned are members of a chamber of commerce and industry and just under 40% are registered at a craft guild, but only about one company in two belong to one or more sector-level employers' organisations.

In the next few years, numerous *Mittelstand* companies will be faced with handing over management to the next generation owing to the advanced age of their founders. Many of them are ill prepared for this step. More than half the entrepreneurs questioned said that they had not prepared for their succession or were unable to answer the question. Handing over to their children might well eventually might become the exception rather than the rule. Such a solution has been adopted by only a third of the companies surveyed. In more than 10% of cases, the sale or closure of the company appeared to be imminent (cf. Mittelstand in Deutschland – MIND, 1999).

B. The German System of Industrial Relations

The German industrial relations system includes two complementary regulatory mechanisms.

1. Collective Agreements

Collective agreements are negotiated by trade unions and employers' organisations, usually at the sector level. Sector-level agreements are usually regional (e.g. a Land). They are mandatory for employees of workplaces whose employer belongs to a signatory employers' organisation. In addition to sector-level collective agreements (*Branchentarifverträge*), there exist a large number of collective agreements at the company level (*Firmentarifverträge*) negotiated by the relevant sector-level union and the employer's representatives in the company (or group of companies, *Konzern*, etc.).

2. The Betriebsräte

The law permits the establishment of works councils (*Betriebsräte, BR*) in workplaces with at least five employees. These bodies representing the employees have rights of co-determination regarding important aspects of daily life in the workplace, such as the procedures for fixing rates of pay and working time, recruitment, transfers and dismissals, the application of collective agreements, and the respect for legal provisions concerning the protection of employees (in matters of health or safety, for example).

Persons elected to the *Betriebsräte* are accorded legal protection against disciplinary measures and dismissal and the law also stipulates the conditions for the exercise of collective representation. The size of these councils depends on the size of the workplace. In those with 5 to 20 employees, the *Betriebsrat* is composed of a single person; in workplaces with 21 to 50 employees, it has three elected members and five in workplaces with 51 to 100 employees. Since the 2001 reform of the Works Constitution Act (*Betriebsverfassungsgesetz*), workplaces with 200 or more employees include elected members who are entirely exempted from their professional duties (previously the threshold had been fixed at 300 employees).

The *Betriebsräte* have a dual function in the production and application of sector-level or company-level collective standards. As the basic representatives of the union, they play an important role in the preparation of collective agreements – such as when they are members of union negotiating committees. As the legal representatives of employees' interests, they have the task of implementing, and of adapting to the actual conditions of the workplace, the sector-level collective standards. Collective agreements contain an increasing number of options to take account of local conditions, which need to be expressed, through negotiation, in detailed standards at the local level. In this connection, people speak of "a second round of collective bargaining in the workplace".

This said, this two-track system of regulation, by sector and by company, is simply one basic model as described for instance in textbooks. The two elements unite effectively only in a proportion of companies. Certain sectors are covered by collective agreements, but lack *Betriebsräte* capable of adapting sector-level standards to local conditions. In other cases, *Betriebsräte* have been set up, but the workplaces are not subject to collective agreements because the employers are not affiliated to the employers' organisation that signed it. Lastly, there also exist workplaces without a *Betriebsrat* and not covered by a collective agreement.

Figure 1. Coverage by collective agreement and presence of *Betriebsräte*:
Typical situations

A	B
Workplaces subject to collective agreement and possessing a Betriebsrat	Workplaces not subject to collective agreement and possessing a Betriebsrat
C	**D**
Workplaces subject to collective agreement and not possessing a Betriebsrat	Workplaces not subject to collective agreement and not possessing a Betriebsrat

How are these four typical situations reflected in actual practice? According to a 1998 study by the IAB (Research institute on labour markets and occupations), the basic model of the dual system – workplaces covered by a collective agreement and having a *Betriebsrat* – is generally in the minority. It is only in workplaces with 100 employees or more that the model at the heart of industrial relations in Germany (Type A in Figure 1) starts to become common and it is only with large companies with over 1000 employees that it becomes universal. According to the same study, in small companies with 100 employees or less the most common pattern is that of a collective agreement but no *Betriebsrat* (Type C). About a third of workplaces are not covered by a not do they possess a *Betriebsrat* collective agreement (Type D). This particular situation, which tends to be the exception in medium-sized and large companies, appears to be very common in small ones (IAB-Betriebspanel, 1998).

Table 4. Works councils and collective agreements: Coverage by size of workplace – West and East Germany

Model	All workplaces West / East	5-20 employees West /East	21-100 employees West / East	101-299 employees West/East	300-1,000 employees West / East	1,001 + employees West / East
Type A:	14%	7%	34%	74%	89%	95%
with CA & BR	12%	5%	28%	66%	85%	98%
Type B:	1.50%	0.80%	3.70%	6%	3%	2%
with BR but no CA	1.60%	0.60%	4.40%	7%	3%	1%
Type C:	55%	60%	43%	14%	3.40%	0.60%
with CA but no BR	40%	41%	42%	17%	8%	1%
Type D:	30%	33%	19%	6%	5%	2%
with no CA & no BR	46%	53%	26%	4%	4%	0%

Source: Workplaces panel, Institut für Arbeitsmarkt- und Berufsforschung (IAB), Nuremburg, 1998.
CA = collective agreement; BR= Betriebsrat.

These figures tend to show that, on the whole, small companies are not well integrated into the official system of industrial relations. Two thirds of those with under 20 employees are indeed covered by collective agreements, but in general do not possess a body representing the interests of employees. In small companies with 20 to 100 employees, this remains the most common situation (40% of cases), but a third of this category are tied to the two-track system of regulation and covered by both collective agreements and Betriebsräte, while a fifth have neither one nor the other.

a. The *Betriebsräte* in Small Companies

In the absence of official statistics concerning works councils, we have to fall back on the findings of representative surveys. According to the figures of the IAB workplaces panel, only 7% of employees in very small companies (5-20 employees) and a third of those in companies with 21-100 employees are represented by a *Betriebsrat*. It is not until we come to companies with 1000 or more employees that we find all employees effectively covered. In all, about 50% of employees in the private sector are represented by a *Betriebsrat* in West Germany and less than 40% in East Germany.

Figure 2. Presence of *Betriebsräte*, by size of workplace. % of workplaces and employees covered

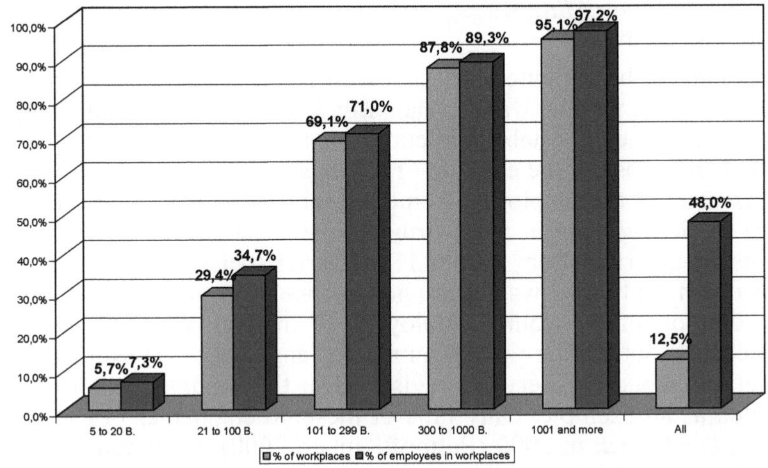

Source: Betriebspanel 2000, (privatwirtschaftliche Betriebe ohne Landwirtschaft und Organisationen ohne Erwerbszweck), IAB-Materialien, No. 1/2002; Figure: Büro für Sozialforschung, Kassel, 2002.

Clearly, the introduction of the *Betriebsräte* system has been very uneven in the various sectors, reflecting company structures and historical traditions. As in the case of collective agreements, company size – as well as its particular legal status and pattern of ownership – play a role here. The IAB data by sector reveal a particularly strong presence of *Betriebsräte* in sectors dominated by large companies and having a long tradition of exchange and coordination between union and employers' organisations (as in the mining industry, manufacturing industry and banking, etc.). On the other hand, the *Betriebsräte* system is weak in sectors dominated by the *Mittelstand* and in small production units (building, trade, private services) (IAB, 2002).

b. The *Betriebsräte* – on the Way to Becoming a Minority Model?

According to another survey, the proportion of employees represented by a *Betriebsrat* dropped from 50.6% in 1981 to 39.5% in 1994 (Kommission Mitbestimmung, 1998). This decline in employee representation is primarily due to the major structural changes that have taken place over the last 15 years. Companies and workplaces have decreased in size as a result of redundancy and staff cuts; a good many industrial companies with long traditions of co-determination have closed down. The splitting up of large companies into a multitude of small firms has deprived the *Betriebsräte* of their organisational base:

the number of elected members has diminished and the 'new' companies, small in size, have not always revitalised such bodies. Lastly, the majority of the companies established in the 1990s are small ones belonging to the *Mittelstand*, traditionally resistant to the co-determination culture.

It should not be forgotten that a wave of new firms does not automatically create a parallel wave of new *Betriebsräte*. As a rule, the body of employees in newly established companies needs several years to get organised and consider the election of a *Betriebsrat* – sometimes against the resistance of the employer. Some authors have deduced from the absence of *Betriebsräte* in most firms in the "new economy" that the organ itself, inherited from the "old" industrial society and an expression of union traditions, was no longer in tune with the structures and mental outlook of the young employees of innovative companies. A survey carried out among young companies engaged in e-business and information technology services registered in the Nemax-50 index has been cited as an example. Only nine of these 50 companies (18%) had elected a *Betriebsrat* in 2000 (Potthof/Kipker, 2000). Such conclusions are nevertheless a bit hasty. For one thing, the proportion of companies with a *Betriebsrat*, nearly 20%, is in fact a bit higher than in the other services sectors. For another, the "tender youth" of most firms in the new economy has not been taken into account. We know from experience that the years immediately after starting up a company are not propitious for the establishment of a *Betriebsrat*, whatever the sector or kind of workplace.

In 2001 an in-depth reform of the Works Constitution Act, which lays down the election procedures and the operation of *Betriebsräte*, was carried out, the first for nearly thirty years. One of the main goals of the reform was to strengthen co-determination in small and medium-sized companies. The establishment of a *Betriebsrat* in small workplaces was to be explicitly facilitated. Even though the concept of co-determination (*Mitbesstimmung*) included in the Act is traditionally modelled on the structures and conditions of large workplaces and companies, the 2001 law sought, for the first time, to take account of the particular situation of small companies. A growing number of small relatively autonomous concerns had, in the 1990s, taken the place of unified and centralised company structures. Among other things, this had resulted in the formation of small units within overarching company networks. The elected members in the *Betriebsräte* found themselves dispossessed, often in the very areas in which they had been active for many years, of the reference points for bargaining with the employer and of their own organisational base. The Works Constitution Act lacked appropriate legal provisions for a reorganisation of the *Be-*

triebsräte system at the small company level. The reform sought to put this right. The election process in small companies would be made easier and a single representative made possible even in workplaces previously excluded from the scope of the law owing in particular to the fragmentation of the company into a number of tiny workplaces.

And yet a reform of the Act focused on small companies, which was socially aware and respectful of the democratic dimension of co-determination in working life, could not be reduced to mere adaptation to the forces of decentralisation and the new company structures. Traditionally, the great majority of employees work in small and medium-sized enterprises. In the 1980s, that is before company structures and the structures of the workplace underwent a profound upheaval, more than 50% of employees in the private sector were to be found in workplaces without a *Betriebsrat* (Kommission Mitbestimmung, 1998: 43ff.). The "blank spots on the *Mitbestimmung* map" were essentially due to small family concerns whose management structures, traditions, and size impeded the election of a *Betriebsrat*. The basic provision of the Works Constitution Act, set down in its first article fifty years ago and providing for the election of a BR in workplaces with at least five permanent employees, had so far not been put into practice. As a result, the reform was expected not only to facilitate adjustment to the subsequent changes in company structures, but also to add a new chapter to the history of the democratisation process in industrial relations.

Available data based on the 2002 *Betriebsräte* elections appear to show that the reform of the Works Constitution Act has, on certain important issues, reversed the tendency by favouring greater stability and representativeness of the *Betriebsrat* system. More employees are now represented by more coherent and better-equipped teams of elected members. The number of women members has greatly increased and the representation of office workers has improved in line with their rising proportion among employees. The evolution of representative bodies is thus proceeding in step with the recomposition of the workforce itself (Rudolph, Wassermann, 2002b).

C. Collective Agreements in the Case of Small Companies

Collective agreements lay down the framework for working conditions in a workplace. Among the key areas of regulation by such agreements are pay structures and amounts, pay supplements and bonuses, working time and leave. Within the hierarchy of standards, the provisions of such agreements are ranked above company-level agreements: local players (such as the management or the *Betriebsrat*) cannot conclude an agreement on rules that deviates from collective agreements in matters covered by the latter. All agreements between the various players in the company must respect the framework fixed by the collective agreement concerned. However, they may negotiate conditions better than the level defined in the collective agreement, such as additional bonuses (to those in the agreement), in accordance with the "preferential" principle (*Günstigkeitsprinzip*).

1. Sector-Level and Company-Level Collective Agreements

The application of a collective agreement may arise from different mechanisms. It will enter into force, immediately and compulsorily, if the employer is a member of a signatory employers' organisation or has signed the agreement him/herself (in the case of company-level collective agreements (*Firmentarifverträge*)) with the union which organises employees in the company.

Coverage in the form of sector-level collective agreements has diminished in recent years. The proportion of employees covered by collective agreements has fallen by about 9% in West Germany and by nearly 12% in East Germany. But sector-level agreements continue to determine the pay and working conditions of 63% of West German and 45% of East German employees (Kohaut, Schnabel, 2003). The proportion of company-level collective agreements steadily increased during the 1990s, rising from 2,000 texts at the beginning of the decade to about 4,500 at the end, for Germany as a whole. The sectors not covered by collective agreements are to be found primarily among the services – associations, organisations affiliated to the Churches, barristers, solicitors, tax advisers, chartered accountants, consultants, advertising agents, private schools, driving schools, dancing schools, sports associations, artificial tanning parlours, video libraries, dental laboratories, software development firms, call centres (with the exception in each case of a handful of company-level collective agreements) (BMA, 2001).

2. Collective Agreements in Small Companies

Collective agreements are generally less widespread in sectors dominated by small companies than in the more traditional sectors in which large industrial and service-providing concerns predominate. Small companies tend to be less covered than larger entities. Only a third of very small companies, with 1-4 employees, are covered by a collective agreement. In the majority of these workplaces, working conditions are fixed in individual employment contracts and employers seldom make use of a collective agreement for reference purposes. As the size of the company increases, it becomes more likely that a sector-level or company-level collective agreement will apply. Thus, three out of four large companies employing more than 1,000 persons are governed by a collective agreement. Small independent family companies are more rarely covered by collective agreements than the small units and subsidiaries of larger concerns. The age of the company appears to constitute an important criterion in that more recently established units are less likely to be covered by a collective agreement than older ones of a similar nature (IAB-Materialien, 1/1999 and 1/2002).

Table 5. Collective agreements: coverage by size of workplace in 2000 (Proportion of workplaces, %)

Number of employees	Sector-level collective agreement		Company-level collective agreement		No collective agreement (% using a collective agreement for reference)	
	West	East	West	East	West	East
1-9	36	15	2	3	63 (36)	82 (39)
10-49	53	31	3	7	44 (53)	62 (48)
50-199	59	45	8	16	33 (53)	39 (49)
200-499	70	57	11	19	20 (59)	25 (57)
500 +	81	65	12	20	8 (52)	15 (47)
All workplaces	41	19	2	4	57 (40)	77 (40)

Source: IAB workplace panel.

Some 41% of West German, but only 19% of East German, workplaces are governed by a sector-level or company-level collective agreement. About 63% of West German employees, as against a little over 45% of their East German counterparts, were in 2000 working in a company covered by a collective agreement. The lower coverage in East Germany is perhaps also due to the forms of company typical of that part of Germany, since we very frequently find that owner-managed independent companies are much less often covered by collective agreements than companies with share capital (*Ibid.*).

However, 40% of West and East German companies not covered by collective agreements are said by management to use such agreements at least partially as a reference for the drawing up of individual employment contracts. It would seem reasonable to presume that the actual impact of the collective agreement system extends far beyond the companies formally covered. Many companies not covered by a formal agreement thus use not only the collective standards laid down in collective agreements, but also the procedures defined therein and the methods and instruments provided for fixing pay scales and job classifications; this was brought out in a 2002 survey of 3,000 companies in the metal and textile industries.

3. The Continuing Impact of Collectively-Agreed Standards

At this point, we cannot explore in more detail the problem of the influence of the labour market on the collectively agreed standards that determine practical working conditions and pay in companies. However, it seems fair to assume that collectively agreed standards concerning pay and working time could not be fixed independently of the situation in the labour market. The agreements policy of the unions rather tends to aim at what it is "possible" to achieve in a given economic context through negotiation with the employers and if necessary through confrontation. The balance of power and the capacity for mobilisation of the players in the negotiations have a big impact on the outcome of collective bargaining. Special situations – regional, industry-wide or company-level – always end up with conditions that are either more, or less, favourable than the collectively agreed standards. But the balance of power between employees and employers also influences the concrete expression and application of collectively agreed standards in the workplace. Labour standards are thus greatly inferior in workplaces not covered by a formal collective agreement. One could get the impression that labour market forces alone determine pay and working time in companies untouched by union influence. But as collective bargaining policies cannot themselves be pursued "against" the labour market, it may be assumed that workplaces not covered by a formal collective agreement and having no collective body representing the employees would find it impossible to elude the general evolution of collectively-agreed standards.

Despite a slight, but apparently continuous, decline in the coverage of collective agreements in recent years, the real influence of collectively-agreed standards over industrial practices in the workplace remains considerable. Survey findings show that collectively agreed standards are referred to even in small companies not covered by a formal collective agreement. This is particularly true for the fixing of pay scales, for working hours per week and for the right to paid holidays. The question is whether the rapidly expanding services sectors, dominated by small companies, will, or will not, gradually join the network of collective agreements during the next few years.

For some years now, there has been an increasingly insistent call, particularly by representatives of the *Mittelstand*, for reform of the law on collective bargaining. In this context, the collective bargaining would be carried out at a more decentralised level – that of the workplace. Where individual firms find themselves in a difficult business situation, the employers should be able to negotiate collective agreements with the *Betriebsräte*, which would take a less favourable stance than the sector-level collective agreement. The supporters of this kind of decentralisation of the contractual system are nonetheless faced with a dilemma: at present, the majority of small companies in the *Mittelstand* do not have bargaining partners mandated by the employees in a position to conclude "in-house agreements". Nine out of ten workplaces do not have a *Betriebsrat*. On the employers' side, these proposals are controversial: the order conferred by collective agreements at a higher level than the workplace is generally regarded as highly legitimate and numerous employers dread the annual confrontation on pay with their own employees. The unions are against such decentralisation to the level of the workplace, which would undermine the principle of solidarity among groups of employees with different degrees of organisation – with those enjoying a favourable balance of power acting on behalf of those in a weaker position. For both employers' organisations and the unions, the decentralisation of collective bargaining would result in a significant loss of power.

II. Small Companies Seen from Within: How Employers and Employees Organise their Relations

A. Selection of Companies and Survey Methodology

1. Scope of the Survey

In order to delimit the scope of the survey in view of the infinite variety and complexity of small companies, it was necessary to choose selection criteria. For example, the companies surveyed should belong to the private sector; they should have not more than 100 employees and not less than 5; they should preferably be independent companies, part of the *Mittelstand*. These criteria therefore excluded from the sample the subsidiaries of large companies. Part of the sample should belong to the traditional manufacturing sector (industrial and craftwork), and another part to services sectors, including recently established ones in the "new economy". Innovative workplaces should be surveyed alongside traditional ones and long-established sites alongside new ones.

For the German sample, two other very important selection criteria were applied. For purposes of comparison, workplaces with and without contractual agreements on the one hand and, on the other, companies with a *Betriebsrat* and those with no formal body representing employees, were selected.

2. Access to Companies

Access to companies in Type A (see Figure 1) was arranged for us by union contacts. The employers were then contacted through the *Betriebsräte* or union officers. Type B workplaces generally fall outside the scope of union interest. Personal contacts and the telephone directory were useful means of making our first contacts. For workplaces in Types C and D, enquiries by telephone usually enabled us to get in touch with employers; in one case, the employers' organisation served as an intermediary.

The fact that the managers of small companies agreed to participate in a survey on structures and relations within the workplace constituted in itself a major filter. Our case studies brought us into contact only with employers open to discussion and who were not afraid of the questions asked by the survey team about conditions within the company. Most of these employers have a "public life": they are active in employers' organisations, political parties, voluntary organisations or other initiatives of a social or cultural nature. The type of small company employer, dear to literature on the subject, who is cut off from the real world and anxious to protect the privacy of his company from outside eyes, is not to be found in our sample.

Table 6. The workplaces surveyed
Information on the companies concerned and the survey

							Interview conducted			
	Workplace	Sector	Legal Status	Number of employees	CA	BR	Owner	Manager	BR	Employee
1	Dental lab (small)	Dental prosthesis craftwork	Private limited company	22	No	Yes	*		*	
2	Dental lab (large)	Dental prosthesis craftwork	Private limited company	70	No	No	*			*
3	Large garage	Craftwork garage	Limited partnership	90	Yes	Yes	*		*	
4	Small garage	Craftwork garage	De facto company	11	Yes	No	*			
5	Business hotel	Hotel and restaurant	Private foundation	120	Yes	Yes		*	*	
6	Hotel - restaurant	Hotel and restaurant	Limited partnership	35	Yes	No	*			*
7	Research agency	Non-profit making research agency	Public utility private limited company	18	No (indirect)	Yes		*	*	
8	Energy research centre	Non-profit making research centre	Public utility association	65	No (indirect)	Yes		*	*	
9	Building company	Construction	Private limited company	43	Yes	Yes		*	*	
10	Software company	Software Development	Public limited company	22	No	No	*			*

In companies of Types A and B, the deliberate decision to conduct interviews with the members of the *Betriebsrat* as well as with the employer was also not without an impact on the constitution of the sample. In every situation we encountered, the employer and the *Betriebsrat* respected each other and maintained an on the whole constructive relationship. In Type D workplaces, not covered by a collective agreement and with no representation of employees, the employers sometimes tended to think that the election of a *Betriebsrat* might pose a threat to the company and its business development.

3. Method and Scope of the Survey

The interviews were conducted in the workplaces; they were intensive and based on an interview guide. In all cases, an in-depth personal interview lasting about two hours was conducted with the owner or the manager of the company. Wherever a *Betriebsrat* had been set up, one of its members – usually its chairperson – was interviewed. In companies without a *Betriebsrat*, we asked the employer to arrange for us an interview with an employee to enable us to supplement the employer's view with that of a representative "from the other side". We managed to do this in three of the four workplaces without a *Betriebsrat*. These interviews were not attended by the employer, were less directed and generally shorter than those conducted with the employers or elected members of the *Betriebsrat*. In most cases, the interviews were conducted in conjunction with the French researchers involved in the research project and occasionally also with the Swedish team. Immediately after the interviews, the researchers held an initial exchange of views on their observations.

B. The Central Position of the Employer: Methods of Management and Dialogue with Employees

1. Management, the Employer's Prerogative

In our observation, the small family companies chosen for the survey had several features in common: the central role of the owner or manager, very short channels of communication, daily contact between management and employees. There is no elaborate hierarchy. While it is true that in most cases official superiors are found in certain departments or sections of the company, substantive decisions are taken by the employer. "I deal with everything" we were told by the owner of a hotel-restaurant with 35 employees. This all-round competence presupposes the sharing of knowledge and transparency regarding the company's situation on the one hand and, on the other, a highly developed sense of responsibility on the part of the owner. This kind of entrepreneur seeks to confront and resolve budding conflicts without delay. Whenever his attention is drawn to situations of tension, he addresses the employees concerned directly. It is he who takes the initiative to clarify a problem: he sees this as a duty and at the same time feels that he is satisfying the expectations of employees. They seldom come to see him on their own initiative "because they are sometimes a bit cowardly". In other words, industrial relations in the company are based on a perfectly patriarchal model. The owner is competent for everything done in the company and he or she feels responsible for everything.

In this style of management without mediation, the employer makes his or her presence felt in every sector of the company, keeping a close eye on the work being done and often giving a helping hand. Quality control of the goods produced and services are part of his job; he or she is ready personally to make any necessary adjustments and to put the final touches. For example, during our interview with the owner of the small dental laboratory (22 employees), laboratory technicians came in repeatedly to show him the work being done or ask his advice. These *Mittelstand* employers are often themselves former practitioners of the craft with many years of experience. In an emergency, they come to the rescue. The employees of the hotel-restaurant, for instance, stressed that their employer would give a hand with all the different jobs to be done and did not consider it beneath his dignity to wipe glasses, the most despised job in the kitchen. The owner of the small garage (11 employees) found a way of applying the collectively agreed reduction in working time by himself doing the job of the sales staff on Saturdays, for whom it had become a day off.

In these companies, emphasis is often placed on the social proximity of employers and employees. What is this proximity based on? The core group of employees have often been working in the company for many years. Many of them come from the neighbourhood. In some cases, they have known each other from their school days. Their family situation is common knowledge; indeed, there may be family links that create parallel structures within the company. Members of the owner's family often hold important positions in the company: his wife may be in charge of bookkeeping and his son or heir in charge of a particular sector, and so on. But there also exist parallel family networks among the employees: it is not uncommon for married couples to work in different positions in the company and, in the recruitment of apprentices; preference is given to the sons and daughters of employees. "Most of our employees have worked for a very long time in the company and are thoroughly broken in like old married couples", said the owner of the small garage.

There is therefore no strict separation between home life and the world of work for either the employees or the owner family. This can be seen, for example, in special arrangements in regard to working time, to take in the family situations of certain employees, for example. "If an employee, for personal reasons, needs to take a day off, I adapt. I will be able to count on him or her when we need to work later in the evening". That is how one employer described his approach to flexible working time in the interests of both parties. The traditional organisation of festive occasions, such as day trips, Christmas parties, drinks to celebrate birthdays, and so forth, play an important role in all companies covered by the survey in maintaining social cohesion.

The owner's immediate authority in all questions concerning the company seems rather incompatible with a mediator body. "I discuss things with everyone in the team and I know them all. We have never had a real conflict. Once a year at the most, there is discussion about a problem that is a bit more important. The staff are content, otherwise it would not work", observed the owner of a dental laboratory. To him, therefore, there is no point in creating a *Betriebsrat*. The owner of the hotel-restaurant likened his style of management to "running a family". For him, being attentive to the personal needs of his employees was an essential condition for creating the atmosphere of trust without which a small company could not survive. In his view, the election of a *Betriebsrat* was essentially for small *Mittelstand* companies that were prone to unresolved conflicts and tensions; it seemed to him quite right that employees should defend themselves whenever they were badly treated. When analysed in this fashion, the demand by employees for the establishment of a *Betriebsrat* is above all a sign of mistakes made by the employer in the organisation and management of the company. This hotel-restaurant owner saw it as a sign of the success of his approach to management that "his" employees had never expressed the wish to have real collective representation.

For the owner of the building company in the survey, the presence of the *Betriebsrat* "was, it has to be said, sometimes a bit irritating". The legal provisions created too many formalities in discussions with it, which did not facilitate the resolving of day-to-day problems. "When problems crop up, I prefer to speak directly to the employees concerned". But this employer naturally claimed to respect the *Betriebsrat* – "once it is there".

But even in small companies of this type, there seems to be room for the formal representation of employees. Once one has learned the ropes and realised that it does not constitute a fundamental threat to the company, it can be integrated into the operation of small companies directly managed by their owners. The head of the building company mentioned not only the irritating aspects of cooperation with the *Betriebsrat*, but also the advantages: he considered it useful for the *Betriebsrat* to be involved in the event of dismissals, in the strict application of the law, "so that things will be completely watertight afterwards". On the whole, discussions with the *Betriebsrat* tended to be relatively informal and spontaneous. "Our approach is not very legalistic but rather informal".

3. Cooperative Management

The bigger companies in our sample possess more differentiated hierarchical structures. This is true for the large garage with 90 employees, the business hotel with 120 employees and the energy research centre with 65 employees. Departmental and section heads with broad responsibilities occupy an intermediate position between the owner or manager and the employees. The concept of overall management by the employer is here modified by some delegation to a lower level. Decisions regarding the staff – recruitment, job classification, bonuses, organisation of working time, holiday schedule – are largely left to the "sectors". Regular meetings between the section heads and the owner or manager constitute an important management tool. The great length of service of the section heads seems to be the key to their relations of trust with the employer. This level in the hierarchy is entrusted to long-serving employees who are as familiar with the company as their employer. Decisions of greater import, such as the creation of posts, dismissals, or reductions in staff remain nevertheless with the employer. Decisions regarding the general conditions governing working time and the operation of technical equipment, the introduction of incentive schemes (bonuses and special payments) or annual increases in pay are treated in much the same way.

In these companies, the employers have ceased to be responsible for everything but they still maintain that they are always seeking direct contact with their employees. This said contacts with each individual employee do not take place as spontaneously as appears to be the case in smaller companies. "One day, I realised that it was an illusion to believe that I knew everything that was happening in my company. I realised that I was getting it wrong when my wife told me about some events in the workshop about which I knew nothing. In a workplace like ours, information gets lost, inevitably". That is how the owner of the bigger garage described the situation. He was trying to remedy it by organising personal contacts with "his people". This strategy is called the "open dialogue policy": the idea is to avoid direct orders and instead to get employees to reach their own conclusions so as to be able to carry out their work independently and responsibly. In such conditions, it is quite possible for small companies to set up discussion "workshops" and quality improvement groups. An attempt is made to get round the lack of transparency and spontaneous contact by encouraging constant dialogue (garage). The manager of the business hotel described his style of management as based on "collegial discussions" with his departmental heads. "I do not simply opt for the 'employer's solution' but try on the contrary to find a 'joint solution' in conjunction the departmental heads and the *Betriebsrat*". The manager of the energy research centre was also aiming at constant dialogue with the heads of each sector, employees, and the *Betriebsrat*. In this case, the management function overlaps at least partly with that of team leading.

In such a context of "bureaucratic" (in the Weberian sense) differentiation of responsibilities, the *Betriebsrat* appears as neither a disruptive element nor a foreign body. It seems to be quite easy to give the elected representatives of employees a problem-solving role within the company, which the employer himself recognises as useful. Whenever management is based on the cooperation of individuals from different sectors or hierarchical levels, the role of the *Betriebsrat* is easier to integrate. It is significant that, in the companies of this type surveyed, the *Betriebsrat* members, or at least its chairperson, themselves hold middle management positions in the company, as site foreman, head waiter, bookkeeper, and head of customer services, etc. These positions generally presuppose considerable length of service in the company. Their position in the hierarchy combined with the mandate given them by their colleagues appears to predestine these employees, in a context of industrial relations based on dialogue and balance, to take on a role of mediator recognised by both parties.

4. From the Founding Team to the Organisation of a Company

The three "scientific" companies are exceptional in regard to their management structures and system of industrial relations. They are young companies, established in the early or mid-1990s, which have expanded greatly in just a few years. The energy research centre is the offshoot of a university research department; in ten years, its number of positions has increased from 15 to 65 and to this can be added about fifty temporary jobs for students. The majority of the employees are professional engineers. The development projects agency was in the public sector before being given an independent structure. Twenty qualified researchers in the social sciences – compared with five when it started – work there. The software company was established in the mid-1990s and today employs 22 specialists, most of them with university training. The employees in these three companies are a lot younger than those in the "traditional" companies covered by the survey.

They all have a similar management structure that has preserved certain features of a collegiate and egalitarian organisation of work inherited from their early days. In the research agency, both the manager and the elected BR member have been in the company since it was founded. Both of them are, so to speak, members of the founding generation. Relations among the employees are informal and in keeping with those in the "new economy". Familiar forms of address are the rule, even between the manager and the *Betriebsrat*. The clothes worn and the style of communication are relaxed and in tune with their generation. All the employees – including the administrative staff – support to some extent the objectives of development assistance. A stricter hierarchy between manager, project heads, researchers, and administrative staff has been introduced gradually, starting from the initial egalitarian team of brilliant experts welded together by shared values and social commitment. This process of growth and differentiation provides the background to a series of conflicts within the company.

In this context, the management function of the manager or of a board member who is not the owner takes time to become accepted, and the process generates disappointment and conflict. These individuals belong to the founding generation; they had formerly worked as a team with their current subordinates and are attached to the collegial atmosphere. In general, therefore, they try to preserve, on the one hand, the freedom of their traditional relationships within the team and, on the other, managerial authority accepted by everyone. Generally speaking, they do not see themselves in the role of the typical entrepreneur but tend to seek a half-way house between head of department and employer. "I am not the owner of the company; I do not define myself as the boss, but rather as a senior executive", said the manager of the projects agency appointed by the board of directors. He compared his role in the company to that of a "libero" in football. He did not have the necessary legal and material basis for acting as an independent entrepreneur. Within the informal environment of this small company, this former member of the team of researchers now has to convince the staff of his leadership qualities and gain true managerial authority. "In the beginning, I expect they said to themselves: 'He's one of us. He'll do what we want to be done. Here we are in direct democracy'. But for me, my problem is keeping order in the company. That calls for clear-cut rules, which can cause conflicts".

The owner of the software company described the process of differentiation and hierarchical organisation that accompanied its growth: "To start with, all decisions were taken jointly. This principle was respected for quite a while, but we paid dearly for it. Now we are introducing a hierarchy". One employee, in the company since it was founded, confirmed the change that had taken place in recent years: "In the first few years, it was almost like a family. We would sit on the floor to reflect on what direction the company should take. There was no distance between management and employees. Everyone shared the same concern, namely help the company to develop". Today, the company is divided into four sectors directed by two heads of department. But the principle of informal management appears to have shifted to another level – important decisions, not the preserve of the owners, are handled by a group of five senior executives, themselves sometimes backed up by tax and management consultants. Today, the newly established hierarchy and the former collegial relationship exist side by side. The "blue settee" – around which they would all meet at the end of the day to dream up crazy projects, some of which would actually come to fruition – was still there. In the day-to-day life of the company, the closeness characteristic of the family business has not vanished, and nor has the employer's case-by-case approach to arbitration. The maxim of the traditional family business – "It's me who deals with everything" – also applies even to a young start-up.

In the two oldest workplaces, there exist *Betriebsräte*. They came into existence as a reaction by employees against uncertainties and conflicts arising from the growth and differentiation process we have just described. The fact that the employees of both of these companies came from the public sector probably had some influence: in the civil service, the presence of a collective representation body (*Personalrat*) is almost a matter of course. Over the years the elected representatives have succeeded in finding their places as mediators between top management, the heads of departments and employees. The managers recognise the usefulness of the *Betriebsrat* in the preparation of collective standards within the company. The process of differentiation in the organisation of the company and the transition from club of founders to hierarchical structure would be almost unthinkable without cooperation between management and the *Betriebsrat*. The increasingly formal nature of industrial relations leads to written collective agreements (*Betriebsvereinbarungen*) between the management and the BR. Sometimes the latter even acts as a sort of "co-manager" of structural changes. The personal relations between the individuals concerned, consolidated over the years, nevertheless continue to impede the development of more formal relations between *Betriebsrat* and management, such as we find, for example, in large companies with long traditions of co-determination. Relations appear to be more marked by a shared past in the company and by the desire for cooperation than by formal ground-rules in keeping with the respective role of each employee. A BR member summed it up: "In a small company, in which many of the people have been there from the start, relations have a very personal touch. Formal and personal relationships are always intermingled".

The software company is more recent. Marked by the ideology of the founder, the owner sees the election of a *Betriebsrat* primarily as a step on the way to bureaucratic decision-making harmful to the business development of the company. He fears a loss of flexibility: "If before every decision I am forced to seek the opinion of the *Betriebsrat*, we will be faced with delays of several weeks. And that the company cannot allow!" The fear that the *Betriebsrat* – synonym or near synonym of the threat to freedom of enterprise – will obstruct necessary business decisions came up repeatedly during the interview. The owner wanted to preserve the non-mediated system of discussions with employees which, in the final analysis, protected his own decision-making powers. At the same time, recent changes towards a more differentiated management structure foreshadow the birth of new communication and decision-making channels. There is now a hierarchy instead of the seemingly egalitarian decision-making structures of the early days. For employees, this could mean the loss, at least in part, of opportunities for informal involvement. It is too soon to tell whether these changes will eventually give rise to a demand for collective representation – in the form of either an in-house participative body or the election of a *Betriebsrat*. In this context, the election of a collective representation would constitute another step along the road towards a company organisation based on the principle of the division of labour.

C. Forms of Collective Employee Representation: "Personal Relations Weigh Heavily…"

According to the Works Constitution Act, workplaces are required to establish a *Betriebsrat* when five or more employees have a right to vote. Surveys conducted in companies in all parts of the private sector reveal that, in 2000, only 6% of companies with between 5 and 20 employees, and less than 30% of those with 21 to 100 employees had organised elections (IAB, 2002). In small companies, therefore, an elected *Betriebsrat* is the exception rather than the rule. How are we to account for this? Why have the majority of small companies refrained from electing a *Betriebsrat*, even though it is an explicit requirement of the law? Some earlier research has already shown that, in this field, a complex interplay of conflicting interests and obstructions led in the end to the failure of the project for an elected *Betriebsrat* (Wassermann, 2002a).

1. Obstacles to the Election of a Representative Body

So long as they lack practical experience in matters of co-determination in the workplace, both employees and employers are generally ill-informed about the main orientations and scope of action of the *Betriebsrat*. "What can and what should a *Betriebsrat* do? What protection does it give in the event of conflict?" As a rule, therefore, people are ignorant of alternative approaches to the current industrial practices, that is, the different problem-solving techniques involving a *Betriebsrat*.

Employees, who are unsure about the practical impact of such a decisive change as the election of a *Betriebsrat* with formal rights, might also show a lack of interest. An individual employee might see in the election a threat to the well-oiled participation machinery or to acquired rights. The fear of having to face reprisals or of being penalised in some other way by their superiors or by their employer constitutes another obstacle. The lack of interest in, or even the rejection of the idea of electing, a *Betriebsrat* are doubtless an indirect result of power structures within the company.

The employer's open or more or less latent opposition is typical of a significant number of companies, the representative body being at best perceived as a bureaucratic impediment to the operation of the company. Union sources show how *Mittelstand* entrepreneurs often use the big stick – such as dismissing the employees behind the election initiative – in order to prevent the creation of a *Betriebsrat*.

The complexity of the election procedure combined with the need to protect the employees engaged in this risky process (likely to have a lasting impact on industrial relations in the company) makes it almost impossible, in small companies, to envisage an initial election without outside assistance. The simplified election procedure that now applies in small companies has not, from this point of view, fundamentally changed matters. In many cases, however, union support is probably not enough. Often the employees in small companies do not know which is "their" union and local union officers often have only a hazy vision of the potential of companies without a *Betriebsrat* in their field of activity. This is clearly true for companies not covered by a collective agreement. Against a background of the decline of large long-established workplaces and the increasing number of small companies with no union presence, the shortage of local union officers – a situation that has worsened in recent years – confronts the unions with practically insoluble problems, given the current means at their disposal.

Potential candidates for election to a *Betriebsrat* in a workplace which has not yet had one are faced with the question of whether they are ready, if necessary, to sacrifice a large proportion of their free time and their energy to a cause with an uncertain outcome, while at the same time running the risk of compromising their own professional future. It is in this area that the situation in small companies differs sharply from that of large companies with established traditions of co-determination. In the latter type of company, the personal risks are often counterbalanced by the prospects of real "co-determination careers" directly related to the exercise of a mandate on a permanent basis. In small companies, the individual and collective advantages of becoming involved in the work of collective representation are much more uncertain than the drawbacks. It is also for this reason that people often prefer to keep their distance from formal co-determination procedures in small companies.

However, the development of the *Betriebsrat* system suggests that small companies and co-determination in the workplace are not always incompatible. Indeed, about half of all BRs are to be found in companies with fewer than 100 employees. Examples show that small *Mittelstand* companies may welcome BRs on a permanent basis and allow them to do fruitful work. After a running-in period often not without conflict, industrial relations in small companies may gradually mature, aided by the cooperation of BR members, employees and the company's management, and thus create a relatively stable culture of consensus.

2. Unofficial Representation

In small companies, the absence of formal representation through a *Betriebsrat* does not necessarily mean that employees are deprived of any instrument or possibility of expressing and defending their interests *vis-à-vis* the employer. In day-to-day working life, small companies appear to be familiar with a wide range of informal channels for working out compromises. In seeking recognition for their individual interests, the various groups of employees are not on an equal footing; their chances of success depend on their position within the staff (level of skill, responsibilities exercised, rank in the company and length of service, etc.). In small companies, the personal relationship between the employee and the employer is crucial.

In a survey of small companies without a *Betriebsrat*, Gerd Syben describes the industrial relations between heads of companies and their employees in the construction industry. A close social relationship among the persons concerned turns out to be the decisive criterion for cohesion among the employees, in an occupational context which, on the work sites, is anything but free of conflict. This closeness is due to the strong emphasis on personal relations between the employer and employees, this relationship being in turn the product of similarities in their careers and personal lives and a frequently similar social background. This is particularly true in rural or relatively unurbanised surroundings. The life histories and social relations of the entrepreneurs and their employees are intertwined; their professional roles and private hopes overlap; presents or expressions of sympathy from the employer in the event of illness or death are all expressions of the close social relationship felt by the head of the company, which is still not necessarily unconnected with forms of traditional paternalism. Just as it seems self-evident to them that employees should agree to work overtime or abnormal hours, the employees for their part seem justified in expecting their personal needs to be taken into account in arrangements concerning working time. In cases where pay remains lower than in the collective agreement, employees will generally be given special forms of compensation. This often includes the use of company facilities or equipment for private purposes. Syben mentions the "arrangement whereby the payment of overtime is abandoned in exchange for the loan of a company car for private reasons" as a typical example of semi-professional semi-private arrangements (*lebensweltlich*) found in small building companies. Even though such arrangements turn out to be rather ineffective ways of representing their interests in the event of conflicts, the author nonetheless considers them as an important reason for the frequent absence of a formally constituted *Betriebsrat* in small companies (Syben, 1997).

Membership of the same social group, attendance of the same schools, activities in the same voluntary organisation and family ties or friendship are all likely to be superimposed on the workplace hierarchy and to "co-determine", so to speak, the income and the status of employees in the company. Alongside these networks of personal relations, mention should be made of more or less implicit practices for the collective representation of interests, which are developed by certain groups of employees in relation to other employee categories and the employer. These forms of collective representation are based on similar views regarding the acceptability of certain working conditions and often occur against a back-cloth of many years of working together. They may engender conflicts: a passive rejection of "arbitrary" changes to traditional work procedures or active resistance in the form of "work to rule" or deliberate delaying tactics.

In their research on industrial relations in small and medium-sized companies, Hilbert and Sperling, as far back as the end of the 1980s, drew attention to the fact that small companies without a *Betriebsrat* do not disregard all forms of participation, even participation not based on institutions covered by the Works Constitution Act. But the informal types of participation identified hinder the establishment of a *Be-*

triebsrat. "Informal participation thus jeopardises the foundations for consolidating (formal) co-determination in small and medium-sized enterprises" (Hilbert and Sperling, 1990).

This said the relations between informal and formal practices of representation through elected *Betriebsräte* are more complex. Within a small staff with no official representation, there are always some employees who act as spokespersons or opinion-leaders, a role they derive from their special position in the company and/or from their personal background (qualifications, interests and values, etc.). This position enables them to act as mediator in the event of conflict in cases where both certain groups of employees and the employer recognise them as spokespersons and interlocutors. The intervention of these mediators recognised by both parties involves a multiplicity of actions in a wide range of areas of a social, organisational, and legal nature, with the emphasis on personal relations. The organisation of a company party, the defence of a colleague against the complaints of the employer, arbitration in day-to-day disputes between employees, consultation by the employer regarding changes in the company may be among the roles played by such spokespersons for the staff. All these rather new functions of representation and mediation are also part of the remit of BR members. It is thus possible to speak of a kind of structural continuum between companies with and without a *Betriebsrat*. It is true that the election of a *Betriebsrat* gives a radically new legal and standard-setting basis for the representation of interests, but it does not fundamentally affect the industrial relations and forms of communication and conflict resolution within the body of employees.

Whenever employees decide to elect a *Betriebsrat*, these spokespersons often play a key role in establishing it. In many cases, they put up as candidates and thus exchange their role of unofficial spokesperson for that of legal representative. In carrying out their new functions, they are in a position to rely on the networks of relations they have built up among their colleagues at work and on their special informal relationship with the employer. However, the first election often leads to significantly more formal relations between the BR members and the employer, especially when it is the result of a conflict that it has proved impossible to resolve through the traditional methods of unofficial mediation. The formal establishment of a *Betriebsrat* does not put an end to informal ways of expressing and defending interests. Formal and informal practices tend to coexist and elected representatives have to be careful not to lose touch with particular groups and with their special ways of defending their interests.

D. Small **Betriebsräte***: Establishment, Status and Organisation of Work*

Six workplaces in our sample possess a *Betriebsrat.* Why were they elected and in what context? Which employees were prepared to involve themselves with the *Betriebsrat*? What are the priorities in the representation of interests? How are the relations with employers organised? What changes in the company were triggered by the existence of a *Betriebsrat*?

1. How Did the Betriebsrat *Come about?*

Half of the workplaces with a *Betriebsrat* belong to the group of traditional-type industrial and craftwork companies. For several generations these firms have been run by a member of the owner family. Another of the workplaces is in the hotel and restaurant sector, traditionally part of the services sector. Two other relatively young companies belong to the research sector. They are run, not by private owners but by managers appointed by third parties. We have come across *Betriebsräte* in workplaces both with and without collective agreements. Although the companies are very different, the history of their *Betriebsräte* is quite similar: in most cases, the BR was set up during a period of turbulent industrial relations, sometimes linked to an open conflict. The initiative could be triggered by periods of business crisis, by a change of owner, or by conflicts within the management at a time of expansion of the company.

In a dental laboratory with 22 employees, a *Betriebsrat* was elected for the first time at the end of the 1980s: a new owner had arrived and the future of the company looked uncertain. A deteriorating business context (due to the first reform of the health system) prompted fears about unemployment; rumours circulated that jobs were to be cut. The employees turned to the local branch of *IG Metall.* It was decided to elect a *Betriebsrat* "because you never know" and "as a precaution" so as to be able to defend the rights of employees in the event of dismissals. An *IG Metall* officer helped with the preparation and organisation of the first election. Not only BR members but also the majority of the employees then joined the union.

In the business hotel (120 employees), the establishment of the *Betriebsrat* resulted from an open conflict between the manager and the staff. In the mid-1980s, the excessively long working hours of apprentices became a source of conflict. "This created a lot of agitation in the company", said the BR chairperson. The parents of the apprentices protested about shifts of 12 to 14 hours forced on their children. For their part, the women service staff contested management's authoritarian methods. They contacted the NGG union dealing with their sector and, with the help of the union secretary, began preparations for the election of a *Betriebsrat*. The manager, who was at first strongly opposed to such a step, adapted to the new situation quite quickly. "He made a U-turn, bought a copy of the Works Constitution Act, and studied it in great detail", we were told by the BR chairperson. The manager came round to the idea that it was preferable to maintain relations of cooperation and trust with the *Betriebsrat*.

Indeed, the manager described the *Betriebsrat* as a useful institution: "In a company, there needs to be a body that employees can consult before approaching the manager or head of department. A *Betriebsrat* can serve a useful purpose on a number of issues. It can help prevent conflicts among the employees. A company like ours cannot afford tensions within it – clients feel their presence and don't come back". It is perhaps a sign of his personal modesty that led the BR chairperson to play down his role in converting the manager from opponent to firm supporter of the institution. However, we gained the impression that a mutual learning process bringing together the manager, the heads of the various sectors and the *Betriebsrat* lay behind the current approach to management and collegial and cooperative decision-making. This example underlines the dynamic nature of industrial relations within a company. Decision-making structures in place for many years – and seemingly effective – based on the employer's authority and to all appearances incapable of tolerating the idea of or making room for a parallel body may, in certain circumstances, break down and fail to adapt to ongoing changes. If employees react in such a situation by electing a *Betriebsrat*, the balance of power will be shaken even more – often against a background of far from minor conflicts. This may be followed by a learning process during which the *Betriebsrat* and management seek common ground and new forms of cooperation. This discovery process may end up in closer ties and mutual respect between the employer and the *Betriebsrat*. In the eyes of the employer, the body representing the employees, initially perceived as disturbing, may come to be seen in a new light as complementing the management's power and ensuring cooperative relations within the company. All this implies a learning process for both parties.

The research agency is one of the very rare cases of a workplace with less than 20 employees that has elected a *Betriebsrat*. The company was founded in 1990 to run development activities formerly handled by the federal ministry for economic cooperation (Ministry of Development Aid). The workplace, a subsidiary of three large organisations of entrepreneurs and employers, is run by a manager. Its work had begun with a small team of committed experts all enjoying the same rights in a lightweight hierarchical structure. The growth of the company was accompanied by the introduction of more hierarchical decision-making structures (in particular by the setting up of departments) and associated conflicts. When, in the mid-1990s, the employees considered that those conflicts were endangering the post held by one of their colleagues, they immediately set about electing a *Betriebsrat* which, in companies of this size, contains only one elected member.

It can be said that a *Betriebsrat* is likely to be set up in a company, including a small one, when the employees are going through a period of major uncertainty, when open conflicts with the employer break out, when long-serving and trusted structures crumble in the face of growing hierarchical organisation or staff changes, or when there is a risk of job losses as a result of certain business developments. The break is likely to occur at very different stages in the company's history. In companies that used to be bigger and are downsizing because of economic difficulties, the purpose of electing a *Betriebsrat* is "to save what can be saved" and to defend in particular the rights of employees to compensation. In younger companies in the midst of rapid growth in staff numbers and its concomitant reorganisation of structures, the election of a *Betriebsrat* may be part of the process of putting employer-employee relations on a formal and objective footing.

2. *Union Help in the Initial Stages*

Our case studies call attention to another factor necessary for the establishment of a *Betriebsrat* in small companies: the support of a union. Owing to the highly formal nature of the elections, the first election at least does not appear to be feasible without the help of independent outside experts. Union support is all the more essential to employees if the employer is against the election of a *Betriebsrat*. During the setting-up period, the union has an influence on the development of the company. This influence is expressed, for instance, in successful recruitment campaigns. At least some of the employees will join the union during this period. During the first months of its life, when the aim is to win concrete acceptance for the rights and legal attributes of the newly created body, the advisory function of the local union structure will continue to be important. And yet, in most of our case studies, close relations with the union did not survive the setting-up period. The number of union members fluctuates, then falls and cooperation between union officers and BR members tends to be reduced to *ad hoc* contacts at ever-increasing intervals.

3. Status and Mode of Operation of the Betriebsräte

The fact that the *Betriebsräte* in more long-established firms are solidly entrenched in the company structures does not mean that the employer recognises an undisputed right of participation. In many cases, their modes of operation and participation practices fall well short of the legal requirements. As for their integration into the company's decision-making structures, two typical situations emerged from our survey.

In small family companies run by their owners, who take all specific decisions in person without any mediation or sharing of responsibility, the *Betriebsrat* has hardly any influence on the management style, at least in day-to-day situations. The head of the company takes the decisions and keeps in direct contact with the employees. The *Betriebsrat* only intervenes from time to time, usually rarely, when more important decisions are at stake. It may, for instance, serve as the initial filter in the annual debate about pay increases. It also appears to play a particularly important role in plans for laying off staff. In this area, the owners affirm their strong desire to find common solutions in conjunction with the *Betriebsrat*. In small companies, the dismissal of an employee is a major event, whether it is for business or for personal reasons. By involving the *Betriebsrat*, the head of the company generally seeks a solution acceptable to the employees and at the same time wants to protect himself against the possibility of a costly procedure before an employment tribunal.

This type of company regards the *Betriebsrat* as a referee and mediator in certain important questions that are in fact relatively few in number. On the other hand, the *Betriebsrat* has no voice in most day-to-day decisions formally subject to the right of co-determination: working hours, overtime, and individual arbitration on pay, etc. This does not mean that its influence in such matters is necessarily zero. But the modes of influence and coordination between *Betriebsrat* and employer are by nature rather informal. On the whole, relations with the *Betriebsrat* are guided less by legal requirements than by forms of exchange specific to the company: "We settle our problems in a less legalistic and rather informal manner".

This quotation could symbolise the way in which most of the BR members in small companies work. The formal representation practices leave a lot of room for informal initiatives. Their working methods and their relations with both the employees and with middle management and the owner are strongly coloured by the personality of the BR chairperson, many of whom personify, as it were, the *Betriebsrat*. The chairpersons tend to personify the institution in the eyes of both employer and employees, even when it contains three or even five elected members. The personal management style of the owner-employer that is characteristic of small family companies seems in this instance to rub off on to the role and mode of operation of the *Betriebsrat*. In small companies, the BR chairpersons often facilitate employer-employee relations. They serve as mediators for a wide range of issues in the life of the company – relations between individual employees, between employees and their superiors, between employer and staff, etc. Most of these acts of arbitration and mediation concern questions, problems, or conflicts that are not settled by collective agreements or by the Works Constitution Act. This mediator status may provide a basis for powers of intervention that can become quite considerable, even extending to the settlement of contentious issues concerning collective agreements or legal matters, so long as it is founded on recognition by both the employer and employees.

In this type of representation of interests, the approach is based much more on private discussions with the employer than on formal negotiations with their demands in writing and the taking of minutes. The given word and handshake often have a greater significance than legal provisions or signed contracts. This does not rule out sophisticated, and even highly formalised, methods of conflict resolution – appeal to the union, appeal to an employment tribunal, convening of an arbitration committee – when the classical forms of exchange do not work. More important conflicts (redundancy plans) which cause the two parties to abandon the path of informal compromise lead representatives in most cases to take a much more formal approach.

The BR's mode of operation is generally speaking as informal as the relations between employer and *Betriebsrat*. In workplaces with between 21 and 50 employees, the latter is composed of three elected members, who do not enjoy the right to be released from their occupational obligations. In the building company, for example, the *Betriebsrat* meets only two or three times a year. After its members have gone through their routine business "they are joined by the owner for an exchange of information". It is quite exceptional for staff meetings to be held more than once a year. They are often held just before Christmas and tend to be merged with the traditional company party, which is probably more marked by the presence of the owner or manager than by the role of BR members.

In these conditions, there is often little room for a more systematic representation of interests to ensure respect for the rights and main legal provisions of the Works Constitution Act. The first task is to win acceptance for the rights of BR members – such as partial release from occupational obligations or the right to continuous training – from an employer who is anxious to reduce as much as possible the costs of the institution and who often finds it hard to understand why BR members might need more freedom of action. This can be illustrated by an episode that occurred in the building company. When the chairperson of the BR, after several days of training by the union, presented the hotel bill to his employer, the immediate reaction of the latter was to refuse to pay it. A few days later, he received a telephone call from the local union officer: "Listen, Gerhard, you are going to be nice and pay for the chap's hotel. If not you might well have to organise in your company the four staff meetings a year required by law". The bill was paid; as before only one general meeting of employees was held each year.

As the larger companies in our sample possess a hierarchical structure that is already differentiated into levels or departments, with formal communication channels between manager/owner and middle management, they clearly offer better conditions for the formal and organisational integration of the *Betriebsrat* into the decision-making structures. The occupational status of the BR chairperson, who is often from middle management, plays an important role in promoting the integration and prestige of the institution. As a senior executive, he is a full member of the official management structure, takes part in meetings of departmental heads, and has access to all information of interest to management. As an elected representative of the employees, he tends, within the company hierarchy, to find himself in a particularly strong position *vis-à-vis* the employer.

In these companies, the *Betriebsrat* functions on a much more regular basis. It often meets once a month and sometimes even more often. Its meetings with management are also on a regular and official basis. It is much more common for the discussions to produce written minutes than in the case of smaller companies.

4. Length of Service and Loyalty to the Company

The active members of the *Betriebsrat* belong to the core group of employees. This is true for all the companies in the sample. As a rule, they have been working in the company for many years, have a long experience of the company and its sector of activity, are highly qualified, and are entrusted with certain responsibilities within the company. Many of them come from middle management. In the two research companies, the BR members belong to the circle of researchers and engineers. The BR chairperson in the hotel-restaurant is head waiter with the grade of head of department. His counterpart in the building firm is site manager, which causes him to make regular visits to the various building sites. The BR members in the dental laboratory come from the body of skilled technicians, the core of the company. In the garage, the BR members come by tradition from the repair shops; when the new generation took over, the role of chairperson fell to an employee in the workshop reception sector. Employees from groups regarded as marginal within the company's social structure – hotel room service personnel, administrative staff in industrial and craftwork companies, drivers and sales staff – were not to be found among the BR members in our sample.

Being in many cases very long-serving company employees, the BR members represent a form of social continuity. Their chairpersons have often been employed in the company longer than the managers, and it is not uncommon for them to have experienced a change of ownership. Length of service, combined with a strategic status of skilled employee appointed to positions of responsibility, appear to all but predestined them to the function of BR member or chairperson. Their rank in the hierarchy – which "inevitably" or almost inevitably rewards a long career in the company – is not an obstacle to working for the *Betriebsrat*, quite the contrary. Their view of the whole picture and the knowledge they have built up on how the company functions tend rather to be seen as assets for effective representation in the eyes of both other employees and the employer. A strategy of discussions with the employer averse to conflict and confrontation could be one consequence of the strong position of such BR members in the company and *vis-à-vis* employees. The BR members have an intimate knowledge of the company; they themselves pass on its informal industrial standards built up over many years; their demands take account of the general context and business possibilities of their firms, with which they are generally perfectly familiar. Thus, in discussing pay increases, the BR members will of course refer to union demands or compromises in sector-level negotiations, but they will "convert" these figures into ones they know to be economically acceptable for the company.

5. The Betriebsrat from the Employer's Standpoint

From the employer's point of view, the *Betriebsrat* is an institution that at bottom serves a useful purpose, though it also raises problems. All employers in the survey spoke of this ambivalence regarding the *Betriebsräte*, a legitimate representative body but at the same time a potential threat to the head of the company's freedom of decision.

"The *Betriebsrat* is a useful institution, even in a small company. I do not share the fears of certain colleagues, who think that it is a threat to the survival of the company", said the owner of the small dental laboratory. "But", he continued, "interference of the *Betriebsrat* in the case of unavoidable decisions can seriously upset procedures. Take the example of dismissals. There is a period of notice to be respected, and you are under the obligation of providing information and giving your reasons before the *Betriebsrat*. This takes time and may hold things up and make the whole business more costly". This did not prevent that employer from highlighting the BR's functional and constructive side. "When involved beforehand in decision-making processes, the *Betriebsrat* can also be an ally". The first example given was the discussion around the annual pay increases: this issue proves easier to resolve with the help of the BR, which negotiates a settlement for the staff as a whole. In companies with no BR, each employee might have to address the employer personally with his or her demands. Cooperation with the *Betriebsrat* and the union has also made it possible, in the case of a dismissal seen as unavoidable, to take precautions against the possibility of a complaint by the dismissed employee before the employment tribunal.

The manager of the business hotel repeatedly stressed the need for harmonious cooperation with the *Betriebsrat* and its members. In his view, problems occur when BR members do not take the actual situation of the company into consideration. "The right people must be elected to the *Betriebsrat*. If that does not happen, the BR, sitting on its legal rights, may more or less bring about the ruin of a small company". The vision of an irresponsible *Betriebsrat* endangering the company was mentioned by most of the employers but could not be backed up by concrete examples.

The owner of the garage spoke of another problem area that in his eyes could be highly dangerous – the BR was at risk of being "remote-controlled" from the outside by the union. In that company, the *Betriebsrat* had existed for over 35 years. In the early days, it had acted under the influence of *IG Metall*. "We went through some periods in which relations with the *Betriebsrat* were strained. The BR chairperson at the time did what *IG Metall* told him to do". The union officer described this chairperson as a "very active person", sometimes effectively engaged in a real trial of strength with the employer. His successor is for his part very attached to *IG Metall*, but appears more willing to compromise with the employer. However, it has to be said that the company was doing well at the time of the "combative" *Betriebsrat*.[4]

6. The Betriebsräte *as They See Themselves*

We always ended our interviews with BR members by asking them the same question: would things have been different had there been no *Betriebsrat* in the company? In the bigger of the two garages (90 employees), whose *Betriebsrat* operates in a relatively differentiated and sophisticated manner for a company of that size, the BR chairperson

4 This company became insolvent 18 months after our visit.

replied with some restraint: "We are admittedly a *Betriebsrat* with five elected members but we do not change much in the company. Without the *Betriebsrat* the situation would probably be different in several areas, but not fundamentally different". He added that the *Betriebsrat* nevertheless played an important role in ensuring that the collectively-agreed job classification system and working time were respected.

"The boss would be able to hire and fire as he liked if there were no *Betriebsrat*! And the collective agreement would probably be less respected if we were not around. Besides, that is what he occasionally tries to do!" "Without the *Betriebsrat* it would be impossible to keep control", said, in very similar terms, the BR chairperson of the building company (40 employees).

The small dental laboratory (22 employees) had had to cut the number of employees several times in recent years for economic reasons. A BR member considered that the owner could have made people redundant much more freely if there had been no representative body. "In other laboratories, it's chaos where redundancies are concerned! When there exists a *Betriebsrat* and the union is present, it is at least possible to limit the damage..."

In the research and development company with 65 for the most part highly skilled employees and with relatively generous working conditions typical of this kind of company, the job of the *Betriebstrat*, according to one of its members, was to ensure respect for social justice within the company. "Otherwise equality of treatment and justice could easily be somewhat neglected. We always try to negotiate transparent rules that apply to everybody. The ground rules can be adjusted a bit – so long as that goes for everybody. We try to avoid the situation where colleagues with a stronger hand always obtain the best conditions for themselves; the quieter ones should also be given their chance".

The single BR member of the small research agency (18 employees), with seven years in the job, had no doubts: the usefulness of the *Betriebsrat* for employees was recognised by all; the manager accepted its role and wanted dialogue, regarding it as a partner in "co-management". The *Betriebsrat* acted as a buffer between management and staff. It was because he was perfectly familiar with the general atmosphere and with the views of the employees that the BR member was able, in cooperation with the manager, to prevent the emergence of certain situations of conflict. He stressed the usefulness of rules worked out in common to replace the manager's unilateral directives. Our interview with him highlighted not only the protective role of the *Betriebsrat vis-à-vis* employees, but also its role as a back-up to managerial and decision-making practices in the company.

7. Better without a Betriebsrat*?*

Without a *Betriebsrat* the situation in the company would be different but, as an employee we interviewed emphasised, not "fundamentally different". Our data are insufficient to compare the situation in workplaces with and without a *Betriebsrat.* In three companies, however, we were able to broach with the owners and the employees the question of why in those cases there existed no *Betriebsrat*.

The owner of the hotel-restaurant (35 employees) thought that there was no representative body in the company because "nobody had asked for one". For him, the issue did not really arise in small *Mittelstand* companies, except in the case of noteworthy staff discontent, which the owner had not managed to detect in time. In such cases, he thought the election of a *Betriebsrat* legitimate. He himself would not oppose such a request by his employees. He ruled out recourse to intimidation, which might well aggravate the situation, and any action whose legality was open to question. Procedures before an employment tribunal could be expensive, as he had found to his cost in the case of a person he had dismissed.

A waiter in this family hotel had previously worked in a workplace belonging to a big hotel chain. A *Betriebsrat* had been established there, though the work it did had not made a big impression. This employee expressed appreciation of the owner's style of management and of the decent working conditions in his present workplace. "Here we manage perfectly to resolve our problems ourselves. There are no conflicts with the employer, who does not for example insist on strict respect for the hours of work. When both sides are flexible, it is always possible to come up with a satisfactory solution". A *Betriebsrat* might well divide people and thus become itself a source of conflicts. A second employee we interviewed, a cook, also stressed the quality of relations with the owner, along with his management style. As a result he was able to be independent and creative in his own field. The possibility of flexible working time played a big part in this positive assessment of working conditions (which doubtless involve overtime, week-end work and late hours). The two interviewees did not regret the absence of a *Betriebsrat* – their views constituted an unequivocal argument in favour of a small private company under attentive management that allowed employees to be independent. Neither of them would like to work in a company belonging to a large catering chain.

The owner of the bigger dental laboratory (70 employees) felt that the business success of the company would be endangered by the presence of a *Betriebsrat*. "I am always having discussions with all members of the staff. This immediately rules out the possibility of major conflicts.

As employees are satisfied it would be pointless to elect a *Betriebsrat*". Although employees for their part consider that a representative body is not really necessary when work is going well, they do not reject the idea in different circumstances. A skilled and long-serving dental technician reacted to our question in this way: "The person I speak to is the boss – and that suits me". Then, after a brief pause, he added: "It is true that what you are not aware of you won't miss either. But it is certainly not bad as things are". A bit later he said that they might well have to elect a *Betriebsrat* if industrial relations broke down. "Things we hear about other dental laboratories confirm our view that our conditions are quite good. In some firms the employer is a little tyrant. Occasionally the apprentices terminate their apprenticeship there and come to us".

In the software company (22 employees), the owner and employees seem to share the same view: they do not need a *Betriebsrat*. And yet they do not place the emphasis on exactly the same points. The owner sees the *Betriebsrat* as a dangerous brake on companies, whose development calls for great flexibility. "If I had first to ask the *Betriebsrat* for its opinion, decisions would be held up for weeks. And that we can't allow".

A head of department with supervisory responsibilities within a recently established hierarchy did not think it necessary to set up a *Betriebsrat*, for the time being. In her view, there were no conflicts or problems in the company that could not be resolved by the in-house style of attentive team-like relations. Things might be different, she thought, in bigger companies with more elaborate hierarchical structures, but in this one everything was (still) on a human scale. But here, too, in opposition to the views of the employers interviewed, formal representation is not refused as a matter of principle. It is the present context that leads them to consider the election of a *Betriebsrat* unnecessary – they do not rule out the idea in all circumstances.

As in "real life", our case studies at least showed the answer to the question to be contradictory. In small companies with no particular problems, employees feel no need for a *Betriebsrat* because they are satisfied with conditions as they are. For employers, *Betriebsräte* are superfluous or even a brake on the business vigour of the company. But they too see the satisfaction of employees as a key to business success. Flexibility *vis-à-vis* the customer is often considered vital to the success of small companies. A small company must be flexible or risk disappearing. For employers, the premise of flexibility is nevertheless ambiguous: for one thing, they expect their employees to display great adaptability but, on the other hand, they cannot really count on the latter's motivation if they do not show themselves to be flexible regarding their demands.

The establishment of a *Betriebsrat* is usually preceded by a conflict. The employees of such companies feel in need of official representation, in order to ensure respect for their collectively agreed rights and legal protection. They are unwilling to give up the *Betriebsrat* even when they see no need for it to interfere in the day-to-day life of the workplace. It is regarded as a kind of "insurance policy" in the event of bigger conflicts. The employers often tend – after a learning period during which both sides mark out their respective territories and test their relations – to discover BR's practical advantages for legitimising decisions, conflict resolution or the motivation of employees. Partnership with the *Betriebsrat* then becomes a normal part of company life. But there subsists a certain malaise: the vague fear that freedom of enterprise will be hampered by inappropriate action by the *Betriebsrat* never seems to disappear altogether.

E. Pay and Working Time: the Application of Collective Agreements in Small Companies

Five companies in the sample are covered by collective agreements concluded at the regional level. We wanted to know how the collectively-agreed standards were applied and, if necessary, modified. This issue was examined in relation to (a) pay and (b) working time. We also looked at the practices of the five companies not covered by a collective agreement: how far did pay scales and working time differ in the two types of company? Special attention was paid to the machinery for implementing collectively-agreed standards, to the particular adjustments made in each company (modifications, additions or misrepresentations, etc.) and to the indirect influence of the sector-level collective agreement on the determination of working time and pay in companies not covered by a collective agreement. We also wanted to know about the role of BR members in the implementation or modification of collectively-agreed standards: to what extent do standards regarding pay and working time differ in companies with or without a *Betriebsrat*?

1. Pay

Five companies apply a collective agreement: two hotels, a building company, and two garages, all covered by regional sector-level collective agreements. This coverage is a consequence of the employer's membership of the employers' organisation for the sector concerned.

In this group, the manager of the business hotel holds a pre-eminent position: as president of the local employers' organisation, he takes part in collective bargaining and explicitly defends the virtues of collective agreements. In his view, collectively-agreed standards at the regional level have a direct impact on working conditions in the companies.

However, at least where pay is concerned, the collectively-agreed standards are distinctly inferior to the actual levels practised in both of the hotels in the survey – and are directly influenced by the regional labour market. Both hotels are located in the region lying between the Rhine and the Main, characterised by extensive tourism facilities and higher than average prices. Skilled workers are, therefore, usually paid at higher rates than the collectively-agreed standards. This is true not only for the business hotel which, in its sector, is considered rather large with its approximately 100 employees. The owner of the hotel-restaurant with 35 employees began by asserting that the collective agreement had no influence in his company and that he only made use of the provisions concerning the rights to paid holidays and the remuneration of apprentices. But it later emerged that the "modest" collectively-agreed pay was not enough to retain or ensure the long-term loyalty of good skilled employees. The "basic rate" is, as it were, limited to small family companies in rural communities away from urban areas.[5]

By awarding pay, which is higher than the collectively-agreed levels, companies covered by a collective agreement have considerable room to introduce pay differentials. Employers, and in some cases heads of department, are likely to award bonuses and other performance-linked extra pay, with the BR's right to oversight limited to the collectively-agreed pay. But, in the interviews, the BR members made it clear that they are not without informal influence in this area. The challenge is less to obtain the highest possible pay than to ensure respect for the principle of justice in the payment of additional bonuses (to those in the agreement): "Whose turn is it? Who really deserves an increase?"

In companies without a *Betriebsrat*, the employer alone decides about awarding additional bonuses. Two methods of approach and modes of decision can be identified. Whereas in several case studies individual pay levels are determined by the head of the company alone, in one of the companies surveyed they involve an effort by the employer to follow objective and general rules. The owner of the hotel-restaurant tends, after each round of collective bargaining at the regional level, to increase pay by a percentage slightly higher than in the collective

5 The collective agreement for hotels and restaurants in Hesse has been extended (*Allgemeinverbindlichkeit*). All companies, whether or not members of an employers' organisation, are subject to collectively-agreed standards that are renegotiated once a year. To our knowledge, there exists no statistical study on the effective application of these mandatory standards in very small companies not belonging to an employers' organisation and, in general, without union representation. Here we find ourselves in a blind spot concerning the standard-setting power of regional collective agreements.

agreement. This annual in-house round of negotiations has taken the place of individual approaches to the employer by employees. "Before, each person came forward to ask for an extra 50 marks! I put a stop to this system by awarding general increases – and thus spared myself a lot of work and problems". The increases are the same for everyone – here again in line with the collective agreement policy of the employers' organisations and unions.

In the two garages and the building company, the approach taken to pay is governed by the collectively-agreed standards. The employers concerned are not themselves actively engaged in the employers' organisations, but "bow to" the compromises collectively agreed. While they criticise union demands, at bottom they approve the order-conferring function of collective agreements. The head of the building company was highly critical of the increasingly widespread use of "low-cost" employees from South and East Europe. Despite the poor economic situation in the construction sector, he was banking on a German workforce. He valued the collectively-agreed pay scales and, if business was bad, made some workers redundant: "it often happens with us that we recruit fast and dismiss fast". The practical application of the pay scales is always a subject of discussion in companies not covered by a collective agreement. A person's job classification at the time of recruitment and collectively-agreed extra pay are two of the most disputed issues that regularly make life difficult for BR members. They have an important supervisory function: "Without a *Betriebsrat*, there would be no means of control", the BR chairperson of the building company told us.

How are pay structures determined in small companies not covered by either a sector-level or a company-level collective agreement? Our case studies tend to show that the immense diversity of workplaces obviously display a wide range of nuances, from the *de facto* application of collectively-agreed standards to the absolute or almost absolute predominance of labour market mechanisms.

The two science-oriented companies in the sample (the research agency with 18 employees and the energy research centre with 65 employees) have a special status where coverage by a collective agreement is concerned. Both companies were the result of outsourcing by public institutions and a considerable proportion of their resources (promotion of research) comes from public funds. This history also explains why they are covered by the collectively-agreed standards of the civil service *via* the "federal employee pay structure" (*Bundesangestelltentarif*, BAT). The employers are not members of employers' organisations and so take no part in the collective bargaining, but they are expected to apply in their private law companies the collective standards pertaining in the civil service. The job classification criteria, pay structure and annual increases are clearly imposed from the outside. The situation of these companies is therefore not fundamentally different from that of other companies covered by a sector-level collective agreement. The BAT reference not only imposes minimum pay levels, but also excludes any additional bonuses.

This constraint leaves far less room for a specific company-level pay policy. It is only through supplementary pay based on age or length of service that managers can attempt to introduce individual differences and thus perform at least in part their employer's role. In one of the companies, management pays bonuses disguised as anticipated age allowances to reward the best performances or finds a way to make up at least part of the shortfall in pay for candidates coming from industry, a gap that can attain a third of the monthly pay packet. In the other company, management regards the BAT as a "ceiling" and uses the resulting room for manoeuvre to introduce limited pay differentials. In both cases, the managers emphasised the essentially "symbolic" side of their pay policies. However small it is, this room for manoeuvre is nonetheless very important for their own image as employer. "It is I who has the last word on pay", we were told by a manager who decides how many percentage points will separate the pay of his employees from the higher rates of their civil service counterparts.

In both cases, the BR members try to fight against the illogicalities or injustices that, in their eyes, sprung from free adaptation of the BAT. "Where we work, the bonuses handed out as personal favours are a never-ending source of tension and conflict!" said one of them. The demands tabled by BR members are always aimed at preventing or undoing discrepancies or standards that are less advantageous than the ones in force in the civil service. However, their legal position is weaker than that of their counterparts in the staff councils (*Personalräte*) of public institutions and services. But they are often able to affirm, informally, the goals of justice and equality regarding pay by, for example, getting in direct touch with the management of such services.

The new information technologies sector (software) has not yet established an employers' organisation, which is in a position to conduct collective bargaining with the unions. The sector has gone through five years of irrational development and growth. Whereas the firms born out of an outsourcing process tend to refer to the collective agreements of the sector they used to belong to (e.g. the metal industry), adapting them to the new sector's working conditions and skill structure, the start-ups begin without the backing of a collective agreement. The creative outlook and devotion to duty of their employees, many of them very young, who place their skills at the service of "their" company, naturally have an impact on the pay structure. "In the beginning we paid miserable wages", the owner told us, "then, year by year, things improved". Current pay is comparable to that of other small companies in the sector; a national compilation of data on pay carried out by the employer's organisation is used as a basis. Basic pay is topped up by performance-related bonuses and by a share of the profits for employees, who hold shares in this firm, recently transformed into a limited company. Higher pay also became necessary in view of the need to recruit skilled employees from firms covered by a collective agreement (such as Siemens). Thus, even in areas with no collective agreement and no ties to an employers' organisation, we find an indirect dissemination of the system of collective agreements among small companies.

What impact can a *Betriebsrat* have on pay in a company not covered by a collective agreement? In the smaller of the two dental laboratories, the *Betriebsrat* was set up in the 1980s, at a time when the workplace was quite a lot larger. The present owner was at that time the technical director. He had experienced the BR as an employee and, as employer, had put on a permanent footing. He personally would be in favour of coverage by a collective agreement. However, no such sector-level agreement has come into being and an attempt is being made in the company to remedy that omission. With the support of the outside union, the employer and the *Betriebsrat* have signed a series of in-house agreements that reproduce essential features of the collective agreement for craftworkers in the metal industry. They include essentially provisions of the framework agreement that determine working time, the right to paid holidays, the payment of overtime, holidays and Christmas bonuses and length of service bonuses, etc. In view of the uncertain economic situation, the idea of including in the agreement some mandatory clauses on pay was dropped. This text constitutes a kind of "social contract" between the employer and the staff: its provisions bind the two parties in spite of its rather uncertain legal status.[6]

After collective bargaining in the metal industry has finished, the employer and the *Betriebsrat* "face up to each other" once a year to discuss pay increases. Usually a percentage increase is granted to all employees. Occasionally, with the consent of the *Betriebsrat*, the staff are not given a Christmas bonus. A few years ago, when faced with business difficulties, the employer proposed replacing the pay increase by one working hour less per week. The *Betriebsrat* has neither the legal status nor the necessary bargaining power to assert staff pay

---

6 Under the law on collective agreements and the Works Constitution Act, companies do not have the right to conclude agreements on matters within the competence of sector-level collective agreements. The union, but not the *Betriebsrat* as in the present case, may if necessary negotiate a company-level agreement.

demands. But it is regarded as the custodian of "industrial relations common sense" in the company and hence a trustworthy link in employer-employee relations, especially during periods of economic difficulty.

2. Working Time

In sector-level collective agreements, working time is precisely defined. The agreements lay down the number of working hours per week, overtime, the organisation of breaks and the right to paid holidays. During the last ten years, the collectively-agreed rules have been supplemented with a multitude of clauses (Öffrungs klauseln) permitting solutions at company level. The practical organisation of reduced working time (the 35-hour week system) is largely based on rules fixed in each workplace, where the practical ways and means of reducing working time – shorter working week, compensation in the form of days off in lieu or accumulated days of holiday – are defined. The collective agreements simply determine the general conditions. This new direction in collective bargaining policies has markedly increased the elbow room of signatories in the workplace, that is, the employer and the *Betriebsrat*.

Although the role of the *Betriebsrat* in implementing the collectively-agreed provisions on pay is essentially concerned with seeing that the minimum standards are respected, it does have a share in the organisation of working time. The BR members have an explicit right of codetermination *vis-à-vis* most working time issues. Changes in the organisation of daily or weekly working time, the recourse to overtime and the holiday schedule require the prior agreement of the *Betriebsrat* (Article 87 of the Works Constitution Act).

The employer and BR members will therefore try to come up with rules enabling the collectively-agreed provisions to be adapted to both the demands of the market place and the expectations of employees as regards leave. This can be illustrated by two examples. In the larger of the two garages, with 90 employees, the opening hours had to be extended in the evening to respond to the changing habits of its customers. In order not to overload the work plan for employees and to limit Saturday work (sales and urgent repairs), the *Betriebsrat* and management negotiated a system of teams with staggered working hours. In the second garage, with only 11 employees, the owner had to battle simultaneously with the reduction in working time and the extension of opening hours. As there could be no question of taking on the extra staff needed for the introduction of shift work, the employer decided to fill the gap himself. He receives customers on Saturday mornings, while his employees continue to enjoy an uninterrupted week-end. In this company, there is no *Betriebsrat* with which the employer could have negotiated, if need be, an alternative arrangement.

In the building company covered by a collective agreement (35 employees), the various teams sometimes work on very distant sites, with the result that the workers only get home at the week-ends. In order to respect the collectively-agreed 40-hour week, long hours on the work site from Monday to Thursday are followed by a longer week-end after the journey back home on the Friday. "This in-house arrangement meets the wishes of employees; so long as the deadlines are respected, the customers have nothing against it", explained the owner of the company.

In the two companies in the hotel and restaurant sector, the debate on working time is taking place against the background of a conflict particular to that sector. The split-shift system is very unpopular with employees and makes the jobs unattractive: waiters and kitchen staff are often required to perform their daily duties in two segments, four hours around midday and four hours in the evening, for example. The working day is thus interrupted by a forced – and unpaid – break of several hours. Some spend as much as twelve hours away from home. In the business hotel an attempt has been made, on the initiative of the *Betriebsrat*, to remedy this drawback by introducing two shifts. But this system does not cover all eventualities, with the result that employees continue to feel penalised in relation to other occupations. The complete abandon of the split shift system would require the recruitment of extra staff on a part-time basis. A policy for the "standardisation" of working time is thus central to the work of *Betriebsräte* in this sector.

In the case of the hotel-restaurant, a solution to the problem of working time appears to have been found without the need for action by the *Betriebsrat*. It can therefore be argued that, in certain circumstances, the management of a company is indeed in a position to take over some of the BR's typical fields of action, or even "to stand in for" that body; this presupposes that the management is able to analyse the points of friction and hence important employee expectations, in order to provide appropriate solutions. To a certain extent this case illustrates the structural conditions likely to lead to the establishment of a *Betriebsrat* by the employees. Whenever the management of a company is either unable or unwilling to search for solutions to problems of a structural nature, the need for a body to facilitate regulation and mediation stands a good chance of emerging. Whenever management gives up the attempt to settle fundamental problems of working conditions, the idea of collective employee representation becomes more relevant.

Companies not covered by a formal collective agreement appear to apply voluntarily certain basic elements in the regulation of working time to be found in a number of sector-level agreements. The number of working hours per week often lies between 40 and 38.5, and paid holidays last six weeks. The five workplaces in this group have introduced "*à la carte*" working time, which has the advantage both of allowing employees a certain degree of freedom and of responding to particular constraints arising from orders or delivery deadlines and requiring a temporary extension of daily working hours. This always concerns skilled staff who, in their occupations, display an independent attitude to the organisation, including the organisation in time, of their work. The business spirit requires that account be taken of employee aspirations in regard to working time in the interests of everybody; thus the planning of paid holidays will be arranged, in order to give foreign employees the possibility of a long absence so that they can return to their own country. An employee of a dental laboratory explained that he did not wait for an explicit order to work overtime: everyone knew the deadlines. If problems arose, they were usually sorted out among fellow employees. "Some like to do a bit of overtime from time to time, if they are building a house for example. It may suit them to take a few hours off the next day to see how the building work is getting on".

Flexible organisation of working time without explicit interference by one's superiors may be regarded as a particularly important element in the employee's relationship to the company and in general well-being at work. The managers of the two firms covered by the BAT civil service pay scales feel that "liberal" organisation of working time is likely to make up for drawbacks elsewhere: "As we cannot offer top-notch pay, we take care to offer at least favourable working conditions. Creative work needs freedom of action". The practices resulting from such a philosophy of working time, which is based on mutual trust and individual responsibility, nevertheless remain rather unclear. When supervisors finally intervene with directives – we were told of disciplinary action against employees missing the fixed time bracket by five or ten minutes – they should expect almost inevitable conflicts with the employees. According to a BR member, the underlying assumptions of the organisation of working time, between trust on the one hand and control on the other, generate latent but lasting tensions and unspoken conflicts concerning discipline and commitment in the work of employees. Where a *Betriebsrat* exists, it cannot avoid taking action.

Conflicts about working time sometimes make it possible to broach more fundamental issues about power in the company. "The behaviour of a head of department was a constant source of stress because he shouted whenever someone was five minutes late", said a BR member. So the *Betriebsrat* took the initiative of advocating more flexible working time. An agreement was signed with management, which put an end to the fixed time bracket: each employee decides his/her hours of work, after consulting his/her immediate colleagues. The employee's signature makes it possible to check the hours actually worked. For the *Betriebsrat*, this change was necessary for reasons of justice and equal treatment. The aim was to prevent practices in the different research sectors from diverging more and more.

In the software company (22 employees) – according to its owner – the 40-hour week serves as the reference. Employees have the right to six weeks paid holidays but must not be absent for more than two weeks at a time. There are no fixed daily working hours. The employees organise their work to a large extent independently. In the end, they decide for themselves if they are going to work late or even set up a "night shift". And yet it is difficult to say to what extent the decision to work overtime is based on free personal choice or rather on the diktat of deadlines. To satisfy certain customers, week-ends are worked repeatedly and an "emergency Sunday shift" has been introduced. Overtime is usually compensated by a "generous" allowance of time off in lieu. Like their counterparts in other companies, the employees appreciate informality in the organisation of working time, regarding it as proof of individual freedom. We also see in this arrangement based on mutual trust and respect between employer and employees a means of making up for the relatively low pay in comparison with other workplaces or regions.[7]

When there is no control of working time, however, the other side of the coin is the tireless efforts of the workforce, a trap that young employees in particular can fall into. The owner of the software company pointed out the dangers to the health and performance of employees of working hours that are not limited. Certain employees are potential "workaholics", he thought. "I have even had occasion to turn off the computer of a colleague myself when paying a late evening visit to the offices". The drift towards irregular and sometimes excessive hours is made easier by the fact that most of the employees are unmarried and very young.

In this company, which is not covered by a collective agreement and does not have a *Betriebsrat* in a position to exercise some control, the organisation of working time and the distribution of work, is largely a matter for the unilateral decision of the employer; if necessary, he can act as he thinks fit depending on business circumstances. At the time of the survey, owing to a long-term drop in orders, management was

[7] A rather vague and informal organisation of working time seems to be a common feature of the sector. See Ahlers and Trautwein-Kalms (2002) and Kluge and Schiemann (2002) on working conditions in the new information technologies sector.

discussing a plan providing for the transformation of full-time posts into two-thirds time ones or, alternatively, reducing paid holidays.

What happens when we compare the methods of drawing up standards regarding pay, on the one hand, and working time, on the other? Questions about pay are usually the direct and undisputed responsibility of the owner or manager. In companies covered by a collective agreement, it is the job classification structure used by the sector-level agreement that applies, supplemented by additional bonuses. The final word on pay – in the same way as decisions regarding recruitment or dismissals – is at the heart of the employer's authority. In companies covered by a sector-level collective agreement, the collectively-agreed standards for pay are seen as minimum standards, thus leaving the employer with some room for manoeuvre. The function of the *Betriebsrat* is to see that these minimum standards are actually applied. In companies not covered by a collective agreement, the pay standards in such agreements nevertheless appear to be used for reference purposes.

Questions regarding working time are more often settled through a system of "give-and-take" between employer and employees. This is less true for the length of the working week or of paid holidays (fixed by the collective agreements) than for their specific organisation in the day-to-day life of the company. The flexibility of the collectively-agreed standards on working time permits variations in response to the state of the company's order book, special requests by customers and the personal or family wishes of employees. The degree of flexibility in working time, observed in the companies covered by the survey, suggests that the collectively-agreed standards are used as guidelines for the design of a company-level system of working time, rather than as unified rules. The *Betriebsräte* play an important role in co-organising work schedules, which take into account labour market pressures and employee interests. In companies not covered by a collective agreement, the basic standards laid down in the sector-level agreements (length of working week and rights to paid holidays) are also clearly used for reference purposes.

F. Employers' Organisations and Trade Unions: Watching from the Sidelines

1. Mittelstand *Employers Jealous of their Independence*

The heads of small and medium-sized companies generally have few links with employers' organisations. Unlike other European countries, Germany does not have employers' organisations specifically for small and medium-sized companies. Guilds (*Innungsverbände*) serve as employers' organisations in the craftwork sector. Membership of local chambers of commerce and industry (*Industrie- und Handelskammern*, IHK) and craft guilds (*Handwerkskammern*, HWK) is complusory. In the 1990s, the *Mittelstand* repeatedly denounced the predominance of big firms in employers' organisations and chambers of commerce and industry which, for that reason, did not pay sufficient heed to the particular interests of small and medium-sized companies. In reaction to instances of collective arbitration unacceptable to them, a number of *Mittelstand* companies have in recent years withdrawn from the employers' organisations. To halt this weakening of their base, which they see as a threat, certain employers' organisations are now proposing membership without coverage by a collective agreement (*OT-Mitgliedschaft*), i.e. companies remain as members of the organisation, but are not bound by the collective agreements signed by the latter.

A study carried out in 2001, "The *Mittelstand* in Germany", looked at the membership of *Mittelstand* employers in employers' organisations and at their ongoing relations with the collective bargaining system. A great majority of heads of *Mittelstand* companies took care to keep their distance from employers' organisations involved in collective bargaining (*Tarifverband*), as well as from any form of centralised collective agreement coverage. Admittedly, according to this survey, 53% of the firms are members of one or more sector-level organisations, but only 23% belong to an employers' organisation with negociating powers (*Tarif versand*) and are thus covered by collective agreements. Collective coverage is particularly weak in the services sector (16%) but a little higher in industry and craftwork (29%) and in commerce (28%). Once affiliated to a *Tarif versand*, the heads of *Mittelstand* companies tend to be reasonably satisfied with their collective representation. Nearly three quarters of them rate the services rendered by their organisations as very good, good or satisfactory. Only 6% express strong discontent with the performance of the *Tarif versand*. However, the upshot is that 83% of all *Mittelstand* employers either keep their distance from all forms of collective agreement or disapprove of the results of the collective bargaining policy (Institut für Mittelstandsforschung, 2001).

What relations do the employers in our sample maintain with employers' organisations and with other organisations representing companies? Apart from the question of formal membership, we wanted to know where and how the heads of companies satisfied their needs for advice and assistance. What outside influences affect the labour standards and management decisions of small companies and help to determine working conditions therein?

Half of the companies in the sample are members of an employers' organisation and are thus covered by sector-level collective agreements.

The manager of the business hotel (120 employees) has responsibilities within the local hotel and restaurant sector employers' organisation and is the employers' representative in the chamber of commerce and industry. He emphasises the order-conferring function of collective agreements, which is essential for the regulation of employer-employee relations in the workplace. The system of sector-level collective agreements at the regional level is not, in his opinion, out of date – quite the contrary. The manager said he was rather against permitting membership of employers' organisations without acceptance of the collective agreement (*OT-Mitgliedschaft*, see above), for it would result in a disturbing loss of influence for the latter; similarly, he rejected the replacement of sector-level by company-level agreements, a step greatly favoured by certain employers.

The owner of the large garage (90 employees) was long a member of the bargaining committee of his employers' organisation, but abandoned his position a few years ago, disappointed by the "rigidities" that in his view characterised his organisation's structure: "Individual companies do not count". However, he has no intention of withdrawing from the representational structure. The alternative – a company-level collective agreement – he finds unattractive as it would enable the union to "get even closer" to the company.

The head of the small hotel-restaurant (35 employees) is also a board member of the local employers' organisation. His involvement, however, is not primarily for militant reasons: it springs rather from his conviction of the necessity of maintaining personal contact with the major employers in the sector, so as not to be left on the sidelines. He does not appear to play a particularly active role in the employers' organisation and does not take part in the region-level collective bargaining. When asked about the impact of collective agreements in his own company he was anxious to stand aloof from the representational structure: "Here, we don't need the collective agreement. Our pay is always higher!" The sector-level collective agreement does, however, serve as a reference for all decisions concerning job classification and pay increases.

The owner of the building company (43 employees) complained of complicated and bureaucratic structures in the sector's employers' organisation. It is true that there are two competing organisations, one bringing together largish companies and the other, smaller ones. Both of them, however, are in fact dominated by big companies with the result that small companies can hardly make themselves heard. This employer also criticised the complexity of collective agreement-based regulation: "There are too many rules. It is typical of Germany. Every six months, some new rule is introduced". He thinks the chamber of commerce system, also, has too many rules. The legal status of his company obliges him to join both the local craft guild and the chamber of commerce and industry – engendering two subscriptions not really justified by the quality of the services provided in return.

In workplaces not covered by a collective agreement, employers – as one might expect – keep their distance from employers' organisations more noticeably than those who are affiliated. The managers of the two workplaces engendered by the outsourcing of two former civil service departments saw no need to join an employers' organisation, an attitude that is perfectly logical in view of the fact that their companies are governed by the BAT (federal employee pay structure) of the civil service. They are in a way the "stowaway" beneficiaries of the civil service collective agreement system over which they have no influence. Nor do they see the advantages of membership in terms of services and advice. The manager of the research agency (18 employees) gets advice, on a case by case basis, from the managers of other firms with which he has professional relations. For instance, he used the example of a large workplace belonging to Deutsche Telekom to sign a company-level agreement on "agreed objectives". The rules worked out in big companies under the co-determination system do not appear to be without a ripple effect, even among employers jealous of their independence *vis-à-vis* employers' organisations. In order to gain access to external advice, this manager has adopted an approach very similar to that of the *Betriebsrat*: over the years both sides have gradually built up networks of contacts and interlocutors in other firms. Thus a small company, which is "isolated" from the official representational structure, does not entirely escape the twin influences of other employers and *Betriebsräte*, which are in turn underpinned by certain trade union guidelines.

In the two dental laboratories, the owners are members of the employers' organisation but are not bound by a collective agreement, which does not exist in that sector. The head of the smaller of the two companies (22 employees) left the employers' organisation a few years ago. He found its contribution to be of little use: "Just childish games". The assistance offered by the organisation is out of proportion to the high cost of the annual subscription. The decision to leave the employers' organisation, however, was taken at a time of business difficulties for the company which forced it to make savings. But the employer keeps in touch with other heads of companies in the sector he got to know during his time of membership.

This employer also turns, through the *Betriebsrat*, to the local union to meet some of his needs for information and advice. The possibility of obtaining information from it and thus avoid having to face the "jungle of regulations" on his own is warmly appreciated. He described his relations with the union officer responsible for the craftwork sector as relaxed, constructive and useful, and he had no hesitation in asking for his help whenever he felt the need. The labour law implications of decisions taken in the company are doubtless a particularly important aspect of such consultations. The arbitration and rules adopted within the company, which may take the form of written company-level agreements, are in this case also underpinned by a quite complex informal network nourished by both employer and trade union influences.

2. Trade Unions with Only a Marginal Influence?

Several criteria can be called into play to measure the influence of trade unions over the employees of small companies in addition to coverage by a collective agreement negotiated by the union concerned. Union density is considered an important indicator of union presence in a company. The existence, or not, of a *Betriebsrat* in the company determines to a large extent the possibility of establishing a formal framework for contacts and discussions between employees and the external union. The union membership of BR members becomes at a later stage essential to the closeness of such cooperation: are the BR members unionised? Do they have union responsibilities outside the company? Union influence over the development of industrial relations in the company depends, in fact, on how cooperation is actually handled and on the closeness of the relations between the leading figures within the *Betriebsrat* and the local or regional union structure.

Table 7. Employers' affiliation and union density in companies covered by the survey

Workplace	Number of employees	Existence of collective agreement	Employer	*Betriebsrat*	Union density
Business hotel	120	Yes	Manager	Yes	About 50%
Large garage	90	Yes	Owner	Yes	83%
Large dental laboratory	70	No	Owner	No	?
Energy research centre	65	Indirect	Manager	Yes	About 10%
Building company	43	Yes	Owner	Yes	13%
Hotel-restaurant	35	Yes	Owner	No	?
Small dental laboratory	22	No	Owner	Yes	80-90%
Software company	22	No	Owner	No	?
Research agency	18	Indirect	Manager	Yes	About 25%
Small garage	11	Yes	Owner	No	?

Union density varies greatly in the companies covered by the survey. It is true that our sample was very limited, but it can be stated that small companies are not in principle impervious to union recruitment drives. Table 7 suggests that there exists no unequivocal link between the union membership of employees and other aspects of the company such as size, sector, coverage by a collective agreement, employer's membership of an employers' organisation and legal status of the company or of its owner or manager. In other words, union density in each individual company reflects each company's history, the product of initiatives and learning processes of both sides.

Nevertheless, there exists a certain correlation between the presence of a *Betriebsrat* and the level of union membership among employees. It should be remembered, however, that, in companies without a *Betriebsrat*, we were able to interview only employers who usually could not – or did not wish to – answer questions concerning the union membership of a proportion of their employees. We cannot therefore exclude the existence of individual employees who keep quiet about their membership of a union. The knowledge of employers regarding union density in their company is sometimes very sketchy: the owner of the large garage put union membership at about 15% whereas, according to the union, it is 83%. The owner of the small dental laboratory gave figures a lot lower than those provided by the *Betriebsrat*. As a rule, employers seemed to underestimate – probably for psychological reasons – the level of union membership in small *Mittelstand* companies.

In companies with a *Betriebsrat*, the latter serves as a bridge between employees and the external union. In the final analysis, the election of a *Betriebsrat* may be regarded as an important condition for the unionisation of employees.[8] In certain circumstances, however, the elected BR members also serve as mediators between the employer and the union.

Local union structures have a decisive impact at the time when the *Betriebsrat* is established. The union officers inform employees about their electoral rights and accompany them in their first practical steps. During these preparations for the election, which might be at a time of conflict, we often find a relatively significant group of employees joining the union. In such situations, the reason for doing so seems evident: "The union helps us to defend our rights against the employer. We must therefore support it by becoming members".

---

[8] An empirical study in the early 1990s on small companies in Hesse has shown that those with a *Betriebsrat* tend to reach a union density similar to that of big companies. The constitution of a *Betriebsrat* may therefore play a fundamental role, even in facilitating dialogue between union and employees (Wassermann, 1992: 29).

During the initial period following the election of a *Betriebsrat*, discussions are usually related to the unresolved tensions and problems in the company, which had triggered the establishment of the BR – in most cases, conflicts over pay or working time. Here, union officers play an important role in providing support and advice. They attend meetings of the *Betriebsrat*, take the floor at staff meetings and sometimes negotiate directly with the employer. For newly elected BR members, union training courses prove very important in giving them the necessary skills and professionalism to carry out their mandate.

The prospects of putting this relatively close relationship with the union, developed at the time the *Betriebsrat* was being set up, on a permanent basis would appear to depend on the ability of the local union structures to integrate the new members into local union activities and to introduce a monitoring and advice system geared to the special needs of small companies. Wherever the union is no longer present in the company and no longer pursues a target of systematic unionisation, the number of members falls, if only as a result of staff turnover; it is not uncommon for the group of card-holders to be limited to a few BR members and their immediate circle.

This is the case of the business hotel (120 employees): at the time the *Betriebsrat* was established, a majority of the BR members and also a majority of the other employees joined the union. Today the number of union members can be counted on the fingers of one hand. The first ones to join have left the hotel and neither the union officer nor the BR members have taken the trouble to recruit new members. The present *Betriebsrat* has only one person who is a union member. The decline in union density seems in this company to be due to a widening rift between the *Betriebsrat* and the union. The BR chairperson criticises the local union for not keeping an eye on the company. He feels "rather disappointed" by the current leader of the NGG union, who is losing interest in small companies, unlike his very attentive predecessor. Discussions between the *Betriebsrat* and the union now seem to be kept to the strict minimum.

The BR member of the research agency (18 employees) spoke of a similar process. When he was first elected the training and advice provided by the ÖTV union had been very useful. Since then relations had become slacker – for one thing, his needs for basic legal expertise had for the most part been satisfied and, for another, the training offered by the ÖTV did not sufficiently target the problems with which he was confronted. "The training courses for BR members are not sufficiently geared to the problems that arise in small companies".

This gradually increasing distance is not an inevitable trend, as the example of the small dental laboratory (22 employees) shows. Here, too, the local union "sponsored" the election of a *Betriebsrat* at the end of the 1980s. Its establishment had taken place against a background of the local *IG Metall*'s policy at the time of systematically seeking to develop links with the very little unionised companies in the dental technology craftwork sector. It supported the election of representative bodies in several companies and enjoyed considerable success in attracting new members. Admittedly, the attempt to negotiate with the employers' organisation a collective agreement modelled on the one for companies in the metal craftwork sector failed but, thanks to training and information directly aimed at employees in this craftwork sector, contacts with the employees of companies with a *Betriebsrat* were stabilised on a long-term basis. The elected representatives of the dental laboratories hold a special working conference once a year. At the national union level, a free telephone number enables the employees of companies with or without collective representation to obtain information on labour law. Two elected representatives of this small company take an active part in the *IG Metall* special committee for dental technicians, whose main function is to facilitate discussions on recent developments in the sector. These persons are therefore directly involved in the work of *IG Metall* in this craftwork sector at the national level. The BR members' close relationship with the union seems to have had a direct impact on the unionisation of employees, some 90% of whom are members of *IG Metall*.

This said, the relations between small companies and trade unions appear on the whole to be rather sporadic, occasional and unsystematic. In the day-to-day life of small companies, the unions tend to be somewhat sidelined. The concrete union backup for the work of the *Betriebsräte* seems a long way from the idealism nourished by experience in large companies, in which union officers are expected to participate regularly in meetings of the *Betriebsrat* and to express the union's demands and policies at staff meetings. It is only in the large garage (90 employees, 83% union members) that we find ongoing links between the *Betriebsrat* and the union. All the elected representatives are members of *IG Metall*. The union officer intervenes regularly at staff meetings and the BR chairperson is able to meet his counterparts in other garages once a month. The BR's relationship with the union is much more informal and "relaxed" in the building company. The union density – 13% – is "not bad" for a company of its size. It is a "unionised workplace" according to the criteria of the sector. But only two members of the *Betriebsrat* are union members. The BR chairperson is not a card-holder; nonetheless he keeps in touch with the union, which is "a very important source of information" for him. He also attends union meetings: "It does not bother the union secretary to find a non-member present". The owner of the building company, for his part, meets the local officer of the construction sector union on a regular basis. The intermittent exchange of information is also facilitated by the familiar style of speech used in the building trade. Mention was made, in particular, of some specific problems related to the application of some complex provisions in the collective agreement.

In order to make up for union advice they consider inappropriate for the particular needs of small companies, the *Betriebsräte* tend to build up networks for informal discussions with their counterparts in other companies. One gets the impression that these networks of informal contacts are important for the dissemination of information and advice and could play a decisive role in the development of collective standards and rules in small companies.

Even though the question of union influence in small companies is considered on the basis of purely formal criteria, such as coverage by a collective agreement or union density, in most cases it will be concluded that the unions play a limited role and have but marginal influence. But the overall picture is much less black and white when attention is paid to informal factors and practices, such as the effect of the dissemination of collectively-agreed standards in companies not covered by a collective agreement or the unofficial channels for obtaining advice and information used by the various parties at very different levels. Admittedly, in the companies surveyed, employees' contacts with the unions are for the most part sporadic, non-systematic and a bit distant. It remains, however, that working conditions and labour standards, as well as internal decision-making in these companies, are, as a result of these informal and often hidden exchanges, probably more marked by union influence than would superficially appear to be the case.

III. "Different, but not Fundamentally Different" – an Overview

A. The Issue of Democracy in Small Companies

The 1990s were marked by the steady erosion of the *Betriebsrat* system. In a context of the decentralisation and restructuring of companies and workplaces, the BRs found their scope and means of action shrinking. The number of *Betriebsräte* and of BR members diminished and many *Betriebsräte* lost some of their permanent members and their power, as workplaces became smaller. Many of the new companies established in innovative sectors dropped the idea of electing a *Betriebsrat*. The overall number of workplaces covered by the co-determination system declined (Wassermann, 2002b).

In 2001, for the first time in nearly thirty years, a reform of the Works Constitution Act, which lays down the conditions for the election and functioning of *Betriebsräte*, was adopted. A central objective of this reform was to strengthen co-determination in small and medium-sized companies. The new law set out explicitly to facilitate the establishment of representative bodies in small companies. Among other things, the Federal Minister of Labour was anxious to facilitate the election of a *Betriebsrat* in very small workplaces resulting from the splitting up of larger companies, hitherto not covered by the law (*Ibid.*).

The 2002 elections to the *Betriebsräte* showed that the 2001 reform did indeed assist the creation of such bodies in small companies with no collective representation. The simplified election procedure, intended to reduce the bureaucratic obstacles in small companies, probably contributed less on the whole than the discussions about the reform. For the first time in the history of the Federal Republic there were public hearings on the pros and cons of democratic structures in small private companies. Immediately after the introduction of the simplified election procedure in the summer of 2001, the unions had to cope with a great many requests, essentially from small companies, asking for information and advice concerning the constitution of a *Betriebsrat*. The 2002 elections saw the number of newly established BRs rise. From this point of view, the reform helped to spread the BR system more widely in small companies.[9] Since the 2002 parliamentary elections, however, the political debate has been once again dominated by the demands of *Mittelstand* lobbies wanting to restrict the rights to representation in small companies. The findings of our study on the relations between traditional *Mittelstand* management structures and the types of employee participation illustrate this ongoing debate for and against democracy in small companies.

B. Decision-Making in Companies: from the Unchallenged Authority of the Employer to Cooperation

Whatever their differences with respect to the traditions of each sector, size and skill structure, the small *Mittelstand* companies resemble each other by a style of management strongly marked by the personality and mode of action of the head of the company. In the smallest compa-

9 There exists no statistical overview on the number of new BRs established. The election statistics of a few union branches indicate a sharp increase in the number of *Betriebsräte*, especially in small companies. *IG Metall* recorded 1,500 new BRs out of a total of 13,000 in its files. It is difficult to know to what extent these new BRs have also triggered an extension of the BR network: *IG Metall* recorded at the same time the loss of about 1,600 BRs since the 1998 elections as a result of company closures and buyouts, etc. (Wassermann, 2003).

nies in our sample (up to about 50 employees), the employer generally claims full direct responsibility for all decisions in the company. In slightly larger companies (50 to 100 employees), we find various forms of differentiated or objective decision-making, such as the use of services or departments with their own hierarchical structures.

Certain forms of mediation between the interests of employees and of the head of the company are to be found even in small companies with a relatively autocratic management. The personality and attitudes of the persons concerned are crucial to the success of such generally informal participation practices in solving more long-term problems. The social proximity of the entrepreneur and employees is an important indicator of the cohesion of the work group; such cohesion arises from the personal nature of relationships in small companies and is often the product of a long shared history in the occupation or trade and in the company and of the fact that they all come from the same social, geographical and cultural background. In such a context, the employer and employees, at least those belonging to a core group of companies, seem able to come up with balanced solutions that are seen by both parties as fair and equitable. On the other hand, authoritarian styles of management that keep employees at a distance make it difficult to mediate between interests. The decision to set about establishing formal representation as provided by the law (*Betriebsrat*) is often made in situations in which the informal modes of mediation between differing interests have proved inadequate.

In a (very) small company in which all decisions tend to centre on its head, we find some competition between this style of management and the functions relating to the collective representation of employees. The system of unilateral decision-making by the employer and of his or her responsibility for everything is challenged by the election of a *Betriebsrat*, which can result in the emergence of parallel decision-making structures in the company. This said, management without mediation by the head of the company does not appear to be incompatible in itself with co-determination by the *Betriebsrat* on the basis of collective agreements and legislation. As time passes, the learning process of each party appears to clear the way for a constructive compromise on ways and means of cooperation.

The conditions under which the *Betriebsrat* is accepted and integrated appear on the face of it more favourable in companies with a more formal organisation and division of labour. Here, the *Betriebsrat* is less often seen as a foreign body and source of disturbance. Whenever the management of the company depends on cooperation between a number of players representing different sectors or hierarchical levels, the *Betriebsrat* seems to find integration easier. It is probably no accident that the BR members, or at least its chairperson, often come from the middle management of this type of company. The combination of higher rank and an elective office appears to predestine such employees for a function of mediation recognised by both parties within a management style oriented towards dialogue and the balancing of interests.

In newly established companies, the organisational and decision-making structures adapt in parallel to the growing differentiation in the organisation of work and the rising number of employees. The egalitarianism of the founding team gradually gives way to a differentiated and hierarchical form of organisation. This growth process is often accompanied by internal crises and conflicts that may trigger the demand for a representative body, either in the form of an *ad hoc* participation structure or *via* the election of a *Betriebsrat.* In such a context, the election of employee representatives may prove a logical step in the transition from the founding team to company organisation, which is based on the division of labour. The *Betriebsrat* serves as a sort of co-management for the change in structure.

C. The **Betriebsrat,** *Mediator and Moral Authority*

In small companies, the *Betriebsrat* is usually created at a time of crisis – a business crisis (falling turnover), change of ownership or disagreements at the top against a background of rapid growth or the threat of job losses. Sometimes the election of a *Betriebsrat* constitutes the employees' response to deteriorating working conditions and sometimes it takes place against a background of open conflict in the company. If the management is either unable or not in a position to find solutions for major structural problems, the particular need is felt for a body, recognised by employees, to handle regulation and mediation. During this period, the local trade structure always seems to act as "midwife" for the creation of a *Betriebsrat.*

The activities of BR members in small companies differ in many ways from both the legal norms and the modes of official employee representation found in large companies. The freedom they need for the systematic performance of their representational duties, which is based on the general rights and conditions defined by the Works Constitution Act, is often very restricted. For example, the rights of BR members to be released from some of their professional duties or to attend union training courses have first to be imposed on the employer. The latter, anxious to cut the costs of the *Betriebsrat*, in many cases does not understand the need for BR members to be given a relatively extensive freedom of intervention. BR members are often not associated with a number of day-to-day decisions that are officially included in the right of co-determination – questions of working time, overtime or pay, for example. This does not always mean that their influence in such matters is nil. Their influence and the forms of coordination with the head of the company are often informal. In many cases, the BR members insist less on their legal rights than on their personal contacts with their superiors, their employer or the owner. Legal rights and formal procedures often take second place to BR-employer relations of a highly personal nature.

Mittelstand employers hardened in the furnace of co-determination appear to regard "their" *Betriebsrat* as an institution that is useful on the whole but not without problems. There is a latent ambiguity underlying their approval – the BR is perceived as a legitimate mediator but at the same time as a potential threat to the entrepreneur's freedom of decision *via* outside interference by the unions – even when the experience of cooperation with it is on the whole given a positive rating. Employers tend to make use of BR members when they need to solve difficult problems with their employees. For some of them, the BR serves as a buffer between management and staff. Others make use of the conflict resolution channels defined in the legislation, in order to confer legitimacy on their decisions in the eyes of employees. When management resources are scarce, the BR quite often lays claim – on the basis of solid relations of trust – to competence in "all industrial relations matters" in the company.

The BR members in small companies without the co-management resources of large ones see themselves primarily as custodians of the rights of employees and as responsible for the transposition of collectively-agreed standards into day-to-day company practices. They highlight their protective function in the event of illegal actions by the employer. The legislation and other provisions intended to protect employees must be respected. This does not mean absolute respect for official standards at all costs. The job of BR members consists rather in defending solutions felt as fair by employees and simultaneously bearing in mind the business realities of the company. In a way, BR members define themselves as "custodians of justice and equity" and as a "moral authority" in the company.

D. Collectively-Agreed Standards as a Set of General Guidelines

In questions of pay, the owners or managers decide for themselves, according to our survey of small companies. In companies covered by a collective agreement, they decide on the application of job classifications and on additional bonuses. This is a crucial power of the employer, who has the last word on questions of pay, recruitment and dismissals. The collectively-agreed standards are regarded as minimum standards in companies covered by an agreement, which leaves the employer room for making adjustments. Here the *Betriebsrat* performs a watchdog function to see that the collectively-agreed minimum standards are respected. In companies not covered by a collective agreement, the collectively-agreed pay standards often serve as an unofficial guideline.

Questions related to working time are more dependent on a system of give-and-take between employer and employees which, however, does not concern the number of working hours or the annual collectively-agreed paid holidays, but rather their practical implementation in the day-to-day life of the company. Collectively-agreed working time is liable to adjustment at any time depending on the company's order book and customer requirements on the one hand and on family problems or the personal needs of employees on the other. The degree of flexibility in working time in companies covered by the survey appears to indicate that the main function of the collectively-agreed standards is to provide guidelines for the system employed in each individual company. They are hardly seen as mandatory directives. In this area the BR has an important role of co-decision at the meeting-point between market requirements and the interests of employees. Companies not covered by a collective agreement clearly take their lead from the basic standards for working time laid down in collective agreements (length of working week and rights to paid holidays).

It should be stressed that the standards negotiated in collective agreements in matters of pay, working time and conditions have a significant impact, through a wide range of indirect links and forms of mediation, on the working conditions in small companies not covered by collective agreements. Our own findings confirm other survey data showing that about 60% of small companies with between 5 and 100 employees and not covered by collective agreements use the collectively-agreed standards for reference purposes (IAB Panel, 2002; Bahnmüller, 2002).

More particularly in small companies not covered by a collective agreement but having a *Betriebsrat*, the BR members often turn to the unions for help in bringing the local standards closer to the collectively-agreed ones. In many cases the employers join them in the attempt to reach verbal or written agreements to make up for the lack of a collective one. Such alternative solutions quite commonly involve more or less unofficial advisory relations between the employer and the trade unions. These "substitute" standards are generally less favourable to the employees and less constraining for the employer than those in the collective agreements.

E. *Trade Unions and Employers' Organisations on the Sidelines*

The links between *Mittelstand* employers and their employers' organisations and chambers of commerce and industry are usually weak and often quite distant. In order to work out local standards, employers do not just turn for information and advice to their respective organisations but also find, through their relatively close personal contacts with the heads of other companies, models or examples for the solutions adopted in their own companies.

Unions also play a somewhat marginal role in small companies. Contacts are limited to companies with a *Betriebsrat*, which usually serves as a bridge between employees and the union. But even in that kind of situation, the contacts tend to be sporadic and relatively informal. For there to be a real relationship been the unions and small companies, the unions would have to provide information and advice geared to the latter's needs. Like the employers, the *Betriebsräte* often make use of a wide range of personal contacts with other companies for the purpose of finding solutions to their own problems of representation.

The attitude of the unions to small companies has evolved considerably in recent years. By tradition they were wont to focus their attention on large companies, but today they tend to recognise the "strategic importance" of small companies for the development of the collective agreement system and more generally for the organisation of union representation. Certain sector-level trade unions have begun to think about ways of improving the integration of small companies – especially expanding private companies in the services sector – in their policies regarding collective agreements, organisation and co-determination at company level. Whether they will, in the future, be in a position to speak and act on behalf of small companies is for them a key issue for their future as representative institutions.

And yet it would be wrong to conclude from the rather marginal role of employers' organisations and trade unions and the absence of formal relations that the collectively-agreed standards of small companies in regard to representative structures and their political and organisational development evolve independently. The collective agreement system, developed by the employers' organisations and the unions, exerts an indirect and often informal influence, even on companies not covered by an official collective agreement. Even in companies belonging to sectors where no collective agreements exist, reference is made to general developments in that field.

F. Labour Standards in Small Companies and the System of Industrial Relations

With the necessary prudence owing to the small number of case studies, we have tried to link our findings and empirical interpretations to the four types of industrial relations described at the beginning of this chapter. We wondered whether companies maintaining different relations with the society's system of collective standards differed fundamentally from each other. The result is presented in the Table below. The oversimplified treatment inherent in this kind of exercise should not lead one to generalise the findings to all companies in the four types of industrial relations. It applies only to the workplaces covered by our survey.

If we compare the characteristics of companies at the two extremes – those covered by a collective agreement and possessing a *Betriebsrat* and those not covered by a collective agreement and without a BR – the following observations may be made.

Table 8. Typical patterns of industrial relations and the drawing up of labour standards in small companies – Findings of the case studies

	Companies covered by a collective agreement	Companies not covered by a collective agreement
Companies with BR	A	B
	Traditional workplaces in manufacturing industry and services	Relatively recent research centers covered indirectly by CA; one traditional craftwork company
	Management based on a hierarchy and relying on cooperation	Management structure based on in-house cooperation Leaves room for cooperation with BR
	BR integrated into in-house cooperation structure	Employers and BR maintain sporadic relations with their representative organisations
	Employers and BR have contacts with their representative organisations	CA in other sectors seek information and advice outside the company
	Collectively agreed standards determine working conditions directly or serve as reference for in-house solutions	Employers and BR seek information and advice outside the company
	The most important company standards negotiated by employer and BR on the basis of the CA	Industrial relations in company based on agreements between employer and BR

	C	D
Companies without BR	Very small traditional companies directly managed by owner	One relatively traditional craftwork company and one start-up with extremely varied structures
	Employers not against BR but find it superfluous in their case	Owners reject BR as restriction on freedom of enterprise and support other more informal methods of mediation
	Membership of employers' organisation of little importance to company, no union present because no BR	Employers keep aloof from collective organisations; no union present
	Collectively-agreed standards serve as reference for organisation of working conditions by employer, who takes account of employee interests	CA framework standards and legislation serve as reference for employer's organisation of working conditions

BR = *Betriebsrat* CA = collective agreement.

G. Small Companies: Gradual Integration into the Industrial Relations System

Companies officially covered by collective agreements and having *Betriebsrat* may be deemed integrated into the industrial relations system. They are involved to a varying extent in the activities of unions and employers' organisations. The collective agreements have a considerable standard-setting impact on working conditions when the latter are included in them. There is an ongoing debate between the two parties on the application and, as the case may be, the local variants of such collective agreements. The standards are sometimes more and sometimes less favourable than the minimum standards laid down in the collective agreements as the result of an agreement between the two parties. The standards defined in sector-level collective agreements often have a more important impact on the day-to-day life of small companies than in large workplaces. Additional formally defined rules included in company-level agreements negotiated by the employer and the *Betriebsrat* are less common in small companies than in big ones.

Just like other types of small family business, management of small companies within the industrial relations system tends to be strongly marked by the personality of the owner or manager. The management structure nevertheless reveals that power relations at the personal level are not altogether subjective – in other words, there is a differentiation of hierarchical levels and of forms of company-level cooperation. The *Betriebsrat* is not perceived as a foreign body but is relatively well integrated into the cooperation and decision-making structures. BR practices and the organisation of its relations with employees and employer include numerous informal actions that may differ sharply from the official standards laid down in the Works Constitution Act.

H. Isolated Small Companies Indirectly Integrated into the Collective Standards System

In companies not covered by a formal collective agreement and with no elected employee representation (i.e. no *Betriebsrat*), the style of management is similarly marked by the personality and temperament of the owner or manager. However, in these cases direct decision-making by the employer tends to predominate. Any hierarchical organisation and diversified decision-making structure will take second place to the direct authority of the head of the company. On the whole, there is no sign of formal cooperation and division of labour in the management structure and organisation of such companies.

These employers, who claim full responsibility for everything that happens in the company, reject the very idea of establishing a *Betriebsrat*, because they see it as an obstacle to freedom of enterprise and prefer more informal and less restricting methods of mediation between interests. They keep their distance from employers' organisations: not many of them become members but informal contacts allow them to keep abreast of developments and issues in the employers' camp. In these companies, unions are not formally represented: if certain employees are members, they keep it quiet.

The definition of labour standards within companies does not, however, occur in a vacuum. Cross-sectoral collectively-agreed standards and legislation serve as guidelines for decision-making by the employer on the subject of local standards. Labour standards and working conditions differ considerably, but not fundamentally, from those areas covered by collective agreements. The characteristics of regional labour markets have a powerful impact on pay scales and working conditions in such companies. What are perceived by employer and employees as acceptable labour standards are usually the outcome of more or less implicit trade-offs between the employer and a few employees, who sometimes act as unofficial spokespersons for certain groups of employees. These companies, not formally integrated into the industrial relations system, nonetheless use collectively-agreed and legal standards as a reference. In-house solutions to problems of pay or working time resemble the collectively-agreed standards. This system of referring to centrally-defined official standards implies that the working conditions for employees in these small companies will gradually deteriorate in relation to those of their counterparts in companies covered by collective agreements. But employees without a *Betriebsrat* are not entirely defenceless in day-to-day conflicts: the conflict resolution methods used by the employer and unofficial spokespersons for the employees succeed with numerous minor problems, but are not very effective in the case of more serious breakdowns.

The companies, which we visited – some integrated into the official industrial relations system and others not – do not, therefore, represent two strictly separate worlds. Our actual findings suggest that non-integrated small companies, which are able to mobilise an extensive network of informal and sometimes tacit relations, find their industrial relations affected by collective agreements and legal standards, though such influence is often sporadic and always results in somewhat inferior standards. The situation in these small companies is "different but not fundamentally different", as one of the persons we interviewed cogently observed.

References

Ahlers E., Trautwein-Kalms G. (2002), *Entwicklung von Arbeit und Leistung in IT-Unternehmen*, edition der Hans-Böckler-Stiftung 62, Düsseldorf.

Auer P., Fehr- Duda H. (Hg.), (1988), *Industrial Relations in Small and Medium-Sized Enterprises*, IAS (Gesellschaft für Angewandte Sozial- und Wirtschaftswissenschaften), Report für die Kommission der Europäischen Gemeinschaften, Berlin.

Bahnmüller R. (2002), "Diesseits und jenseits des Flächentarifvertrags, Entgeltfindung und Entgeltstrukturen in tarifgebundenen und nicht tarifgebundenen Unternehmen", *Industrielle Beziehungen*, Heft 4/2002.

Bundesministerium für Arbeit und Soziales (BMA) (2001), "Tarifvertragliche Arbeitsbedingungen im Jahr 2000", *Bericht des Bundesarbeitsministeriums*, Bonn.

EUROSTAT (2001), *Unternehmen in Europa, Sechster Bericht, Daten 1987-1997*, Luxemburg: Europäische Kommission.

Hilbert J., Sperling H.-J. (1990), *Die Kleine Fabrik; Beschäftigung, Technik und Arbeitsbeziehungen*, München: Rainer Hampp Verlag und Mering.

Institut für Arbeitsmarkt- und Berufsforschung, (IAB) (1998), "Beiträge aus der Arbeitsmarkt- und Berufsforschung", *IAB-Betriebspanel*, 5. Welle West, 2. Welle Ost (1997).

Institut für Arbeitsmarkt- und Berufsforschung (IAB) (2002), "Betriebsräte in Kleinbetrieben – ein bislang eher seltenes Phänomen", *IAB-Materialien*, No.1/2002.

Institut für Mittelstandsforschung (1999), MIND – *Mittelstand in Deutschland*, Gruner + Jahr & Co AG, Wirtschaftspresse, Köln: Zeitschrift Impulse und Dresdener Bank.

Institut für Mittelstandsforschung (2000), *SMEs in Germany, Facts and Figures*, Bonn: Hans-Eduard Hauser.

Institut für Mittelstandsforschung (2001), MIND – *Mittelstand in Deutschland*, Zweite Untersuchung 2000, Bonn.

Kluge N., Schiemann V. (Hg.) (2002), *Mitbestimmung in der digitalen Wirtschaft – (k)ein Widerspruch*, Gütersloh: Bertelsmann Stiftung.

Kohaut S., Schnabel C. (2003), "Zur Erosion des Flächentarifvertrags: Ausmaß, Einflussfaktoren und Gegenmaßnahmen", *Industrielle Beziehungen*, Heft 2.

Kommission Mitbestimmung (1998), *Mitbestimmung und neue Unternehmenskulturen – Bilanz und Perspektiven*, Gütersloh: Verlag Bertelsmann-Stiftung.

Kotthoff H., Reindl J. (1990), *Die soziale Welt kleiner Betriebe*; *Wirtschaften, Arbeiten und Leben im mittelständischen Industriebetrieb*, Göttingen.

Müller-Jentsch W., Seitz B. (1998), "Betriebsräte gewinnen Konturen – Ergebnisse einer Betriebsräte-Befragung im Maschinenbau", *Industrielle Beziehungen*, Heft 4/1998.

Müller-Jentsch W., Ittermann P. (2000), *Industrielle Beziehungen, Daten, Zeitreihen, Trends 1950-1999*, Frankfurt/New York: Campus Verlag.

Observatory of European SMEs 2002/ No. 1: Highlights from the 2001 Survey, European Commission.

Potthoff H., Kipker I., (2000), *Job-Maschine Neuer Markt, Personal-Erfolgsfaktoren deutscher Wachstumsunternehmen*, Frankfurt/M: Deutsche Börse AG.

Richter W. (1997), "Der Mittelstand: Motor der deutschen Wirtschaft", in Icks, A. Kaufmann, F. Menke, A., (Hg.) (1997), *Unternehmen Mittelstand*, München: Chancen im globalen Strukturwandel.

Rudolph W., Wassermann W. (2002a), *Trendreport Betriebsrätewahlen 2002*, Kassel.

Rudolph W., Wassermann W. (2002b), "Neue Betriebsräte in kleinen Betrieben – Die Reform zeigt erste Wirkung", *Arbeitsrecht im Betrieb*, Heft 3/2002.

Rudolph W., Wassermann W. (2002c), "A Promising Future? – Works council elections 2002", *Mitbestimmung*, Heft 8/2002.

Syben G. (1997), *Interessenvertretung in Kleinbetrieben im Baugewerbe*, Bremen, Eine Untersuchung im Auftrag der Hans-Böckler-Stiftung mit Unterstützung der IG Bauen-Agrar-Umwelt, BAQ Forschungsinstitut.

Wahsner R., Horstkötter I., Bögenhold D. (2000), *Arbeit und Recht in Klein- und Mittelbetrieben*, Köln: Bund Verlag.

Wassermann W. (1992), *Arbeiten im Kleinbetrieb; Interessenvertretung im deutschen Alltag*, Reihe der Hans- Böckler- Stiftung, HBS Praxis, Band 4, Köln: Bund Verlag.

Wassermann W. (1994), *Kleinbetriebe in Europa. Materialien zu Fragen ihrer "Europatauglichkeit", zu Perspektiven der Firmenkooperation und zur Rolle der Gewerkschaften im KMU-Bereich*, Graue Reihe – Neue Folge Nr. 69, Hans-Böckler-Stiftung (Hg.), mai 1994.

Wassermann W. (2002a), *Die Betriebsräte – Akteure für Demokratie in der Arbeitswelt*, Münster.

Wassermann W. (2002b), "Perspektiven gewerkschaftlicher Betriebspolitik nach der Betriebsverfassungsreform 2001", *WSI-Mitteilungen*, Heft 6/2002.

Wassermann W., Rudolph W. (2003), *Das Zahntechnikerhandwerk zwischen Gesundheitspolitik und Markt*, Eschborn: Problemstudie zur Entwicklung einer Branche des Gesundheitshandwerks, RKW-Verlag.

Wassermann W. (2003), "Betriebsräte gestärkt – Gewerkschaften geschwächt?", *Mitbestimmung*, Heft 7/03.

CONCLUSION

Differences and Specificities that Distinguish Small Companies from Each Other and from Larger Companies

Christian DUFOUR and Adelheid HEGE

This concluding chapter focuses on the three aspects that underline the national chapters, while also providing a comparison between the three countries visited.

The definition and breakdown of small companies are dealt with first. An international comparison underlines differences in definitions. What methodological lessons and consequences can be drawn from comparing admittedly incompatible definitions but which, in all cases, give pre-eminence to the number of employees and therefore implicitly to industrial relations?

Attention then focuses on the role given to small companies in the organisation of industrial relations in the three countries. The original institutional structure in each of the countries produces varied patterns of differentiation between small and large companies. What is the scale of these differences and how can they be described? Small companies carry more weight than might be imagined in devising collective labour standards.

Lastly, special attention is given in this final chapter to the field surveys. On the basis of such research, we have put forward a series of proposals regarding what the specificities of small companies are based on in industrial relations terms. While recognising the diversity of situations and contexts, we endeavour to identify factors that are specific to these companies, in each country as well as in all three. In our view, both the relationship between these entities and external labour standards and the process of drawing up internal labour standards would seem to stem from identifiable common sociological phenomena.

I. Small Companies – the Real Facts and a Fragile and Fragmented Notion

An inventory needs to be made of small companies if they are to be compared to each other, or compared to larger ones, and all the more so, on an international scale. The three national chapters highlight the specificities of these assessments. Each country conducts enumerations according to a variety of specific principles. Within each country, a multiplicity of coexisting and non-coherent definitions has to be cross-checked if an accurate picture is to be obtained. The obstacle to a quantitative comparison of small companies on an international scale is the mobility of definitions within each country. The European standard for listing small and medium-sized companies is no exception to the rule; it provides a supplementary original definition rather than a standard that can be used in the comparison.[1]

A. Three Variable and Unequal Criteria

The statistical definitions refer to three essential variables which combine to define exactly what is understood by the term, small companies: the number of employees, their legal status and their economic importance. This combination and the definition that was chosen for each of them outline the range of possibilities in producing definitions. These three criteria do not enjoy the same privileges. The number of employees, even when equal to zero, is always chosen for defining a small working unit; it is combined with the criterion of legal autonomy for defining a company, whether small, medium-sized or large, according to the chosen threshold. The criterion of legal autonomy defines a company in the strict sense but it is not always used for counting small companies but small establishments instead, an area of cohabitation between work units of identical size but with different legal statuses. This approach groups together workplaces, which are dependent on larger economic units, and autonomous companies on account of the identical number of their employees. Economic importance, measured in terms of turnover or the balance sheet, is used essentially to distinguish "real" small autonomous companies from those that provide a legal refuge for controlling other companies.

---

1 According to the European directive of 3 April 1996 (96280/CE), an SME is a company with a workforce of 0 to 249 staff, whose turnover does not exceed €40 million and whose total accounts must not exceed €27 million. For a maximum workforce of 249 employees, this definition stipulates a turnover of €0.15 million per employee, which would seem rather high. National definitions do not necessarily stipulate accounting features. For a brief overview of questions relating to industrial relations in small and medium-sized enterprises in Europe, see EIRO (1999), "Industrial relations in SMEs", www.eiro.eurofound.eu.int/1999/05/study/tn9905202s.html.

The Number of Employees – a Central but Indeterminate Criterion

The number of employees – the most central of the three criteria – is used both for national and international statistics and in definitions for employers' organisations that specialise according to the size of the company (small companies and/or craftworkers). The central nature of this criterion means there is considerable flexibility in the quantitative levels retained. When counting companies, the absence of employees is not an obstacle. For an adequate breakdown of companies according to size, there are significant variations in the limits according to the country and the source of data. These variations illustrate the specialisation of the subjects listed and require a degree of caution in the use of the aggregates obtained outside their respective constituent areas.

In the midst of this maelstrom of definitions, the volume of employment is commonly perceived as the key factor in distinguishing between companies. This privileged status suggests a preference, an orientation in differentiation within companies. The volume of employment, and subsequently employment relations, play a key role in the identity of companies. This interpretation is confirmed by the existence of the category of "very small companies", in which the volume of employment alone is the criterion. Nevertheless, this acknowledgement of the role of the number of employees does not give any precise indication of the nature of the differences.

Size, Legal Status and Economic Autonomy – Porous Principles of Differentiation

The legal description of what is a small company would seem, a priori, to be more selective than variations observed in the definition based on the number of employees. Does the site constitute an autonomous company or not? The purest definitions of small companies focus on the status of legal independence. This convention is based on economic history which has invariably brought together the notions of legal entity, economic entity and social entity. Behind it can be perceived the image of the "real employers" or the "Herr im Haus".[2] This warrants two remarks. Firstly, legal autonomy brings together various social principles: Uni-nominal companies (Ich-AG, which appeared recently in Germany), companies with or without limited liability, cooperatives and associations, whether profit-making or not.[3] On the other hand, the same

---

2 "The boss is the master".

3 We have accepted here the rather imprecise term that gives a company the legal status adopted by the social group that controls it: limited liability company, associa-

legal independence is combined with very varying degrees of economic autonomy and industrial relations management of the designated company; groups are made up of a multiplicity of small companies that are economically dependent on each other, and of small companies attached to centralised brands *via* franchises. Relationships of economic dependence, whether upstream or downstream, have long been commonplace (Boccara, 1998).

For sociological research focusing on industrial relations in such entities, it is worth pointing out that the notion of a "small company" can be confused with that of a "small workplace". It is possible to assimilate entities with different legal statuses on the basis of the volume of employment. Does that justify attributing to them similar practices with regard to the management of industrial relations? What is the origin of these differences?

A preliminary inventory of available definitions for small and larger companies emphasises their specialisation and therefore the difficulty of transposing them (Torres, 1997), both nationally and internationally. In all three countries, small companies are distinguished from larger ones essentially by the number of employees: the definition of "small" varies. With the impact of industrial regulations that govern job markets, the notions of company and workplace have been porous, thereby leading to the assimilation of unequal legal situations: the notion of company is therefore contaminated. Simultaneously, a number of legally autonomous companies are dependent on more powerful groups *via* their capital or their inclusion within a system of productive relations.

B. The Number of Companies: Variable Results but always Plentiful and Polymorphous

Companies can be counted and classified principally according to the number of employees. Regardless of the chosen definition, the distinguishing feature of the workforce of small companies in the three countries is its size and the heterogeneous nature of the situations involved.

So many Companies…

In the three countries surveyed, the entities included in definitions of small companies considerably outnumber those that are classified as larger companies. In spite of differences between countries and between sectors, over 90% of the companies listed have fewer than 100 employees and frequently more than half of them do not even reach the thresh-

---

tion, cooperative, etc. On the legal debate surrounding the notion of a company, see Roussel-Verret (2004).

old of 10. In Germany, among the 2.2 million companies listed in the *Mittelstand* – therefore within a population of companies selected according to criteria defining what are small (and medium-sized) enterprises with a relatively high threshold – 60% employ fewer than 10 employees and 8% more than 50.[4] In France, among the 2.4 million companies in industry, commerce and the services – therefore a definition that includes all types of companies – almost half do not have any employees. Among the others, 86% have between 1 and 9 employees, 11% between 10 and 49, 1.8% between 50 and 199, 0.33% between 200 and 499 and 0.17% over 500 employees.[5] In Sweden, in 1999, 95% of companies in the building sector had fewer than 20 employees; the same size of workforce was to be found in 93% of companies in wholesale and retail trade and the hotel and restaurant sector and 50% in other private services.[6] From that angle, large companies are marginal. Entrepreneurial activities are, above all, pursued by small-scale entities.

... Heterogeneousness Being the Common Feature?

Tracing a (fluctuating) boundary between "small" and "large" companies will not suffice to construct *ipso facto* two categories that include individuals with common features. The large number of small companies suggests the presence of substantial differences within that group.

They are to be found, naturally, in all productive sectors. They often offer a range of more varied specialised activities than is the case of larger companies. Their means of access to markets are very diverse; they include both situations of dependence and niche effects which larger companies rarely experience. They are supported by very heterogeneous capitalistic structures: the irony of delineating this category lies in the fact that some of these companies host the controlling bodies of major companies (holdings). A distinguishing feature between small companies and between small and large companies is the length of their activity. Long-established companies and recently founded ones stand side by side in this category. A new company is almost inevitably a small one, except for cases of legal scission, merely because companies need time to grow. A long-established company is not necessarily a large one and the range of "seniority" among small companies, which account for virtually all newcomers, is more varied than that of larger ones.

Therefore, a feature shared by all small companies is that of variety. Indirectly, this observation may reveal once again that a feature of

---

4 See the chapter by Rudolf and Wassermann.

5 INSEE, Siren, 31 December 1999.

6 See the chapter by Murhem.

larger companies may, conversely, be more limited diversity in their circumstances, if not greater similarities.

The Practical Categories of Internal Differences

This extreme diversity is a result of statistical appraisal whereby companies are classified according to the number of employees alone. The economic and social history of each company has produced sub-categories that correspond to features specific to some small companies or which include some of them in specific socio-economic entities. Some features stem directly from the organisational methods of the companies, while others reflect measures to codify industrial relations in companies.

The German Mittelstand is a fluctuating category for differentiating companies (Wassermann, Rhode, 2004). It rests essentially on the notion of the entrepreneurial autonomy of company owners and includes companies with relatively large workforces, even if most of the companies involved are small.[7] It is separate from, but includes, companies listed under the Handwerk (craftwork sector) which it cannot be mistaken for as the Handwerk has an organisational structure that makes of it a readily identifiable, active and representative body. There is no equivalent of the Mittelstand in France. Employers in small and medium-sized enterprises have organisations, which are quite separate from those of larger companies, a feature of which, in some cases, is their representation of "real employers". In France, the craftwork sector is nearer to the German Handwerk although the French concept has a lower maximum employee threshold than its German counterpart; it also has organisational and representative structures. In Sweden, the statistics reveal a concentration of small companies among those with the smallest number of employees, but the organisational principles are based more on unity than on differentiation, according to the particular sectors of activity.

The criterion of size comes into play according to variable forms of logic and pace in each country for distinguishing between companies in their relationship with labour legislation. France and Germany, the two countries with a dual representation system in our comparison, have laid down thresholds for the establishment of employee representation according to the number of employees: five in the case of Germany, more than ten in the case of France. In both cases, this threshold does not apply merely to companies (*Unternehmen, entreprises*) but workplaces as well (*Betriebe, établissements*). Small companies are therefore

7 The *Mittelstand* may also identify the middle classes in the political sense of categories belonging neither to the nobility nor to the proletariat.

assimilated by the number of employees to workplaces belonging to larger companies. Reciprocally, dependent sites are assimilated to independent economic entities according to their size.[8] In Sweden, an initial limit of 25 employees is laid down by law for the presence of their representatives on company boards, which does not lead to lumping workplaces and companies together.

Every country therefore has its own definitions, based on administrative classifications (statistical definitions) or on the outlines of company and/or employer organisations. The plurality of national notions reflects unequal, mutually incoherent conventions. They are sometimes cut across each other, but never enable immediate comparisons to be made. They are always close to data concerning small workplaces (*établissements*, *Betriebe*), but assimilation of the two is obviously impossible without running the risk of changing the subject under review.

The difficulty of identifying small companies on a common basis within each country and between countries highlights the risk of letting a definition establish itself by default and implicitly. By default, it refers to a group of smaller companies. Implicitly, it confers on them common features.

The temptation to attribute identifying features to smaller companies on the basis of grouping them together by default comes up against the heterogeneous nature of an empirically grouped population in such conditions.

This leads to a basic conclusion in methodological terms. As heterogeneousness is an inherent feature of the category of small companies defined by the number of employees alone, it is necessary to specify the purpose of this classification and to indicate the criteria for inclusion in such a group. This process specifies a subpopulation and indicates the relations that exist between the designated group and the populations and subpopulations that are excluded from it, namely other small companies and larger ones.

II. Small Companies and Industrial Relations

From an industrial relations standpoint, assimilating small companies with each other would seem justified up to a point. In the three countries, the industrial practices of small companies possess features which distinguish them from larger ones. Globally speaking, pay is lower, the workforce includes more women, recognised qualifications

8 The two categories are often assimilated by the public authorities when local workplaces are identified without any reference to their legal autonomy for fiscal or social contribution reasons (the case of UNEDIC in France).

are lower and employee representation is less common if not totally absent.

Does this mean that small companies "escape" labour standards that concern larger ones?

In fact, the existence and specificities of small companies are often mentioned to justify arbitration conducted by industrial interlocutors or by the legislature when such standards are devised: at the same time as legislation in France on the reduction of working time made a distinction in legislative standards according to company size, the debate continued in Germany on the relevance of sector-level agreements for the smallest companies and on the conditions of employee representation in medium-sized companies. Devising labour standards produces simultaneous effects of exclusion and inclusion of small companies. The staggering of industrial relations systems plays an essential role in the construction of this inclusion/exclusion relationship.

A. Reservation and Intervention of the Law in the Differentation Process

The Individual Rights of Employees

In the three countries, laws governing industrial relations make no fundamental distinction as to employed status according to the size of the company in which the employer-employee relationship exists. Any employment contract is equal to any other. The first employee in a small company has the same legal status as any additional employee in a multinational group, even if the employee has close extra-professional links with his/her employer.

Basically speaking, labour regulations apply equally to the employees of companies of all sizes. In Germany, however, protection against dismissal (Kündigungsschutz) describes employees' rights according to the size of the companies. In France, the legal working week has, since 1998, been different in companies with more or less than 20 employees. As from the summer of 2005, a new employment contract – the new recruitment contract offering a very insecure employment status – is available only for companies with fewer than 20 employees. In addition to this lack of differentiation between various forms of individual status, there are various specific modes of intervention of the law in industrial relations in small companies. Labour justice, as it exists in Germany with the labour courts (*Arbeitsgerichte*) and in France with the employment tribunals.

Prud'hommes, is an example of specialised structures, whose identity is not immediately perceptible. These legal bodies, which are theoretically open to all employees and employers for settling individual conflicts, are essentially used by employees in the smallest companies against their employers. They are externalised methods of managing industrial relations, particularly in the event of breach of contract, for workplaces that do not have internal mediation capacity; in the three countries, evidence shows that in those instances where unions exist, external intervention is less frequent.

France is the only country of the three that possesses a sophisticated labour inspectorate administered by government. It applies to all companies, although the contact procedures with smaller ones are significantly different from those that apply to larger ones. It offers employees and employers alike legal recourse based on government legitimacy. Sweden does not possess a system of this kind. In the field, union structures, their acceptance by employees and employers and their contradictory contacts with employers' representative bodies, would seem to play a similar role. They are called upon by employees or employers for advice on the interpretation of rules or in the event of an open conflict. They may attempt to be summoned to a site when they have been informed of questionable practices. The differences in the capacity of intervention of trade unions on sites that are not directly covered by union representation is more clearly understandable through this difference in trade union roles. In France, employees and trade union officers can call labour inspectors to the rescue, whereas Swedish employees and union representatives refer matters to their union bodies. Swedish trade unionists seem to be better welcomed in companies than French government officials. Formal and informal contacts maintained between trade union and employers' organisations have established a method of regulation that is external to companies, with the consent of the parties, to settle internally insoluble conflicts.

Collective Representation Rights

Conversely, the law draws a clear line between large and small companies with regard to employee representation, at least in France and Germany. In both of those countries, elected representation institutions are only compulsory when a company has at least five (Germany) or more than 10 (France) employees. In both countries, this obligation applies as much to companies as it does to workplaces reaching such thresholds. Here is evidence again of the distinctions referred to earlier between the legal status of various work entities. In Sweden, there is no indication of a minimum number of employees with regard to union representation, but a threshold of 25 employees is required for representative participation on the company board.

In all three countries, the experience of practitioners, confirmed by field surveys, shows that the presence of representatives occurs above legal thresholds. In fact, it is only well above such thresholds that such institutions are established durably and even more so if they are to play an effective role. This joint observation, backed up by data in each of the national chapters, is the central subject of the analysis presented below on the basis of field surveys.

B. Collective Agreements, the Cornerstones of Inclusion and Gateways towards Exclusion

In the three countries under investigation, the State grants trade unions and employers' organisations the task of negotiating pay, the pay structure and changes in work schedule and working time arrangements. France is the only country of the three that has a minimum wage laid down by the State. Germany, however, has been investigating since 2004 the introduction of a minimum wage the links of which with collective pay agreements have yet to be defined.

In all three countries, however, sector-level collective agreements are considered to be the keystones to labour standards.

Collective Agreements, Production of Labour Standards and Small Companies

It would seem that Germany has the purest form of sector-level agreement policy: only those companies that belong to employers' organisations are bound by implementation of the agreements which the latter have signed. There is no government minimum wage nor any cross-sector national policy aimed at ensuring the equal development of wages per sector. Consequently, companies, whether small or large, which do not belong to an employers' organisation and do not conduct internal negotiations with a union, implement the pay standards they wish; the State rarely intervenes for requiring parties to accept the extension of agreements. Accordingly, employees in road transport, in the absence of collective agreements and union representation, have particularly low pay levels while working long hours (Dufour, Hege, 2003). The rate of collective agreement coverage is approximately 60% with substantial differences between West and East Germany.

In Sweden, sector-level pay is also the subject of negotiations in the absence of any State minimum wage and without any extension procedure. A sector was traditionally part of a pay solidarity policy that limited its contractual autonomy. Swedish pay and the way it is fixed continues to be the heir of the pay solidarity policy conducted over several decades, even though, in recent years, trends towards the decentralization of bargaining have become the rule. The membership rate of employers' organisations has continued to be very high, which has led to more than 90% of employees being covered by collective agreements. Employers and union organisations have conducted an efficient policy with regard to industrial practice. Employees, who are unionised to over 90%, have easy access to local union structures, which are accepted by employers, thus making unions a true agent for the diffusion of pay standards for any loopholes in collective bargaining; the labour market is duly informed through union influence, which employers and employees know how to take account of and refer to where necessary.

In Germany, as in Sweden, collective agreement pay and its development constitute standards whereby real pay is visible throughout a sector. In France, the system specifies minimum levels, quite remote from pay actually awarded in most of the larger companies and particularly those that have union representation.

France does recognise the right of sector-level trade unions and employers' organisations to enjoy a similar capacity to bargain, while diluting the importance of the representativeness of the players involved. However, the State systematically extends sector-level agreements to all companies, without taking account of their membership or non-membership of their respective organisations. A lively debate is under way on the conditions of representativeness of trade unions in these circumstances. On account of this systematic extension, France has a high percentage of employees covered by collective agreements (over 93%), although the rate of trade union membership is very low. Furthermore, the State has established a minimum wage applied to all companies and serves *de facto* as a reference to negotiators for fixing sector-level minimum pay (CSERC, 1999). Lastly, the right is acknowledged by law to negotiate pay at sector- as well as company-level.

Sectors and the Threat of "Exit" of Small Companies

In all three countries, sectors can be seen as centres of bargaining between employers and employees and of compromise between companies with varying business results. The standards under discussion apply to all participating companies, regardless of size and market position. The negotiation of collective agreements that separate companies according to their size, as in Germany in craftwork, is much less frequent.

These standards make up a range of economic constraints that govern the selection of companies according to their productivity. The bringing together of standards between East and West Germany provided a perfect illustration of the effect of collective agreements during the 1990s. When the implementation of an agreement standard is linked to each company's membership of a negotiating body and its signing of an agreement, the representativeness of the employers in the negotiation is a vital factor in the results of that negotiation.

Viewed from that angle, sector-level bargaining has meant that small companies are not only the basic targets of the content of collective agreements, but also decisive players in the production of such agreements, even though they do not seem particularly active at the negotiating table. Acceptance by employers of the specifications of these compromises gives greater meaning to such agreements which the largest companies could easily avoid. The sustained presence of small companies within employers' organisations is therefore an essential factor in collective bargaining. Germany has already experienced their partial absence for many years. In France, the minimum wage and minimum requirements laid down in collective agreements have meant that the latter have become management tools essentially for the least efficient companies, therefore many small companies among them. A decrease in membership of employers' organisations is threatening the relevance of the sector. Their presence is of more vital importance than that of their employees. The latter are considered to be more legitimately represented by employees in large companies than small employers by their colleagues in larger companies.[9]

In each country, in various ways, collective bargaining takes account of the tension between the differing circumstances of companies, their size playing an important though not uniform role in determining their position in such circumstances. Sectors such as rail and air transport, chemicals, the production and distribution of electricity and telecommunications are almost exclusively made up of large companies. In other cases, such as the hotel and restaurant sector, small companies make up the vast majority, while larger ones remain the exception. The latter, however, are often part of powerful groups, which are very influential by their very existence on industrial relations practices and standards. Trade union strategies must adapt to this. In Germany, differences of focus between *IG Metall* and *IG BCE* (chemicals) are often put down to the composition of each of these sectors: the number of global chemical oligopolistic companies contrasts with the multiplicity of metal industry companies (Dufour, Hege, 2000). Sweden describes its economic fabric as being composed of large companies and very small ones, without the presence of the German *Mittelstand*; and the regula-

9 On the composition, representativeness and recent changes in employers' organisations, see *Chronique internationale de l'IRES*, No.72, September 2001 and Traxler, Franz, "Employers and Employer Organisations in Europe: Membership Strength, Density and Representativeness", in *Industrial Relations Journal*, 31: 4, 2000: 308-316.

tory role of national agreements has for many years avoided the question of adaptations according to sectors.

In its canonical form, the legitimacy of the sectors rests on their ability to distribute fairly the greater part of employment and pay conditions between the various companies in that sector, providing thereby a tool derived from a process intended to be integrating.[10] When viewing the three countries, three different models of the role of sectors come to light. In Sweden, a sector acts as an intermediary between a national equalising pay policy and the real practices of companies. In Germany, sector-level bargaining at regional level aims at being sufficiently adapted to the field so as to leave little room for complementary workplace negotiations. In both of these countries, a sector-level agreement is recognised as playing a role of substitution for the internal management of companies, which is both rational and economic in internal constraints. In France, the State minimum wage and the systematic extension of sector-level agreements combine to set minimum conditions, which in many companies do not even serve as a reference as they are so remote from everyday practice. Collective agreements – and their minimum pay, which is closely linked, in particular, to the national minimum wage – would seem first and foremost to be devised for small companies and to leave most employers with the upper hand in internal industrial relations management (Barrat, 2002).

In the three cases, far from being exempted from standards, small companies lie at the very heart of their construction, but in accordance with astutely devised modulations that force the players to produce original institutional developments (Saglio, 1991).

C. Company Agreements, Local Arrangements, Player Participation and the Labour Market

In each of the three countries, collectively-agreed standards do not constitute rules regarding ultimate practices. In small as well as large companies, local arrangements modify and complement external agree-

[10] Small companies are represented as such in sector-level bargaining in France. They can be involved in employers' sector organisations in Germany through the intervention of specialised federations. In none of the three countries studied is there any basis for employee organisation linked to the size of the company that provides the employment. This feature is to be found within trade unions, indirectly, through sector specificities. The chemical industry is naturally more concentrated than the hotel and restaurant sector. In Germany, in 1995, 26% of those working in the hotel and restaurant sector were owners, compared with only 5% in industry. The matter of company size is therefore related to objective features that are external to trade unions whose forms of organisation are therefore negatively affected by these features. This process dictates the "natural" hostility of small companies to the introduction and intervention of trade unions.

ments. In small companies, these arrangements and the way they are acquired play a significant part in the life of companies, with strong international similarities.

Employee Representation in Small Companies, a Sign of Specificity

All three countries have standards specifying conditions for employee representation in companies. They are varied in nature and involve the size of companies in different ways.

In Sweden, stipulations regarding codetermination of employees in decision-making bodies lay down an obligation for workforces of 25 employees and over. This obligation is accepted but surveys offer a more precise view of how it is implemented. Conversely, employees are free to designate union representatives in the daily life of companies without taking account of any thresholds related to company size. Nevertheless, in small companies, employees seem reticent to designate their representatives although union density is high and employers fully accept that local trade unionists, following agreements entered into with employers' organisations, can operate in their company.

The pair of similar countries with twofold systems – France and Germany – have legislation that provides for a gradual process of access to various forms of employee representation governed by the size of the workplace rather than the company. Both countries therefore confuse in this regard what statistics and the law distinguish in other instances. A workplace with four employees in Germany or nine in France within a company with several tens of thousands of employees is therefore treated on an equal footing with a company of a similar size: it is not compulsory to establish an employee representation body within it.

In Germany, on the basis of the threshold for the creation of the *Betriebsrat*, a series of complementary rights and means come into play as the company's size evolves. A threshold of 200 employees has to be reached, for example, for an elected representative to be authorised to be available full time, which means a sort of qualitative leap. Regardless of the size, a union can conduct negotiations in a company if there are members and if the company does not adhere to a sector-level agreement.

France has refined the subtleties of employee representation and union presence rights, combining the effects of size and distinctions according to duties and forms of representation. employee representatives (DP) do not have the same rights as the works council (CE) and union representatives (DS). But single employee representation (DU) may enjoy these rights concurrently. DPs are entrusted with less sensitive duties than elected members of works councils (CE).

Neither in Germany nor in France are representative bodies designated once the planned thresholds have been reached. Significantly higher thresholds often have to be reached and "founding" events (strikes, dismissals, restructuring) have to occur for legal rules to begin to apply. In Sweden, employees do not make use of the possibility of designating a representative any earlier than their colleagues in the other two countries.

The very different legal principles for each country are therefore applied in a very unequal fashion in each country. In all three, however, small companies prove reticent about the obvious presence of employee representation. This common factor is certainly more structuring if we are to understand the specificities of small companies in this regard rather than the diversity of legal principles.

According to available estimates, the gaps between legal standards and real practices are considerable. In Germany, a survey in 2003 recorded a rate of presence of *Betriebsräte* of less than 7% in workplaces with 5 to 50 employees. In France, according to the *Réponse* survey, the vast majority of companies with more than 20 employees had no representation structure (Dufour, Hege, *et al.*, 2004).

Local Arrangements – a Structural Component of Industrial Relations in Small Companies

Theoretically, in the three countries concerned, the local arrangement may take the form of a company agreement, the legitimacy of which is based on the relationship it should entertain with leading players in the given sector, at least as far as the employees are concerned. In Sweden and Germany, there is no minimum size of workforce for company bargaining, as it is conducted *via* the union that is external to the company (in liaison with an elected body if that exists). In France, a union representative or employee representative acting in that capacity only intervenes where the workforce comprises several score of employees, which justifies mandating. It would seem, therefore, that employers have a free hand in running their companies. Evidently, they do not have to report to their relevant employers' organisations to justify their decisions. The interaction of players at local level is not a copy of that conducted at a higher level.

A local arrangement, whether collective or individual, more often than not takes the form of informal practices. These are of particular importance in small companies. For employers and employees alike, they represent the specificity of practices in entities of that kind. In no way are they accidents or aberrations; they are the product of relations between players specific to these small groups as will be shown later. They can be seen as a mark of originality, not marginal but structuring in industrial relations in small companies. Informal practices are also to be found in larger companies but they exist in parallel with formal systems which claim to structure most of the interaction between employers and employees.

Systems of Representation Subject to Change

Both of the countries with twofold representation systems recently experienced legislative changes that were deliberately targeted at small companies. In 2001, through the impetus given by the unions, the Social Democrat and Green coalition government modified the legal framework regarding possible development of the *Betriebsräte* within the smallest companies, giving rise to a vigorous debate. At the elections in 2005, questions regarding the future of the *Mitbestimmung* were at the heart of the debates. In France, the mandating system was instituted in 1998, before an agreement was signed in 2001 between all the representative trade unions and the Craftwork Employers' Association, UPA, in order to encourage dialogue in those companies. In 2005, modifications to the employee counting procedure pushed back the legal boundaries to the introduction of representation bodies and an employment contract specific to small companies was created.

These modifications divided the industrial parties and have been a constant subject of political controversy. It is still too early to assess their consequences in France and in Germany. The concern in Germany will be to observe whether the law can modify practices considered to be shortcomings by comparison with the standards recognised in large companies (Rudolf, Wassermann, 2002). In France, it is expected (or feared) that mandating will help the unions to obtain a foothold in these small companies. Will these two experiences confirm the theories according to which union presence in small entities incurs too great an expense for the initiative to be profitable, in terms both of influence and membership? From a sociological standpoint, it will be noted that these experiences seek to influence – with contradictory aims – what undoubtedly constitutes one of the most striking features of small companies, namely their resistance to systems of representation that are well tried in larger companies. There are those who believe that the absence of such institutions is a sign of the ill-will of employers which can be fought against in the name of democracy and law. There are others for whom such systems hamper the employers' freedom of action and the opportunities of business development of these companies. Why has Sweden spared itself this debate? Even when the possibility of designating a union representative in companies is not adopted, the intervention of an external trade unionist does not seem to raise any problems and no change to the current rules is envisaged.

The reasons for these different types of behaviour are no doubt to be found in the structural features that are specific to the size of such companies.

III. Internal Industrial Relations, the Interpretation of External Rules and the Production of Individual Company Standards

The previous pages describe the industrial relations environments which, through processes specific to each country, have a strong impact on small companies and fit them into a regulatory framework which would appear to leave them with little autonomy.

The field surveys, however, provide a different view of the situation. They show small companies that display a degree of originality in the rules they adopt; they give importance to internal interaction within companies, both for adapting external rules and for implementing internal ones which are not merely those drawn up externally. This internal activity constitutes a decisive if not vital resource for small companies. What is at stake is a constant dialogue between employers and employees as well as between employees themselves. This exchange can take forms that are as varied as are small companies themselves.

The variety of solutions, their plasticity and the domestic nature of their elaboration are factors which differentiate small companies from each other. This variability, detectable in the three countries, must be recognised as a factor that describes industrial relations practices within small companies. It is not in fact anomic.

There are three factors, common to the three countries, which govern the rules of this internal interplay and its various forms: the role of the employer in the company, the status of the employees' group in relation to him/her, and relations that both parties entertain with external parties. Each of these points will be analysed below. They act invariably according to combinations in which the specificities of small companies in industrial relations are revealed.

A. The Role of the Employer: the Conflict of Closeness and Distance

The life of small companies and that of their employees are directly linked to the personal intervention of the entrepreneur/employer. His/her individual characteristics – personality, which is so often referred to when accounting for a local situation – have an almost direct effect on the business as well as the industrial relations conduct of a company, the two being scarcely dissociable. This feature can be expressed differently. The lifespan of a company, its size and its field of activity become features of secondary importance in determining the characteristics of industrial relations in these limited groups.

The smaller the structure, the more important the entrepreneur's personal commitment becomes; in correlative terms, the lesser the distance between the entrepreneur and the socio-economic entity. It depends on the personality (and disposition?) of the entrepreneur rather than any explicit, carefully devised policy or objective procedures that internal relations are more or less cooperative, more or less authoritarian or more or less paternalistic. The scale of possibilities is very wide and the multiplicity of cases makes any proportional assessment of the various types of possible behaviour hazardous.[11]

The Continuity of the Company and of the Entrepreneur...

The existence and survival of a company in the short or medium term underlie any description of internal industrial relations, whether provided by employers or by employees. This is clearly evident in companies run by their founder, particularly in the period shortly after their creation. More long-standing companies are not necessarily free of this, as they are often particularly concerned with the transition between generations of entrepreneurs. In mature companies, which have shown what they can do and have a potentially long-term leader, the question of succession frequently emerges when mention is made of a possible accident. This same theme is brought up in all instances through the capacity of adaptation to external business conditions. It is always linked to the personal ability and individual commitment of the employer. The latter is expected to have an indispensable capacity for adaptation as a personal quality linked furthermore to his/her own commitment. In long-standing companies, employees often make comparisons between the various generations of employers they have known.

Divergent points of view on the conditions of survival and/or development of a company, as well as the personal commitment expected of its leaders, account for any break in alliance that may follow on shortly from the co-founding of a company. These breaks, attributed to "differences of character", reflect first and foremost the combination of the entrepreneur's personal characteristics and the operating conditions of the company in such small entities. The very same strong personal

---

[11] The report on Sweden presents the typology of behaviour of small business leaders (Goss, 1991), which corresponds quite well to observations made in all three countries.

commitments of entrepreneurs are often an obstacle to attempts at alliance during the existence of a company.

... Under the Vigilant Eye of Employees

The employees of small companies are constantly aware that, even when markets are robust, the continuity of the company and of the jobs it provides requires specific intervention, as if it were an extension of that provided by the individual or family entrepreneur when the company was created. They are quite aware of the frailty of small companies, a feature that is inherent to their size. Local events concerning them make up a virtually daily chronicle of neighbourhood news. Employees are watchful and take part directly in the intricate phases of the virtually inseparable lives of the company and the entrepreneur. The arrival of a son-in-law, who is a technician in the profession, reassures the employees of a building company. In a garage, when the son and successor to the company is ordered by his father to suspend his literary studies, the employees are both reassured and anxious. The founder of an insurance company convinces her only son to interrupt his military career to manage mobile, enterprising commercial staff. The chambermaids of a hotel are quite aware of the solicitations of a competitor nearing retirement who wishes to sell up his hotel. The equity needs of a charismatic leader of a computer start-up causes concern as to how long he will remain part of the management. The financial difficulties of a major client are soon common knowledge, just as the profitability of an unexpected market is assessed. The longer-serving employees preserve and pass on a memory of these crucial moments, particularly when they have led to dismissals. They do not hold the keys to the situation but they know and can comment on the circumstances, among themselves, among which the family circumstances of the entrepreneur take pride of place.

While many small companies – following the example of larger ones – leave their employees without any opportunity to react when changes occur that affect them,[12] in many cases the attitude of the employees of small companies is decisive in crucial circumstances. They are a credible source of information on their company, rather more so than in more complex workplaces where activities are more divided and abstract. Legislation does not give them access to the accounts but news travels, often thanks to them; they entertain direct relations with customers and suppliers and, among them, a number have a sound idea of the technical processes brought into play. Whether they are building companies or subcontractors, certain services and trades of a technical nature, com-

[12] Several creators of small companies whom we met were former executives who left large companies where they felt excluded from the decisions that concerned them.

puter or mechanical engineering companies, the employees – without being invited to discussions where the future of the company is debated – intervene directly or indirectly in their companies in a variety of ways.

As employees, they can enhance the value of their fidelity to their employer and the company on the labour market. According to their skills, they can envisage becoming entrepreneurs themselves and position themselves as potential competitors to their employer or threaten to cooperate with competitors. The owner of a small company of plumbers, for example, is well aware that the value of this company rests on the professional skills of such and such an employee. In a small building company, the accountant and the best craftsman went off with the customer file, leaving the elderly employer and his incompetent son with the least-skilled employees. In a computer company, for example, as the consultants were being recruited by clients, the founder of the company gave them access to the company equity; in restaurants, the kitchen is often established as an opposition force and the chef negotiates his cooks' pay with the employer. But in the case of the garage, which will have to close through pressure from the major car manufacturers, the employees know that they could not do any better than their employer who, like them, is more of a mechanic than a financial expert.

The employees of small companies who come into contact with trade unionists from larger companies often refer to the latter's lack of awareness of the central part played by the employer and his position in the company's survival. This difference is sufficient to justify the distance they maintain with trade unions. Trade unionists, on the contrary, interpret the reaction of the employees in small companies as psychological dependence on their employer, which reveals a lack of understanding of their economic dependence.

Small Structures and the External Entrepreneurial Principle

When the manager of a small company no longer combines the duties of entrepreneur and employer, the part he plays in the company's continuity changes. This can be clearly seen in associations and cooperative societies. These companies – although small – rest on organising principles which the managers cannot abuse. They themselves are employed, although that does not mean that they are necessarily on good terms with the other employees. In such cases, the company managers cannot be confused with company leaders, which are social groups that play an essential part in the durability of the company. The former are themselves employed and cannot identify with the continuity of the institution that justifies the existence of the company, even if the personality of the manager plays a key role in the capacity to intervene of decision-making bodies in which the entrepreneurial principle is concentrated.

A number of subtle aspects can be observed which delineate the position of entrepreneurs in the durability of a company. Consequently, in the three countries, garages – which have a small number of employees and are legally independent – have shifted from the status of independent entrepreneurs to that of franchisees (dealers) with very limited initiative as regards their markets and products. Car manufacturers keep a close eye on developments among their dealers, force them to merge and are ready to substitute themselves for them. In many cases, the way industrial relations are conducted internally remains one of the last attributes – or last responsibilities – left to the local employer's initiative.

The Entrepreneur/Employer – the Mainspring of Industrial Relations

The same image is used internationally by the parties concerned for describing relations in small companies and for distinguishing them from larger ones: the image of the family. This image, which is an easy target for jibes, is perfectly acceptable if family models are conceived as being diverse, unequally subscribed to, not chosen by those who share them, but invariably focused on their founders. The image of the family adapts extremely well to this diversity of real situations. It becomes false if reduced to a purely idyllic or authoritarian version.

The diversity of industrial relations in small companies and that of their principal organisers is at least as great as the diversity in the economic situations they experience, regardless of the system of external standards. The image of the tyrannical employer of a small company is false when applied systematically, just as much as that of the invariably benevolent employer. Reality is a good deal more subtle, because, in small companies in particular, the entrepreneur, a specific not interchangeable individual, must constantly take account of the employees' ability to intervene in the professional field, as well as in negotiating compromise. There is evidence to show that relations in most small companies are those that develop in groups of a limited size formed under more or less assertive leadership that is varied in origin.

Whether entrepreneurs like it or not, industrial relations in these small structures centre around their own personality and professional practices. They only distance themselves from this in conditions that it is impossible to bring into play at will. This can be illustrated by a paradox. In all three countries, in spite of significant differences in external standards, those employers who are most cooperative with the employees all admit to having difficulty in setting up the representative bodies they would like in order to comply with the law. It could be said that representative bodies are less useful when the employers display open-mindedness and a degree of savoir-faire with their employees. However, the creation of representative bodies does not necessarily respond to a demand from the employees alone. "Cooperative" entrepreneurs seek to institute a form of mediation which would release them from personal commitment, and even create a regulatory process quite independent of themselves. Employees often deny them this release, by displaying neither readiness to lose the advantage of direct contact with the employer nor acceptance to take on the risks of a more or less successful delegation of power.

The Assertion and Maintenance of Leadership

The technical skills for running some small companies channel the employers' intervention but does not limit their influence. Each chartered accountant or lawyer imposes their influence within their firm as original individuals, who must implement the professional standards by which they are bound, however rigorous and uniform they may be. The same goes for labour standards – as regards equivalent pay and employed status, for example, all building firms are not equal. Employees are aware of such differences and assess them; they frequently motivate a change of jobs or the fidelity that employees display to the employer.

These surveys do not deny the existence of a form of "employer authoritarianism", but they do put it into perspective by underlining that it is neither systematic nor specific to small companies. Furthermore, it applies to a great variety of cases. It can go hand in hand as much with the perfect professional mastery of a seasoned patriarch as with the lack of professional authority of an entrepreneur who feels insecure in the face of his/her troops.

Cases of authoritarianism should not conceal the fact that they are often a reflection of an employer's difficulty in asserting his/her leadership within his/her own company on account of the small size of its workforce. Relations between the parties concerned are governed by specific rituals rather than institutionalised mechanisms. The small businessman must show himself to be indispensable in the running of the company in order to assert his authority over his employees. In the smallest companies, the sharing of tasks is not sufficiently great for professional superiority to warrant spontaneous support to the claim to leadership. The employer has therefore to be a professional paragon, whose superior skills underpin his claim to authority. Any questioning of this skill constitutes a serious rupture which inseparably opposes the individual and the status alike. As soon as a company expands in size, however, the entrepreneur is faced with a concentration of managerial and financial tasks. S/he performs them in addition to productive tasks, without necessarily possessing any proven skill in their regard. Executing such duties is seen as much as an obligation and a concession that have to be conceded to the community (various government departments and the workforce, etc.),[13] all the more so as they are remote from the founding professional skills of the entrepreneur. They ensure his/her control over the company if s/he masters them, while distancing him/her from employee colleagues. They often require the intervention of costly specialists (a chartered accountant and a lawyer, who are often better paid than the entrepreneur) who perform vital duties in a company that would be ideally free from their intervention.

The specialisation of the employer in tasks that are not directly productive is often experienced by employees in very ambiguous terms. They see this as a debt they owe to the status of entrepreneur which they have no wish to take on themselves. It justifies the hierarchy that exists between them and their employer as the entrepreneur has the advantage over them of dual professional skills, thereby making him/her more remote. This establishes acknowledgement of his/her leadership and of social and economic distance between cooperating parties. Once the company has expanded and the sharing of tasks has been more clearly instituted, the memory of the entrepreneur's professionalism continues to endure.

This difference with the employees can also be found in personal commitment to working hours. The entrepreneur is the person who "never spares his efforts". France provides a clear example of this. Negotiations on working time have always highlighted this gap, which becomes an issue in any exchange between employees and the employer. This issue is all the more powerful as it affects the symbolic order of closeness[14] and distance.

B. Variations in the Work Group

The stages that underlie the transformation of the role of entrepreneurs/employer correspond to disparities in the creation of a distinct work group (*collectif*). Both processes are part of the single industrial relations system that links the two parties concerned. Any reciprocal changes are dialectic rather than mechanical. In order to exist as such, employees must make up a group within the company while the em-

---

13 "The boss of a very small company often has a deep-seated mistrust of any external interference, especially when it comes from government departments and, even more, from trade unions" (Charpentier, Lepley, 2003: 102).

14 The notion of closeness is given another meaning by some authors in analysing small companies (Torrès, 2003).

ployer sets himself/herself apart from this group to identify with the company.

The Thwarted Invention of "Employee Status"

The legal form of employee status is something small companies discover very early on in their existence. It may, however, be part of a personal relationship which confines it within a formal framework as in the case of the entrepreneur's wife who looks after the accounts as a part-time employee, for example. The next of kin may also be part of the company without their employed status interfering in any way in the rationale of a family relationship. Calling upon the family circle delays the transition to "real" recruitment. A degree of hierarchy would seem to emerge between the various types of relationships underlying the same legal status of the employees: the employer's wife and his children are not related in the same way to employed status and to the company as are members of the wider family circle. Another circle encompasses friends and neighbours. Person-to-person relations in the company reproduce varied social patterns that durably envelop the employee-employer relationship.

The "real employees" entertain very varied relations with their employer according to their occupational status in the company. Either they can share with the employer his/her professional skills of which they are a sort of technical double, or they can provide individual expertise which the company needs[15] or else they seek to obtain their future skills in the company through apprenticeship. Their working contribution can be easily replaced or enhanced, they may have more or less seniority in the company, etc. The combination of personal relations and professional characteristics frequently leads to a mosaic of individual statuses. The employees observe, comment on and assess these systems of interdependence. The more complex a relationship between employee and employer may be and may depart from one of pure subordination, the more difficult substitution may become. It is more difficult to dismiss a trusty "old hand" or a close associate than an anonymous employee. Bearing that in mind, employees do not necessarily want the relationship that links them to their employer to be reduced to merely one of employee-employer, which would not necessarily be to their advantage. In this regard, the actual location of the company matters a lot. In small towns, the relationship cannot be anonymous and the labour market is more limited. This complexity may be to the advan-

15 The accountant has a very specific outline in this regard; the outline as such may change if the accountant is a member of the family (often the employer's wife) or an external employee. The chartered accountant and the services s/he provides may offset temporarily the appointment of an outsider.

tage of the employees and the employer alike even if small companies that one may hear about from outside are usually those in which such relations are outrageously to the employer's advantage.

The growth of the company represents a threat to this direct link between employees and employer which employees identify as a source of positive individualisation by comparison with a more collective, commonplace employee-employer relationship. Even in small companies with difficult industrial relations, a large company with its reputed financial and statutory advantages is not necessarily so attractive. Industrial relations there are often seen as quite impersonal, governed by bureaucratic, immutable rules, therefore somewhat inhuman, and ultimately more brutal than direct confrontation and its injustices.

Neither this interdependence nor the sharing of the ritual constraints and gestures between employer and employees can do away with the boundary that exists between them in a company. Nevertheless, they do attenuate the acuteness of such interdependence and push legal formalism into the background, especially if the employer is not inclined to highlight the difference in status.

As far as new recruits are concerned, a degree of adaptation is required in order to be integrated within the rules of the small groups. Those who cannot succeed in this "leave of their own accord", as emphasised in each of the three countries. Dismissals can take on all the more dramatic dimensions if the distance from a strict employee-employer relationship (and legal rules) is greater.[16]

Establishing a Distance: Intermediation

The employer is an integral part of the group (or "family") by virtue of specific duties which establish the company's cohesion and organise the various types of status within the workforce. The relationship between employer and employees is not therefore the sum of individual relationships between them. These duties set the employer apart from the outset without necessarily entailing a collective identification of the employees. When the industrial relations are appreciated by the employees, they consider the employer to be "one of them" and s/he has a specific function to fulfil.

This original distance becomes formalised with time and the growth of the company, according to a process of reiteration and debate through the various channels and timescales specific to each company. Even though sudden events may reveal it, the distance is the result of a slow

16 All witnesses of such events (employees, employers, trade unionists, labour inspectors and employment tribunals, etc.) refer to the particular traumas that are caused by dismissals in small companies.

process of change, rarely shared unanimously by all of the employees who are frequently divided on this matter. It occurs in very limited groups whereas larger ones are unaware of it. Larger companies experience this more frequently as their longer history has created more circumstances likely to encourage it. It may be the responsibility of the employer who may appear increasingly aloof because of ostentatious signs of wealth (company cars and business lunches, etc.), different working hours, a more confidential organisation of business, arbitrary behaviour in relations with employees, and misuse of company property. It can also be the fault of employees who fail to adapt to the company culture and resist exclusion. It may also stem from external circumstances such as expansion or succession, etc.

When an employer distances himself/herself from the direct management of collective and "person-to-person" relations, distancing takes on an organic function that will ultimately become a human resources management function. Intermediaries (who are on the payroll) intervene, bringing to light a structuring of the group that was more or less latent earlier: the skilled worker closest to the employer becomes foreman, a forewoman is appointed, a project manager is recruited who supervises the longest-serving employees, an accountant handles the payroll, etc. The entrepreneur is replaced by these intermediaries, or at least one of them, for discussing daily incidents and subsequently pay conditions offered to one or other of the employees. Each employee's job no longer depends on the immediate appreciation of the employer who steers away from this dual relationship and adopts the position of arbiter. Without the actual matter at issue changing, the nature of any demand is transformed by the very process of distancing *via* a person delegated by the employer. The personal nature of the relationship disappears and presupposes a more objective approach. New procedures are implemented, implicitly at first, carried through by individualised roles rather than by permanent structures.

Getting round the intermediary is still possible. The ease with which one can deal directly with the employer, where necessary, nurtures a distinction between various employees, according to their length of services and/or skills. Distancing from the employer does not therefore automatically create a common identity for the employees. It may in fact contribute to fragmenting what was previously a more homogeneous group.

From Intermediation to Autonomous Representation

Unequal access to the employer generates a form of intermediation which may be seen as a transition towards more explicit forms of representation. Team leaders speak on behalf of "their" people; the accountant takes on the role of spokesperson to "help everyone out"; the long-standing, faithful employee is consulted by the employer. For new recruits, this structuring brought about by expansion takes on the aspect of "natural" organisation. Neither for the employer nor for the employees is it aimed at bringing about a rupture between them. The intermediary is the spokesperson for one or several individuals, but not for the group as a whole. The employer acquires a functional advantage in the process which does not, nevertheless, exclude his/her direct intervention so often preferred by employees.

Exercising intermediation involves certain requirements. The mediator, regardless of his/her identity within the group, must accept to convey any requests to the employer. Even if s/he makes no commitment as to the outcome, s/he lends legitimacy to the approach. Reciprocally, s/he must provide the employer with justification for having taken on the claim. An account of his/her meeting with the employer requires him/her to explain how s/he had access to the latter and what was the basis for the decision. Was the request submitted and carefully presented? Why was it accepted or rejected? How does the mediator assess the outcome? And lastly, what is the validity of such mediation duties?

Rather than any functional or transitional form, intermediation is an ongoing process in the life of limited groups which find any open conflict or assertion of separate interests difficult to bear. This is why, in all three countries, it is often difficult to identify real practices in representative institutions and it is also illusory to perceive in the development of such institutions any sign of a change in the nature of internal relations. In both of the countries with twofold systems, in which such institutions must be established by law once a particular number of employees has been reached, it is not unusual that an elected member of the *Betriebsrat* or employee representative (DP) should be the very employees who already perform intermediation duties. A pre-existing role has been sanctioned by a vote without being transformed. The elective mandate operates within intermediation conditions, previously established, rather than through changing its very nature. Meetings with the employer can on occasion be conducted in a corridor, or *via* a telephone conversation; neither the employer nor the employees see any need to modify this practice. This also explains why it is difficult to find candidates for election: the poll as such cannot grant the desired legitimacy for carrying out such a function. Many representative institutions of small companies can be analysed as more or less living forms of intermediation. They reflect a particular state of industrial relations in which the employees do not wish to delegate their own ability to intervene, thereby being in full agreement with employers who do not wish to see such institutions established. When they do exist and operate along consensual lines, they are not subordinated to the employer. The desire for a consensus also emanates from the employees as each of them is afraid of the institutionalisation of conflicts, which the group could not take on. The "elected" representatives cannot stray durably from this line of conduct even if they have been chosen because of their capacity to resist pressure from the employer or earlier intermediaries. Employees take a very severe view of any attempt to make of such facilities anything other than what they were designed for. In particular, they do not give their support to elected representatives who would seem to impose on an employee group an identity that it does not have. In those conditions, neither the elected representatives nor the employees can have the type of relations with the union that are maintained by those working in big companies. The basic reason for this is that they do not maintain between themselves, with their work, with the employer or with the company itself, the type of relations that make the presence of a trade union functional and socially productive as in a larger-sized company.

The situation gradually changes in nature when, after many incidents, successive, noisy resignations of discontented employees, and permanent failures in "natural" intermediation, the employees or some of them wish to distance themselves markedly from the employer. An open conflict is often an occasion to take the plunge and institutionalise this distance. It is a difficult task. The change that transforms a "family" company into a "normal" one is rarely experienced as totally positive. The paroxysm of the conflict does not ensure the permanent positioning of the various parties concerned. The emergence of employees' leaders comes up against the leadership of the entrepreneur and any cleavages amongst the employees. The desire for a more formal distance from the employer is often felt differently by the various groups coexisting within the company. A request for the establishment of the *Betriebsrat*, employee representatives (DP) or a union representative (DS), for long postponed beyond legal requirements, becomes the subject of controversy amongst the employees. Such contradictions hamper an initiative to refer to general law – external to company standards – for bringing about a qualitative change in the system of internal relations. An attempt by an individual to be invested with an official role of representative cannot rest solely on the legal arguments for such a requirement. The viability or rejection of the desired institution depends on the quality of support the representative may enjoy at least among part of the workforce. His/her insertion in the industrial relations of a company and the survival of employees' leaders in the company are also dependent on this.

Once again, the scenarios that prompt this initiative vary considerably. The occurrence of an open conflict is not infrequent, but the existence of legal representative institutions in no way guarantees the nature of the collective initiative undertaken. The creation of such an institution does not mean that the employees will abandon former practices and adopt the new path open to them.[17] Reciprocally, the least cooperative employers may well set up legal procedures which they can control easily and instrumentalise to the detriment of any representation that is independent of them. A vast area of uncertainty exists in which representative institutions do not signify the existence of cohesive employees' group, whereas their absence does not show in principle that the employees do not react to being under their employer's thumb.

The autonomy of the body provides a clearer distinction between companies than its mere existence. The smallest companies have no access to it, but the threshold for its introduction is unspecified. Size plays a part as well as how long the company has existed, but the sociological features of the groups of employees and the conditions for their leaders' emergence count even more. To display its autonomy *vis-à-vis* the employer, the representative body must also be able to distance itself from individual pressure from employees and conflicts between groups. The smaller the company, the less the representatives can take advantage of their status in order to conduct collective arbitration; representative delegation would appear abusive, an anti-democratic *coup* on the part of the elected representative against those who elected him. In medium-sized companies, the various groups of employees can neutralise each other in the leadership process.

C. External Standards, Internal Standards and the Role of Unions

These considerations provide a better grasp of the trade union intervention model in each of the three countries. A union's intervention in small companies must find its path in the interplay of internal regulations. Globally speaking, all three countries differ substantially from this point of view, even if similar practices are detectable. The differences seem to be related to the differing abilities of unions in the three

---

17 In France, an employer of this type in computers has lost hope that his employee representative will attend the trade union courses "that he needs". Every time there is an election, he is afraid that there will be no candidate. The employees, whether representatives or not, tend to prefer discussing things round the table in the canteen than doing so in management's office where some of them meet. In Germany, the director of a research institute has observed the relatively unsuccessful efforts made by the chair of the Betriebsrat to position his institution at the centre of industrial relations exchanges, without being hostile to it.

countries to ensure the transition between the various phases in internal industrial relations in small companies.

In Sweden, trade unionists have a capacity of intervention in companies, including small ones, that is not to be found in the other two countries. The high level of individual trade union membership among employees and companies, combined with the reciprocal role of employers' organisations and trade unions in devising employment standards, enables unions to be called upon more easily to interpret collective bargaining agreements and to mediate in internal debates. Employees see this service as their right. Employers derive the advantage of an internalised regulation system that focuses on the substance more than the form of industrial relations in their company. An open or latent conflict can be settled within the company through external intervention based on the appropriate dual legitimacy. Employers therefore limit the risks of tense individual intervention of one or more employees on the work group. As one employer puts it, "I would rather have the intervention of an external trade unionist in the event of a problem rather than the permanent presence of a union represented by an employee in the company". Employees should not have to cope with any conflictual confrontation with the employer, with its inevitable train of individual and collective consequences. A union's capacity of intervention would therefore seem to be based on its acknowledged dual capacity: that of being a proven interpreter of external standards, which it has helped to devise, and that of a regulatory agent for internal procedures. The union validates the originality of the procedures while placing them in a framework for interpreting general standards. The employees are not, however, expected to manifest themselves as such *vis-à-vis* the employer. The latent internal conflict can be deviated towards externalised arbitration between negotiators whose legitimacy is recognised within the company.

France and Germany have no experience of this practice of expert trade union intervention. The low rate of union membership in small companies means that union intervention is a more alien and more provocative gesture, for employers and employees alike, even though it may be for different reasons. In both countries, there is a trend, on the contrary, for one or more employees to show their distance with regard to the employer, the dominant operating principles of the company and, possibly, some of the employees themselves. In such conditions, initial trade union intervention frequently occurs on the occasion of an open conflict that undermines the delicate balance of power within the company. This intervention is seen to be a perilous operation for the very survival of the company or for the career of some of its members.

The union that intervenes for the first time in a small company in the event of an open conflict finds itself in a difficult position, whether it likes it or not. It is called upon to preside in judgement over certain internal practices without possessing the means to ensure the durability of its intervention. Its position is all the more fragile if it appears to be the instrument of a small proportion of the employees, who are responsible for the conflict. In that case, it is likely to be instrumentalised and to hamper its chances of establishing itself more widely and durably in the company. The establishment of a union presence in such conditions, initially heroic, often proves to be ephemeral and costly in industrial relations. The case of France is interesting in an international comparison as a degree of competition may arise at that juncture between the various procedures for transition to representation. The union or unions can designate a representative and organise an election for employee representatives or the works council. However, election and designation can be contradictory instruments in any struggle for influence that may occur in that instance. An employer may well respond to the appointment of a trade union representative by organising an election which, to his/her own advantage, will reveal the fragile nature of the union representative's position. An election is not necessarily to the advantage of those employees with the closet links to the union. Such links may actually be the cause of failure.

A union may succeed more easily in establishing a long-term relationship with the employees if it accompanies the development of internal relations without adopting a judgemental stance with regard to the quality of such relations. So long as the internal standards remain dominant in the company and the representative bodies do not have enough autonomy with regard to the employer and employees, the trade union can have but a discreet advisory role. The contradiction in France and Germany lies in the fact that support of employees is not guaranteed and may even be postponed indefinitely.

D. An Equivocal Position, Original but Requiring Valorisation

By highlighting similarities in the situations in the three countries, an international comparison can help to identify features that are specific to small companies with regard to industrial relations. Three of these deserve closer consideration by way of a conclusion.

The first refers to their integration in industrial relations systems, the second their internal forms of social interaction, and the third their differences by comparison with larger entities.

A Central and Equivocal Position in Industrial Relations

In all three countries, small companies play a central role in devising labour standards regardless of whether they are formulated through collective bargaining or legislation. While they may be less comprehensively organised than larger companies, they nonetheless feature in any public debate but through other channels than in the latter. Neither employers' organisations nor lawmakers can fail to take account of the existence of these companies. For the former, they constitute, through their threat of defection, a risk of delegitimising the industrial relations systems, even if the stakes are unbalanced depending on whether they are observed from the employer's or from the employee's point of view. For the latter, by their very number and by their geographical and economic importance and finally by the number of entrepreneurs involved, they represent an economic, social and political influence that is all the greater as it is more diffuse. For the former and the latter alike, the diversity of the interests of entrepreneurs and companies means that it is much more complicated to take account of them in striking a balance between social and political considerations. Collective standards, even when aimed at being more adapted to small rather than large companies, are inevitably poorly adjusted to small ones by virtue of their diversity. This leaves scope for local adaptation for which employers are always ready to strive. As far as trade unions are concerned, the employees in these companies, who constitute a minority of all employees, are less well catered for in collective references and objectives than those who work in bigger companies. Nevertheless, it is indispensable that these employees be taken into consideration, if only to exercise a minimum of control over the risks of competition that they represent on the labour market. Such justification is rather weak, however. The economic activities of small companies are not necessarily in competition with those of larger ones. As suppliers, small companies readily provide opportunities for valorisation for their clients and contribute indirectly to consolidating the internal industrial relations systems in big companies, by externalising some of their obligations (flexibility, job insecurity and lower pay). For the trade union movement, this is undoubtedly a contradiction that will have to be tackled in the future (Dufour, Hege, 2005).

Specific Forms of Relationships

Small companies are not small-scale models of large ones which, only for want of being bigger, cannot provide the same context for industrial confrontation. While they share common structural features in spite of their diversity, it is not by default, by escaping collectively the features of larger companies.

They cannot conceal the signs of their emergence and are constantly reminded of the question of their survival. This common basis underlies their industrial relations whose homogeneousness and differences are linked to the central role played by the employer. His/her essential position depends on the very structure of these companies; the diversity of industrial relations stems from the very diversity of the profile of the entrepreneurs and their environment. The various occupations and the infinite variety of social and economic circumstances guarantee diversity with similar structural fragility. The same relationship of employees' dependency on the employer manifests itself therefore in heterogeneous but not anomic practices. Relations between employees and employers, which are dominated by the requirements of adaptation to the specific features of the company, labour standards and economic circumstances, are conducted in the three countries according to two quite distinct models.

The first of these, more specific to very small companies, involves direct confrontation between individuals whose resources are sometimes similar or sometimes unequal. The social roles – internal or external to the company – are not structurally distinct; professional considerations govern the sharing of work while outlining the distinct profile of the entrepreneur. His/her leadership may find it difficult to steer the course, either by encouraging an authoritarian approach or by opening the path to professional companionship. These two forms reveal a quest for indisputable unity. The same active principle manifests itself in contradictory forms.

The other model appears in companies where a certain distance has been established between entrepreneur and employees. Various roles in the company are diversified. The implicit or explicit quest for redistributing relations is incumbent on the whole range of social roles to be found in the company. The need for industrial mediation cuts a tentative path through individual and occupational interests. Mediation displays a trend towards differentiation which cannot break with the principle of unity. This model, however uncomfortable for its participants but lasting in its effects, involves the cohabitation of contradictory structuring principles, creating an intimate mixture of conflict and merging.

Transitions from one to the other of these models are ill-defined. The number of employees is not the only explanation, as the myriad of different contexts excludes this criterion from being the only decisive one. This may help to understand why the diversity of standards of employee thresholds retained in the three countries leads nevertheless to comparable practices.

Original Features to Be Valorised in Order to Understand Big Companies

Small companies are governed by their own standards of industrial relations conduct. They cannot be expected to boast of collective procedures that rest on the interaction of more numerous groups and occupational practices that are rooted in their industrial environment. The lack of research on small companies, their own difficulty in defining themselves, and the use of inappropriate methods of evaluating their practices may leave the impression that they are by essence intolerant of any confrontation of divergent interests. This would not seem to be so according to our surveys, in any of the countries. Conversely, it is true that this confrontation does not manifest itself in the canonical forms of representation – in the sociological rather than legal concept of the term (Dufour, Hege, 2002) – that prevail in the largest companies where managers and employees' representatives enjoy statuses that exceed their individual characteristics in order to organise the industrial relations of groups, which are capable of acquiring their own identity. When so-called institutional forms of representation exist in small companies, they are usually used differently from those in larger ones, thereby revealing their different sociological roots.

As has been shown above, the observation of small companies requires focusing on the more informal manifestations of confrontation and daily practices within the companies. This process provides a description of the specific conditions in which small companies conduct their industrial relations. If the conditions underlying this process are special, is the process itself their exclusive domain? Can it be said that within larger companies the established institutional forms generate decisive arbitration in their industrial relations? We might well ask whether hierarchical individual relations and their rituals and the mediation procedures are not part of a permanently available arsenal, made transparent through its daily use and left in the shadows of specific structures that attract our attention. Is not the bringing into play of this daily, informal arsenal a condition for access to efficient representation and the success of institutions dedicated to representation? Small companies are very different from big ones. Care must be taken not to overlook the spirit of their practices by imposing on them criteria devised for bigger ones. Much could no doubt be gained from recognising in any analysis of industrial relations in large companies that they themselves rely on informal practices, for groups whose identities are of unequal consistency, with complex leaderships. The whole cannot be boiled down to the explicit interplay of institutions. Much of the rationale at work in small companies is matched by that to be found in bigger ones, even if the latter officially ignore it.

References

Barrat, O. (2002), "La négociation collective, le statisticien, sa lanterne et le débat social", *La Revue de l'IRES*, No.39. 2002/2, p.3-32.

Boccara, F. (1998), "Emploi: mythes des PME et réalité des groupes", *Économie et statistique*, No.319-320, p.137-161.

Charpentier, P., Lepley, B. (2003), "Les TPE face aux 35 heures", *Documents d'Études*, Paris: Dares, No.65, janvier.

CSERC (1999), *Le SMIC, salaire minimum de croissance*, Paris: La Documentation française.

Dufour, C., Hege, A. (2000), "Les négociations dans la métallurgie et la chimie: quels enseignements européens?", in ministère de l'Emploi et de la Solidarité, *Bilan annuel de la négociation collective en France.*

Dufour, C., Hege, A., (2002), *L'Europe syndicale au quotidien, la représentation des salariés en France, Allemagne, Grande Bretagne et Italie*, Bruxelles: PIE-Peter Lang.

Dufour, C., Hege, A., (2003), "Les négociations dans les transports routiers", *in* ministère de l'Emploi et de la Solidarité, *Bilan annuel de la négociation collective en France*, Éditions Législatives, ministère des Affaires sociales, du Travail et de la Solidarité.

Dufour, C., Hege, A. (2005), "Emplois précaires, emploi normal et syndicalismes", *Chronique internationale de l'IRES*, No.97, novembre, p.5-22.

Dufour, C., Hege, A., Malan, A., Zouary, P. (2004), *Des institutions et des acteurs dans les entreprises pour quelles relations sociales?*, Rapport pour la DARES, avril.

Meidner, R. (1994), "Succès, faiblesses et perspectives d'avenir du mouvement syndical suédois", *La Revue de l'IRES*, No.14, p.3-25.

Roussel-Verret, I. (2004), *Les IRP face à l'éclatement de l'entreprise*, Rapport CFE-CGC pour l'IRES.

Saglio, J. (1991), "La régulation de branche dans le système français de relations professionnelles", *Travail et emploi*, 1/1991, No.47, p.26-41.

Torrès, O. (1997), "Pour une approche contestable de la spécificité des PME", *Revue internationale PME* (RIPME), vol.10, No.2, p.9-43.

Torrès, O. (2003), "Petitesse des entreprises et grossissement des effets de proximité", *Revue française de gestion*, No.144 mai-juin, p.119-138.

Wassermann, W., Rhode, W. (2004), *Konfliktfeld Kleinbetrieb, Mittelstand zwischen Alleinherrschaft und Mitbestimmung*, Bund Verlag Köln.

Rudolph, W., Wassermann, W. (2002), "Neue Betriebsräte in kleinen Betrieben. Die Reform zeigt erste Wirkung", *Arbeitsrecht in Betrieb*, Heft /2002.

"Work & Society"

The series "Work & Society" analyses the development of employment and social policies, as well as the strategies of the different social actors, both at national and European levels. It puts forward a multi-disciplinary approach – political, sociological, economic, legal and historical – in a bid for dialogue and complementarity.
The series is not confined to the social field *stricto sensu*, but also aims to illustrate the indirect social impacts of economic and monetary policies. It endeavours to clarify social developments, from a comparative and a historical perspective, thus portraying the process of convergence and divergence in the diverse national societal contexts. The manner in which European integration impacts on employment and social policies constitutes the backbone of the analyses.

Series Editor: Philippe POCHET, *Director of the Observatoire Social Européen (Brussels) and Digest Editor of the* Journal of European Social Policy

Recent Titles

No.59 – *Changing Liaisons. The Dynamics of Social Partnership in 20th Century West-European Democracies*, Karel DAVIDS, Greta DEVOS & Patrick PASTURE (eds.), 2007, 268 p., ISBN 978-90-5201-365-7.

No.58 – *Work and Social Inequalities in Health in Europe*, Ingvar LUNDBERG, Tomas HEMMINGSSON & Christer HOGSTEDT (eds.), SALTSA, 2007, 538 p., ISBN 978-90-5201-372-5.

No.57 – *European Solidarities. Tensions and Contentions of a Concept*, Lars MAGNUSSON & Bo STRÅTH (eds.), SALTSA, 2007, 355 p., ISBN 978-90-5201-363-3.

No.56 – *Industrial Relations in Small Companies. A Comparison: France, Sweden and Germany*, Christian DUFOUR, Adelheid HEGE, Sofia MURHEM, Wolfgang RUDOLPH & Wolfram WASSERMANN (eds.), SALTSA, 2007, 229 p., ISBN 978-90-5201-360-2.

No.55 – *The European Sectoral Social Dialogue. Actors, Developments and Challenges*, Anne DUFRESNE, Christophe DEGRYSE & Philippe POCHET (eds.), SALTSA/Observatoire social européen, 2006, 342 p., ISBN 978-90-5201-052-6.

No.54 – *Reshaping Welfare States and Activation Regimes in Europe*, Amparo SERRANO PASCUAL & Lars MAGNUSSON (eds.), SALTSA, 2007, 319 p., ISBN 978-90-5201-048-9.

No.53 – *Shaping Pay in Europe. A Stakeholder Approach*, Conny Herbert ANTONI, Xavier BAETEN, Ben J.M. EMANS & Mari KIRA (eds.), SALTSA, 2006, 287 p., ISBN 978-90-5201-037-3.

No.52 – *Les relations sociales dans les petites entreprises. Une comparaison France, Suède, Allemagne*, Christian DUFOUR, Adelheid HEGE, Sofia MURHEM, Wolfgang RUDOLPH & Wolfram WASSERMANN, 2006, 243 p., ISBN 978-90-5201-323-7.

No.51 – *Politiques sociales. Enjeux méthodologiques et épistémologiques des comparaisons internationales / Social Policies. Epistemological and Methodological Issues in Cross-National Comparison*, Jean-Claude BARBIER & Marie-Thérèse LETABLIER (eds.), 2005, 2nd printing 2006, 295 p., ISBN 978-90-5201-294-0.

No.50 – *The Ethics of Workplace Privacy*, Sven Ove HANSSON & Elin PALM (eds.), SALTSA, 2005, 186 p., ISBN 978-90-5201-293-3.

No.49 – *The Open Method of Co-ordination in Action. The European Employment and Social Inclusion Strategies*, Jonathan ZEITLIN & Philippe POCHET (eds.), with Lars MAGNUSSON, SALTSA/Observatoire social européen, 2005, 2nd printing 2005, 511 p., ISBN 978-90-5201-280-3.

N° 48 – *Le Moment Delors. Les syndicats au cœur de l'Europe sociale*, Claude DIDRY & Arnaud MIAS, 2005, 2nd printing 2005, 349 p., ISBN 978-90-5201-274-2.

No.47 – *A European Social Citizenship? Preconditions for Future Policies from a Historical Perspective*, Lars MAGNUSSON & Bo STRÅTH (eds.), SALTSA, 2004, 361 p., ISBN 978-90-5201-269-8.

No.46 – *Restructuring Representation. The Merger Process and Trade Union Structural Development in Ten Countries*, Jeremy WADDINGTON (ed.), 2004, 414 p., ISBN 978-90-5201-253-7.

No.45 – *Labour and Employment Regulation in Europe*, Jens LIND, Herman KNUDSEN & Henning JØRGENSEN (eds.), SALTSA, 2004, 408 p., ISBN 978-90-5201-246-9.

N° 44 – *L'État social actif. Vers un changement de paradigme ?*, Pascale VIELLE, Philippe POCHET & Isabelle CASSIERS (dir.), 2005, 2e tirage 2006, ISBN 978-90-5201-227-8.